"A real game-changer. I've been fascinated with this particular field of leadership development for quite some time. However, like many people, I've found it hard to apply the existing theory to my work. This book is the key to changing that and I gained a tremendous amount from reading it. It weaves together this wide web of new, complex ideas, then presents them in a way that is simple, accessible, practical and highly insightful.

I've been able to apply the various concepts, tools and practices immediately, both in my work developing others and to help develop myself. There's something in the style of the book that struck me, too: in reading the book, you're not just benefiting from the authors' insights, you're experiencing their humanity."
Rebecca Stevens, Head of Leadership and Learning at Clarks

"A fresh and engaging approach to get you building your capacity to lead in the modern 'VUCA' world. The authors provide a range of practical methods to help you take charge of managing your own upgrade and helping others with theirs. It's an infectious set of concepts that you'll recognise from your day-to-day work and want to share with the people around you."
Michael Borthwick, Director of Planning & Acquisitions at Claranet

"There is gold here - both for leaders and for those who coach or mentor them. For if it's true that 'we see the world not as it is, but as we are', then one of the most pressing questions facing leaders is how we consciously evolve both what we see and what we are. *Upgrade* is a really important book, a timely and vital contribution that does what previous authors in this field have tried and failed to do. It's nothing less than a practical user-guide to building the human capacities needed to address the complex and seemingly intractable issues of our times. Expect an uncommon combination of accessibility, profound depth and immediate application."
Peter Young, Director at Bladon Leadership

"A fascinating book that I really enjoyed. I love the 'operating system' concept, how easily relatable it was and the idea of then upgrading it. The case studies really brought it to life and it's great to interact with the content personally throughout."
Gareth Rogers, CEO at Farnborough International, home of the world-famous Air Show

"This book really worked for me and would be a great entry point for even the most cynical of people. The practices are excellent: just the right level of intellectual and personal challenge. I would recommend this book to anyone who wants to understand their current skill levels and how to develop them to deal with issues thrown up by career progression, organisational change and the impact of technology on their operating environment. It gives you the tools to manage and survive in an uncertain world by learning how to anticipate and control events, rather than being controlled by them."
Caroline Britton, Non-Executive Director at Revolut following 18 years as a partner at Deloitte

"*Upgrade* really made me think differently about my approach to leadership. The book provided a completely unique perspective when considering how you need to operate in a 'VUCA' world. For me, personally, it's a compelling idea that you need to upgrade your personal operating system to have sufficient capacity to function effectively. Add to that the various case studies and practices and you have a fascinating approach to developing the capacities required to lead successfully."
Matt Hale, Academy Manager at Southampton Football Club

"An incredibly timely book that resonated with my experience of working in the public sector. I felt it really brought something new to the leadership literature, and has challenged me to think about my approach to leadership in a much more fundamental and holistic manner."
Catherine Poyner, Deputy Director in the public sector

"*Upgrade* is not for the faint of mind. It answers questions most of us won't even have thought to ask. I'd recommend it to anyone facing dilemmas, frustrations and bewilderment in seeking to lead themselves and others. It's a book that will reward the reader with practical new tools for thinking, learning and taking action."
Phil Hayes, Chairman at Management Futures

"If you're wondering why things simply don't seem to be working, this could well be the book for you. It provoked a host of powerful new questions for me – both personally and professionally – then helped me answer them. It's an essential resource for L&D professionals, too, who will find it fills the gap many practitioners in this field have been struggling with. The authors have done a great job of integrating and distilling a vast amount of research into something very, very practical."
Claire Davey, Partner at Latitude-Six, formerly Head of Coaching and Leadership Development at Deloitte

Praise for *ARC Leadership* and *The Boss Factor*

"This book has had a real impact on me... Business schools in particular would do well to pay attention... given what's gone on in corporations, they need to take greater responsibility for producing future leaders who aren't simply able to profitably grow a business, but are – to their core – Authentic, Responsible and Courageous."
Karen Lombardo, formerly Worldwide Head of Human Resources at Gucci Group

"An incredibly useful and accessible book that has transformed my thinking and approach to both managing upwards and leading my team... It's a book I know I'll read and refer to more than once and the author

makes that easy: there's a lot to reflect on and the way *The Boss Factor* is written is like having him in the room with you."
Simon Haskey, Consulting Practice Lead at Dell EMC

"A rigorous, intelligent book that challenges us to make a fundamental shift, to make ourselves better – both as leaders and as people."
Adam Burns, Editor at MeetTheBoss TV

"A refreshing book that takes a new perspective on the relationship between leaders and the people they lead. I really loved the practical tools and exercises, which made this book a directly relevant, interactive and memorable experience where so many are a passive stroll through theories that are all too easily forgotten. This book actually made me think far beyond just reading it. It made me do something. It made it stick."
Geoff Morey, Learning and Organisational Development Consultant at Macmillan Cancer Support

• ● •

UPGRADE

●●●

Building your capacity for complexity

RICHARD BOSTON
&
KAREN ELLIS

Cover and interior graphics: Jason Flinter at The Flint
Production: Alison Rayner

Published by LeaderSpace
Harwood House, 43 Harwood Road, London SW6 4QP
All enquiries to: publications@leaderspace.com

First published 2019

ISBN: 978-0-9929445-6-8 (Paperback)
ISBN: 978-0-9929445-8-2 (eBook-ePub)
ISBN: 978-0-9929445-7-5 (eBook-Kindle)

From Karen

To my guide, mentor and teacher, Anthony Lunt
You made the world an enchanted place and
helped me inhabit it more fully

• ● •

From Richard

To Evie, Jane and my dad
There are no better reasons than you
for me to keep working on my own OS

• ● •

Also by Richard Boston

ARC Leadership: from surviving to thriving in a complex world

The Boss Factor: 10 lessons in managing up for mutual gain

Also by Karen Ellis

A forthcoming book, as yet untitled, helping people in complex roles that span multiple contexts to lead truly 'systemically' – due in 2019 and written with Joe Simpson

Contents

● ● ●

1

About this book and our approach to writing it

● ● ●

THIS BOOK IS ABOUT two poorly understood, little discussed but utterly vital aspects of human life at work: our ability to make sense of the complexity that surrounds us in our day-to-day lives, and our different ways of 'making meaning' within that complexity.

It is an attempt to distil the most useful practical wisdom from a wide range of theories within the relatively obscure field of 'adult constructivist development', otherwise known as 'vertical development'. Our intention is to enable you and your colleagues to use that wisdom to support your own development. In doing so, you'll enhance your internal 'capacities' for understanding and working with complexity. Whatever your starting point, you'll develop a more insightful, nuanced and comprehensive understanding of the situations that face you every day. You'll also translate that understanding into action, upgrading your approach to innovating, collaborating and making decisions in high stakes situations.

So, in essence, this is a book about you and how to make yourself a 'bigger' you!

Most authors would get to know each other and *then* perhaps experiment with writing a book. In our case, it's this book that has brought us together. We'd spent no more than three or four days in each other's company when we decided to combine our mutual love of this field of vertical development and create something

> **"Collaboration on a book is the ultimate unnatural act."**
>
> Tom Clancy, author[1]

3

new – something that would take this very important body of ideas and make it much more accessible and practically useful for everyone, not just academics and people working in leadership development.

We focus here on four capacities that emerged from research Karen[a] has been doing in this niche field of adult development since the late 1990s – research that underpinned her work as a consultant and coach. Prior to meeting Karen, Richard had been circling the world of vertical development for several years. He'd found it fascinating on an intellectual level but was struggling to work out how to make much practical use of it in his own work.

The door his first chance encounter with Karen opened was both personally and professionally enlightening. On one hand, a topic that had been intellectually interesting for years now offered him some of the most profound development he'd had to date. On the other, the four capacities totally nailed it for him. They offered an answer to the questions he'd heard (and asked) far too many times when introducing these ideas to others[2]:

- So what?

- Now what?

So we decided to bring our ideas and experiences together to see if we could show people how we can all consciously and deliberately develop these four internal capacities in our day-to-day working lives – without the need for training programmes, corporate retreats, coaches or consultants. Not that we don't believe in those 'offline' approaches. We've made careers out of them, and authentically so. They can be fantastic accelerators. They're just too slow – and too narrowly and infrequently deployed – to create the kind of step changes we need in our organisations if we're going to operate more effectively in our rapidly changing contexts.

---

a   Karen is pronounced with the 'kar' rhyming with 'car'.

4

In writing this book, then, we've sought to weave decades of diverse research into a single coherent story. We've translated what can be highly academic, abstract and esoteric literature into something that's far less exclusive and far more accessible to all. We've brought it to life with case studies[b] and our own personal experiences in order to show how this stuff works in the real world. Then we've gone beyond all that to offer you a wealth of practical ways to 'upgrade your personal operating system' and help the people you work with to upgrade theirs.

Like any two human beings, we don't always agree. What you'll find here, though, are the benefits of distilling our shared beliefs and few disagreements into something better than either of us had considered before. It's been a thoroughly enjoyable experience and we look forward to sharing it with you.

---

b   To respect the confidential nature of our work, the case studies are amalgams of real people, rather than actual individuals, unless we say otherwise.

PART 1

• ● •

Why and how to read this book

Why we need these four capacities

• ● •

- The essence of these capacities
- Why we need them in an increasingly complex world
- The difference between 'upgrading' your internal operating system and simply 'adding more apps'
- Whether this book is for you

IF YOU'RE READING this book you're looking for something that'll help you, your people and your organisation survive and thrive in a fairly challenging environment. Like most of us, you're probably finding you're asked to deliver more, faster and to higher quality than often feels reasonable. You're expected to do so despite the confounding variables being more numerous, interconnected and changeable than they used to be. You're also probably doing so under greater internal or public scrutiny than ever before.

You are not alone.

In this book, we're offering four areas of focus that make a *massive* difference to people's ability to survive and thrive – not just at work, but in their broader lives, too. You have these four inner 'capacities' already. You wouldn't have made it this far through life without them. You just might not have developed those capacities to their full potential. It's the same as with the muscles in your body: they're there but not all of them are as strong as they could be.

For each of the four capacities, we'll introduce you to four 'levels' of development, each based on consistent thinking from the field of 'vertical development'. There's no sugar-coating this: the more developed the level at which we're operating in a given moment, the better prepared we are to cope with the challenges of a complex world. So we'll offer you practical tools to help you work out

"Much of the stress I now see in leaders has less to do with workload and more to do with the strain of trying to make sense of an environment that has become too complex for their current [level] of development. The waters are rapidly rising and many leaders are finding they are in over their heads."

Nick Petrie, the US Center for Creative Leadership[3]

the level at which you're currently operating, then upgrade – where you choose to do so – from that level to the next. You'll want to pick one or two upgrades at a time, as trying to upgrade all four capacities at once risks diluting your learning or overloading yourself. That's true for everyone, no matter how driven they are or how quick they are to learn.

We believe the most effective leaders have learned that they too are in the business of developing others. True, they often bring in professionals to help them do so, but they remain actively, passionately and artfully involved throughout. So we'll also show you how to use the tools in this book with the people around you – to help them develop as individuals and to enhance the work you're doing collectively. Some readers will find it's enough, for now, to focus on developing themselves. If that's you, that's fine. The tools for developing others will be there for you to use when you decide the time is right.

This raises the question 'Who is this book for? Is it for managers and leaders or for people whose job it is to develop those managers and leaders?'

The answer is 'both', but our primary audience is people who lead, manage or work in teams or organisations. Our secondary audience is the coaches, mentors, facilitators and trainers who support the development of those people, teams and organisations. We're speaking, too, to people responsible for attracting, selecting, leveraging and developing 'talent' and people with 'potential'. These are common terms in organisational life, but they've proven hard to define and codify. We believe that's because the words 'talent' and 'potential' are attempts to point towards these inner four capacities without a clear understanding of what they are, how they work and how we come by and develop them.

Given our primary audience, this book is written to be easily accessible to people who are keen to dip in and take something useful and highly practical, then apply it quickly to themselves and move on. It's also written to include additional material, easily accessed, that enables those who want to dig deeper and go further to do so. For instance, you'll find we skip over much of the research behind our work but return to it in the endnotes.

We're talking about something quite different here

One critical thing to remember as you step into this book: upgrading isn't the same as developing a new skill or absorbing new information, knowledge or ideas. Taking your phone as an analogy: adding new skills, information, knowledge and ideas is like adding new apps. When we're talking about upgrading these four capacities, it's the equivalent of updating your phone's entire Operating System (OS).

Most workplace learning and leadership development focuses on adding apps. That's important. After all, with no apps, your phone, tablet or computer isn't much use to you. However, if you'd had the same phone for ten years and hadn't updated its OS, your phone wouldn't be able to keep up with the pace of change. Some apps would run poorly, some not at all, and as you loaded more and more apps your machine would slow to a crawl.

Update to the latest OS and, suddenly, those apps all run faster and more effectively. You can also run more apps simultaneously. Not only that but doing so uses up far less of your battery.

It's the same with upgrading these capacities, which are four key components of your own personal OS. Your operating system determines your ways of understanding, relating and responding to yourself, other people and the world around you. As you move from one level to the next you'll find you're better able to:

☐ Be more resilient and adaptable in a wider range of situations

☐ Find hidden opportunities in fiendishly complex problems

☐ Apply your existing knowledge, skills and qualities in increasingly diverse situations

☐ Cut through the confusion to what's most important

☐ Translate complex ideas into simple, compelling messages

☐ Weave multiple concepts and perspectives into a coherent whole

☐ Navigate strategic, ethical and commercial dilemmas

☐ Work with diverse stakeholders with competing needs

☐ Respond to tensions and conflicts

☐ Create, co-create and innovate

☐ Help others to grow, deliver and succeed

☐ Trigger genuine, sustainable transformation in individuals, teams and organisations

☐ Progress your own career, whatever 'progressing' means for you

When we're stuck using an out-dated OS, we get used to working harder and harder as it struggles to cope with an increasingly heavy and increasingly complex load. Too many people we've met have been focused on simply ploughing through it all. In doing so, they're taking unnecessary risks for themselves, their people, their organisations and the people who love and depend on them. There's a reasonable chance in an increasingly complex world that failing to keep up-to-date with your upgrades will mean that eventually you'll fall foul of a challenge you're simply not equipped for. It could be something none of your apps can help you with, but it could equally be that those existing apps *could* have saved you, if only they'd been running on the right OS.

Four keys to surviving and thriving in a complex world

Your phone's operating system is made up of various components or chunks of computer code – one dealing with memory and data management, one with connectivity to other devices via Bluetooth and wi-fi, and so on. Together, these components dictate how your phone:

- Gathers and interprets data in the world around it

- Interacts with that world, including you

- Monitors and manages itself, including updating its own OS

- Reacts to conflicting commands from different apps or inconsistencies in different pieces of data

The four capacities at the heart of this book do much the same thing. They're the four components of your internal OS that make the biggest difference to your ability to survive and thrive – and your ability to help others survive and thrive, too. Together, the four capacities make up our ways of making (or trying and failing to make) sense of ourselves, each other and the world in which we're operating. Collectively, at their core, they're capacities for making meaning.

We'll describe them each in detail later, with case studies. In summary, though, these are the four capacities:

Sense-making	observing, understanding and processing the complexity of a situation – e.g. getting your head around all the different interconnected topics, data, issues or causal relationships
Perspective-shifting	'zooming out' to benefit from a more realistic and multi-faceted understanding of a situation or relationship – e.g. understanding the perspectives and agendas of the various stakeholders
Self-relating	observing, understanding, regulating and transforming yourself – e.g. making sense of your own reactions, thoughts and feelings
Opposable Thinking	responding to the dilemmas and conflicting ideas that can create tensions within us and / or between us and other people – e.g. working with opposing views

One way of grasping the four capacities is to think of Sense-making as mainly cognitive, Perspective-shifting as primarily interpersonal, and Self-relating as *intra*personal – that is, looking *within* ourselves. It's not a perfect fit, as in reality all three capacities are interconnected and affect how we operate intellectually, interpersonally and intrapersonally. Nevertheless, it helps many people grasp and remember those first three capacities, so if it helps you then stick with it.

Opposable Thinking feeds into all three areas. It's the capacity that helps us when we are personally conflicted or struggling to choose between two or more seemingly opposing courses of action. It helps us tackle interpersonal challenges that emerge when people become (or are at risk of becoming) polarised. Opposable Thinking also helps us deal with conflicting data, seemingly incompatible diagnoses of a problem and competing ways of making sense of the world.

Another, complementary way of distilling the four capacities is that each focuses us on one of the following sets of questions:

Sense-making	What on earth is going on here? How do I diagnose all the important elements that make up this situation so I can deal with it most effectively?
Perspective-shifting	How is everyone else responding (or likely to respond) to the situation? What do I see when I step back and look at it from a neutral point of view? How objective am I *really* being when I do that stepping back?
Self-relating	How do I need to manage my own reactions to this situation? In what ways am I getting in my own way, in this situation and others? How do my beliefs and values shape how I am responding here?
Opposable Thinking	How do I respond to differences of opinion regarding the nature of the problem and how we should proceed? How do I bring the opposing sides together to forge a productive, sustainable way forward?

Importantly, the capacities apply equally well to groups and teams. You simply replace the 'I' in the questions above with 'we'.

Why focus on upgrading these capacities?

We appreciate that, if you've decided to read this book, you're probably already fairly convinced there's a case for trying an upgrade or two. If so, maybe you don't need to read this next section. You'll find it helpful, though, if you're looking to inspire others to try an upgrade of their own and you're anticipating a degree of scepticism.

The reasons for upgrading are rooted in what's happening in the world around you. So we'll touch briefly on two ways of looking at that world, then return to the role of the four capacities.

Welcome to VUCA.
You might well have been here before...

There are many ways of describing what's happening in the world of work and the world more broadly. We hear words like 'exponential', 'global', 'interconnected' and 'complex' all the time. One acronym we find particularly helpful is 'VUCA'[a]. It's a word that itself polarises people. For some it's ubiquitous; to others it's utterly alien; for some it's no longer fashionable; for others it's a term that triggers a lightbulb moment that explains everything they're finding difficult. For us, it's a useful concept that helps our clients map the messiness they're dealing with on a day-to-day basis.

VUCA stands for Volatile, Uncertain, Complex and Ambiguous. It's a term apparently coined in the 1990s by the US Army War College[4]. It proved so helpful on the modern battlefield that it's found currency in many civilian organisations.

---

a   Most commonly pronounced 'voo-ka'.

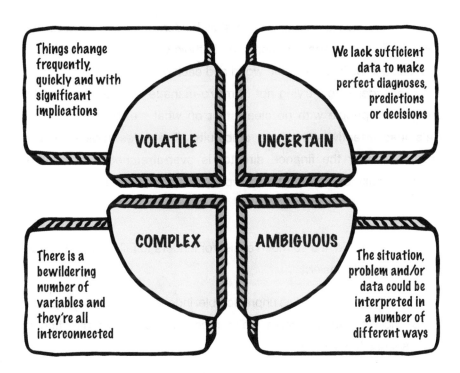

Things change frequently, quickly and with significant implications

VOLATILE

We lack sufficient data to make perfect diagnoses, predictions or decisions

UNCERTAIN

COMPLEX

There is a bewildering number of variables and they're all interconnected

AMBIGUOUS

The situation, problem and/or data could be interpreted in a number of different ways

The manufacturing company that's struggling to get a consistent flow of water and power to its factories because of persistent outages? That's a volatility issue, as is the fluctuation of exchange rates that affects the profitability of companies trading internationally.

The middle manager waiting on the results of a consultation process that could mean she has to make several of her team redundant? That's some truly uncomfortable uncertainty. Uncertainty also kicks in when an election puts a surprise candidate in a position of power or you're waiting for the results of trade negotiations between your government and the governments of other countries in which you're trading.

The team that's working on those trade negotiations, navigating a web of political, economic, legal and cultural considerations in pursuit of a favourable outcome? They're working with complexity. So, too, is the inner-city social worker whose stakeholders have varied roles and come from diverse socioeconomic and ethnic groups, all with their own agendas and beliefs about the world and each other.

The leader who's trying not to micro-manage but has gone too far and left his people with no clear steer on what's expected of them? He's inadvertently stirring up ambiguity. The sales director who's unsure whether the finance director is over-stretched, incompetent or intentionally defrauding the company. She also has a problem with ambiguity.

In this VUCA world, it's so much easier for leaders to fail or appear to fail. For example, it's easier:

- For us to come across as unpredictable, indecisive, weak, incompetent or lacking integrity when we're repeatedly changing direction in response to volatility

- For people to question our authority or competence if we admit there's uncertainty or say "We just don't know at the moment"

- For others to judge us if we're grappling with the *complexity* of a situation that they think is merely *complicated*

- For us and the people we lead to doubt our ability to overcome an obstacle when even the nature of that obstacle remains ambiguous

It's little surprise then that the Corporate Research Forum cites the ability to deal with VUCA-style problems as key in today's and tomorrow's working world[5].

We need to talk about Cynefin

The difference between 'complicated' and 'complex' situations is summed up well in Dave Snowden's 'Cynefin'[b] framework[6], often used as an alternative to VUCA. Snowden encourages us to try to gauge which of the following categories best describes a given challenge or opportunity and to choose our approach accordingly.

- *Simple / obvious:* the relationship between cause and effect is easy to see and repeat

- *Complicated:* the relationship between cause and effect is less obvious because there's a significant delay or distance between one and the other, but it is discoverable and replicable, so sufficient research will reveal the best way forward

- *Complex:* it is not humanly possible to track the myriad dynamics of cause and effect, so the only way to progress is to experiment and course-correct as things evolve

- *Chaotic:* things are moving so swiftly and with so many moving parts that we need to act immediately to stabilise things and then analyse what happened later

Snowden's model provokes a great deal of useful thinking for us, but we'll focus on two things here. Firstly, the word 'obvious' comes from the Latin *ob viam*, meaning 'in the way of', which is a great way of remembering one of the most important lessons to learn in a VUCA world: if something seems 'obvious' it might be, but it could also be hiding something – i.e. 'in the way of' something – far less obvious (see 'The secret to changing shift patterns').

---

b   Pronounced 'ki-nev-in'. It's a Welsh word often translated as 'place' or 'habitat', but it has far richer connotations than that, referencing the uncertainty, complexity and ambiguity of our environments.

The secret to changing shift patterns

A manager in one of our client organisations treated changing workers' rotas as a simple problem with an obvious solution. He took a mechanistic approach and came up with what looked like a more efficient way of managing people's time according to their stated preferences. On the face of it, the new way of doing things should have been better for everyone.

He hadn't accounted for the complex nature of group formation at work. For example, he'd no idea that the people affected had formed strong social bonds around a board game they played with those who shared the same shift. The new rotas broke up those groups, so they bitterly resisted the change even though it made life easier for each separate individual. This resistance had a significant impact on engagement, efficiency and overall performance.

A second thing Snowden's model highlights is the general lack of differentiation, in business at least, between complex problems and *complicated* ones. The terms are often used interchangeably.

Elective heart surgery is complicated. Doing it well requires deep, continually updated expertise. It's done by a team of people who have fixed, clear roles and behave pretty predictably. They, and the patient's body, are following a set of rules codified via the collective wisdom of the medical profession. These rules might change over time, but they do so in an orderly fashion based on new information that is rigorously examined before it becomes canon. As long as you recruit, train and retain a team of experts your patients will be in safe hands.

By way of contrast, deciding how to respond to the sudden explosion in obesity-linked circulatory disorders is a complex challenge. As individuals and societies we find ourselves unsure who should even own the challenge, let alone how to fix it. Should primary responsibility fall on our health services? Or on our national or local Government? Our schools? Supermarkets? Communities? People's families and friends? Individuals themselves? And who in this interconnected system has enough 'control' to solve this issue? Indeed, who has sufficient will to tackle the social taboos of healthcare rationing; the rights and responsibilities of individuals versus corporates when it comes to health and nutrition; the existence of 'food deserts' in certain areas? There are so many interacting variables, stakeholders and causal links that it's difficult to know where to start and the most obvious courses of action often produce further problems.

In case you still need convincing

You might have a preference for VUCA or Snowden's Cynefin framework, or something else. You might be exercising your Sense-making capacity already by weaving those frameworks together. Either way, the more VUCA / complex the world around you, the more you'll depend on the four meaning-making capacities at the heart of this book and the more you'll benefit from upgrading to the next level.

The evidence is pretty compelling. DDI[7], a global HR consulting firm, found that organisations with 'VUCA-ready' leaders outperform their competition threefold.

Harvard luminaries Robert Kegan and Lisa Laskow Lahey provide a number of other studies with similar findings[8]. By way of example, one focused on the CEOs and middle-managers of 21 large, industry-leading companies with revenues averaging US$5 billion per year. Those who'd essentially developed our four capacities

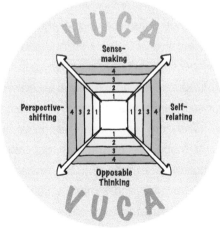

to a 'higher level' were rated more effective in independent performance assessments. They challenged the status quo more effectively. They were better at solving complex problems and they were more able to inspire, empower, successfully delegate and build relationships with others[9]. Similarly, Kegan and Lahey offer case studies of three very successful companies that put their success down to their ability to embed what are essentially 'higher level' practices into *everyone's* day-to-day activities[10].

If we focus on each of the four capacities in turn, Sense-making is a foundation stone for 'contextual intelligence'[11] and what DDI calls 'leadership agility'[12] – both cited as critical to success in VUCA environments[13]. It's worrying then that DDI found that leadership agility is high in only 18% of leaders[14]. After all, it's often Sense-making that tells us that the problem we're facing is more complex or VUCA than we initially assumed – without it, we risk assuming things are far simpler than they actually are and thus massively underestimating what we're dealing with. It's Sense-making, too, that enables us to play out numerous possible futures in parallel as a means of responding to uncertainty[15] – an activity that quickly overwhelms us if we've yet to develop this capacity to a high enough level.

DDI's research[16] also places particular emphasis on communication and the ability to see things from different perspectives. The more uncertain, complex and ambiguous a situation is, the more important it's going to be to put ourselves in the shoes of the various different stakeholders so we get a 360° view of the 'field' we're playing on. Doing so relies on Perspective-shifting. As we develop that capacity, we're increasingly able to lift ourselves above that field so we can examine and weave together those different viewpoints ever more comprehensively and insightfully.

The data we've seen[17] and our own experience in the field suggest a lot of people struggle to consistently deliver what we call Level 2 Perspective-shifting. Far too few are operating at Level 3 and beyond. While Levels 1 and 2 might suffice in a fairly simple, stable environment, there's a strong argument for leaders and their people upgrading their individual and collective capacity for Perspective-shifting if they're to meet the challenges of an increasingly VUCA world.

If there's one capacity that gets less attention from most people than the other three, it's Self-relating. However, it *is* getting a lot of attention from some really big hitters in the fields of psychology and leadership development. Nobel prize-winner Daniel Kahneman[18] shows us how illogical our decisions are when we're working on automatic pilot, letting our subconscious and unconscious take the lead. Steve Peters[19], a medic and coach to elite athletes, shows how our 'inner chimp' derails our best intentions and sabotages our relationships with others. Daniel Goleman[20], the world's leading proponent of emotional intelligence, highlights the need for leaders to get much, much better at actively managing where and how they direct their attention. Psychologist Robert Kegan takes this a step further, showing how – as we develop – we shift from having 'the book of our lives' written for us to taking up the pen for ourselves. More on Kegan later.

Upgrading the four capacities will also make you more resilient

Stress and issues with mental health are typically exacerbated by five factors that respond particularly well to an upgrade:

- *Cognitive overload:* when the complexity of the situation surpasses our existing capacity for Sense-making

- *Mind-reading:* the result of sub-optimal Perspective-shifting

- *Catastrophising:* failing to use Self-relating to notice and address negative thought patterns, or Perspective-shifting to look at other possible interpretations of the situation

- *Black-or-white thinking:* a failure to engage higher level Opposable Thinking

- *Unrealistic expectations of ourselves and others:* the rigid adherence to stereotypical 'musts' and 'shoulds' that has its origins in under-developed Self-relating

The 'perfect storm' of volatility, uncertainty, complexity and ambiguity can lead to confusion, frustration, stress and misery. Each of us can handle different amounts of that cocktail, but eventually any of us could drink too much and suffer the consequences. Our capacity for Self-relating determines our ability to monitor and manage how much VUCA we're consuming and how we're responding to it. For instance, when we're under pressure, Self-relating helps us notice when:

- We're acting as though the situation is less (or more) VUCA than it actually is

- We're overcompensating by trying to control everything, which generally makes things worse

- We're failing to access the other three capacities as effectively as we usually do, which is limiting the contribution we're making across the board

Finally, where Opposable Thinking is concerned, a Heidrick & Struggles CEO Report[21] notes that the ability to work within a series of leadership dilemmas is now seen as a core requirement for CEOs. They – like many of us – are increasingly called on to establish direction when there's no 'one right way'. More and more, these CEOs and their people find themselves navigating the opposing needs, agendas and world views of multiple stakeholders.

The more volatility, uncertainty, complexity and ambiguity we face, the more likely it is that people will form wildly different interpretations of the situation. From this spring disagreements, disputes and even outright conflict. Leaders, teams and organisations that develop their capacity for Opposable Thinking are better than those that don't when it comes to surfacing, understanding and finding value in conflicting views. They're better at taking what appears to be a dilemma and using it to shape a way forward that is better than anything either faction could have come up with on their own.

Doesn't this just mean
we need *cleverer* leaders?

The more *complicated* the problem, the greater the contribution your IQ will make to solving it. Even then, though, your interpersonal and intrapersonal capacities will play a mediating role. A team of highly intelligent experts tackling a complicated problem will often underperform if they're below par when it comes to Perspective-shifting, Self-relating and Opposable Thinking. They simply won't collaborate effectively, so they'll be less than the sum of their parts.

Even the judgement of an individual working in isolation is affected by their physiological and emotional state at the time – remember, for instance, the last time you made a poor decision because you were ill, stressed or over-tired.

When we're faced with situations that are VUCA, not just complicated, those challenges are amplified. We're required to do a whole load of things that require so much more than a high IQ. For example:

- Understanding the cognitive and emotional constraints faced by the people dealing with the problem

- Gauging the extent to which the problem takes us beyond our current skills, knowledge and ways of thinking

- Challenging our assumptions and questioning our understanding of the situation, the system, even the way the world works.

We do still need leaders who are good at understanding and describing their organisation's context, establishing direction and setting objectives, securing people's commitment and holding them to account. We do still need leaders who ensure their people, teams and organisations have access to the knowledge, skills and resources required to get the job done. We do still need leaders who act as custodians of their organisations' cultures and values.

However, we need leaders who can do those things in a VUCA world, not just one that's relatively stable, certain, simple and clear. We need leaders who can differentiate the challenges that *are* VUCA from the ones that aren't, then adapt and learn accordingly. People who can 'nudge' the system through constant, incremental changes rather than labouring under the illusion that they can measure the current state of the system, define the ideal future state, then create a reliable roadmap for the journey from one to the other.

We need leaders who can communicate simply enough about the complexities of their business environments for their people to take action. We also need them to know when they're oversimplifying. If they don't, their people will lack sufficient understanding to make good autonomous decisions when things don't go as planned.

It's this extra layer of VUCA-driven needs and expectations that lies behind our clients coming to us saying:

**"We know our leadership capability framework
is no longer helping us find and develop the people,
qualities and skills we need in order to succeed.
How can we ensure our leaders have what it takes
to cope with this new world?"**

The four capacities at the heart of this book are one response to that question. It's a response we and the people and organisations we work with are finding increasingly compelling. We're hoping the four capacities will prove as useful to you as they are to the rest of us.

So this is another call for better people skills?

Recent years have seen an upsurge in calls for leaders to develop their 'softer skills', including being more compassionate, authentic and socially responsible. On the face of it, those are quantitative changes: requests for an increase in things all of us have within us to some degree. What we're talking about in this book, with these levels, is a *qualitative* shift – a true upgrade, not just an increase.

Putting aside authentic and responsible leadership for now, let's focus on compassion. What we're certainly *not* saying is that people operating at lower levels in these capacities lack compassion. Many show intense degrees of empathy and sympathy for other people. However, when we've yet to develop these capacities to their potential, our compassion often operates like a laser beam – highly focused on certain kinds of people, usually those we perceive victims or underdogs. The more we upgrade our Perspective-shifting and Opposable Thinking, the greater the breadth and variety of people with whom we're able to empathise. We're more likely to have compassion for people who are very, very different from us, live very different lives in very different places and even in different times from us – even people who have very different values from ours. This enables us to empathise and sympathise with people who are no longer around but seem to be carrying the blame for 'causing' our current difficulties. Similarly, we start to care more for people who've yet to join our teams or organisations – even those who've yet to be born – who will suffer or thrive as a result of the decisions and actions we take today.

Having compassion requires us to manage our own biases. Not only that, but it's an exhaustible resource for most of us, meaning we need to manage and replenish the energy required to maintain compassion over time and under pressure. Plus many would argue that we need to show ourselves compassion if we're to thrive and be able to help others do the same. Thus compassion relies heavily on our capacity for Self-relating.

What if my world's really not that 'VUCA'?

Maybe you're right. Maybe your world *is* entirely 'SCSC' – stable, certain, simple and clear[22]. If it is, then upgrading the four capacities will still give you an unfair advantage but it'll not be as critical to your survival.

However, it may be that your world is a little more VUCA than you realise. Perhaps it seems pretty stable but there are complexities and ambiguities lurking beneath the surface, undiscovered or undiscussed. Perhaps your day-to-day is mostly 'SCSC' but is punctuated by periods of heightened volatility, uncertainty, complexity or ambiguity, such as those in the image below.

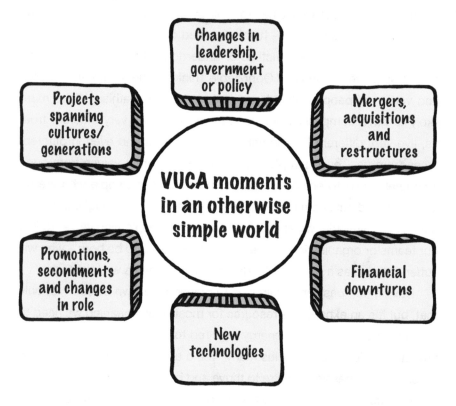

Most people's worlds have that sense of being SCSC most of the time, with periods of lumpiness and challenge. If that's you, then this book will help you prepare for and manage those VUCA periods. You'll also find that life, in general, gets easier.

You'll also be better equipped to deal with evolution of people's attitudes to leadership and the world of work. It's happening at different speeds in different cultures and organisations, but we have less faith in the leaders around us than people did in the past – whether those leaders are running our corporations, governments, public services or even charities. Since the 1990s, there's been growing scepticism regarding our traditional model of organisational leadership: a hierarchical pyramid of heroes who establish both the direction we head in and the pace at which we progress. It's a model that sees organisations and their people as machines, a metaphor that drove previous industrial revolutions in which work was increasingly standardised, compartmentalised and ultimately automated. It's a model that has its roots in the formal hierarchies of the earliest large organisations – the civil services and armed forces of stable countries dating back more than 2000 years to early China, Egypt and beyond.

It's a model that served humanity relatively well[c] in a world that was relatively steady, certain, simple and clear. Hence, it's not surprising that it's a model to which the vast majority of large, long-established businesses and public-sector organisations still adhere. The disruptors are doing things differently. New entrants are experimenting with new structures and entirely new paradigms. Iterative and experimental strategy development, self-organising teams, some versions of Agile thinking, scrum delivery and design-thinking processes are all nibbling away at the traditional linear 'vision, strategy, plan, implementation' model for getting stuff done. The need to get better and faster at scanning the horizon, innovating, pleasing customers and saving lives is driving all sorts of new ways of doing things – and not just at the margins.

---

c   We say 'relatively' because it could be argued that one of the model's weaknesses is that it doesn't serve all parties equally well. How could humanity have made the model work better? Perhaps by using our four capacities more effectively, or at the very least being better at Perspective-shifting and Opposable Thinking!

Perhaps – if it currently feels pretty stable, certain, simple and clear – your world will stay that way for the rest of your working life. Or, perhaps, your world is living on borrowed time.

I'm not really a leader. Is this book for me?

Probably, yes. When we talk about leadership in this book, we're talking about the activity of leading, which doesn't necessarily come with a position of formal authority. You might not have a team of people who've been placed 'under your command' for a number of months or years. You might be leading an Agile team formed for a matter of weeks or have found yourself stepping up to lead a group of peers who've tacitly nudged you into that position without anyone really mentioning it. You might be managing people in a matrix who also report into other leaders elsewhere in the organisation.

You'll also find that much of this book applies equally to people who aren't leading at all. It's a sad reality for authors, though, that if you're asked whom your book is for, it's generally unacceptable to reply 'anyone'!

What if I'm a practitioner working in HR or Learning & Development?

If you are a talent developer, learning and development professional, coach or facilitator, you may also be asking if this book is for you. You also know full well that it is much easier to take other people down a road you have already travelled. So, you can read this book in one of two ways:

1. As a 'diagnostic guide' and 'practice handbook' to help you work out where your colleagues and clients are in their development, then tailor your interventions more closely to their needs

2. Focusing on your own development first, getting to grips with the ideas, assessing yourself and trying out the relevant practices for the upgrade(s) you're looking to make

We highly recommend the latter. Take that route and you'll develop a much clearer understanding of the joys and frustrations of working with, and breaking through, your own meaning making.

Whichever approach you try, you will see that we've done our very best to bring some complex theories within the grasp of lay managers. You'll also find the practices a rich source of inspiration even if you ultimately decide the world of 'vertical development' is not for you.

So what's next?

In the next two chapters, we'll look at what it means to 'upgrade' in these capacities and how best to use this book to support you in doing so.

After that, we'll dig deeper into each capacity and its four levels of development. We'll briefly name-check the people whose research we've leaned on most for that capacity, then bring it to life using case studies and help you link what you're reading to the reality of your own day-to-day. We'll help you work out which of the four levels in that capacity best represents your (and colleagues') current ways of working. Then we'll offer a collection of practices to help you upgrade to the next level. Finally, we'll offer advice on using those practices to help others effect an upgrade of their own – whether you're a leader, a Learning and Development professional, or both.

Summary

The world feels messier and more tightly intertwined than ever. Increasingly, surviving and thriving requires us to lean on and develop four 'meaning-making' capacities:

- **Sense-making**   observing, understanding and processing the complexity of a situation – e.g. getting your head around all the different interconnected topics, data, issues or causal relationships

- **Perspective-shifting**   'zooming out' to benefit from a more realistic and multi-faceted understanding of a situation or relationship – e.g. understanding the perspectives and agendas of the various stakeholders

- **Self-relating**   observing, understanding, regulating and transforming yourself – e.g. making sense of your own reactions, thoughts and feelings

- **Opposable Thinking**   responding to the dilemmas and conflicting ideas that can create tensions within us and / or between us and other people – e.g. working with opposing views

We'll be focusing on four levels of development in each of those four capacities. You'll work out your 4 x 4 'capacity profile', then we'll show you how to upgrade to the next level in each, should you wish to do so.

● ● ●

2

What does an 'upgrade' really mean?

● ● ●

- The essential upgrades we know you've already made
- The kinds of things that trigger an upgrade
- How you can tell if you've already started
- Where these four levels come from
- How they differ from what's come before

YOU'VE PROBABLY NOTICED that babies and tod-dlers think they can

hide from you simply by covering their eyes. To an adult, it's a ludicrous notion. To the child it's utterly logical and as effective as a fully-fledged game of 'hide and seek'.

Why is this?

It's because they have no idea that other people see the world from a different perspective. They have no concept that other people's thoughts and feelings are separate from their own. So their underlying – entirely unconscious – assumption is that

> "Faced with the choice between changing one's mind and proving that there is no need to do so, almost everyone gets busy on the proof."

John Kenneth Galbraith, economist and diplomat[23]

whatever happens to them also happens to you. If they can't see, you can't see.

At some point in their development, the penny drops. The game is over and a new game begins. In this new game, you stand at one end of the kitchen table and the child you're experimenting on[a] stands at the other. You give the child an easel, or maybe just a piece of paper. Then you place three items on the table between you – in this case, an apple, a bowl and a coffee mug.

Then you ask the child to draw what they think *you are* seeing. They're not allowed to move to your end of the table, or even up the sides. They have to imagine what you're seeing and draw it.

There's a certain age at which they can only draw what *they* are seeing and a certain age at which they can draw what *you* are seeing. The age at which the flip happens varies from child to child, just like with that earlier game of 'hide and seek', but once they've got that capacity for Perspective-shifting it is available to them whenever they choose to switch it on.

---

a   Okay, you might not be a psychologist and the child might not have given written consent, but it's still an experiment.

The levels we're talking about with these four meaning-making capacities work in exactly the same way. Once you get it, you get it. Once you bed-in a specific level through practice, it'll always be there for you. You might not use it all of the time. You might forget to switch it on even when it would be helpful, but it's there.

By the same token, when you're operating at one level, the next one up might be on your radar but feel a little bit slippery, like a bar of soap you're trying to get hold of. You're probably moving toward it of your own accord. If you are, it'll be because you've been finding that your old ways of thinking and operating aren't quite cutting it and you're trying to up your game. The levels beyond that next level, though... they'll feel increasingly alien.

This is not a metaphor; this is your reality

When we liken your progression through these levels to those stages of child development, we're not using an analogy or a metaphor to make a point. These levels are *actual psychological stages of development*. They're as real and observable as the ones we went through as kids. The two transitions we described above are the earliest stages of development when it comes to our capacity for Perspective-shifting. They sit *below* the levels we're talking about in this book.

It's the same for the other three capacities: the four levels of adult development we're focusing on in relation to each capacity are four slices of a developmental continuum. In any given capacity, most people in organisations – and most people who'd pick up a book like this – will have reached Level 1 already. Many will have reached Level 2. Fewer will have reached Level 3 and hardly any will be at Level 4 in any of the capacities, let alone all of them. Very, very few people ever go beyond Level 4. So, while we might occasionally allude to what constitutes Level 5 and so on, it's not territory we're intending to cover in this book.

Where did this idea of a developmental continuum come from? It has its roots in child psychology but its more recent advances come from the field of 'adult constructivist development', which also draws on a range of other disciplines, including sociology, anthropology and psychotherapy. As you might expect, this diversity has created a fair amount of debate when it comes to the finer details. However, they all agree that adults' development, like children's, happens continuously but is punctuated by a consistent, seemingly universal set of plateaus. These plateaus are separated by periods of transition which are like gates that we pass through – sometimes turbulently, sometimes slowly and calmly. Each gate takes us to the next level of development.

What is it that makes the sequence of those gates – those upgrades – so universal and non-negotiable? It's that each upgrade builds on the foundations laid by the last. Not only that, but the *reasons* for upgrading to the next level are rooted in the limitations baked into whichever one we're currently at. Our motivation to upgrade comes from our direct, often visceral experiences of the shortcomings of our existing ways of thinking, feeling and interacting with the world around us. Common examples include finding or worrying that:

1. Your technical expertise doesn't produce the right answer as often as it used to

2. You can't manage the complexity or volume of your work as well as you need to (or as well as someone else seems to)

3. You've missed a critical factor when making an important decision

4. You're plateauing in your career or being leap-frogged by people who were once your juniors

5. You're locked in a pattern of behaviours that are reducing your effectiveness, happiness or ability to fulfil important responsibilities, including those outside of work

It's these kinds of experiences that prompt some leaders to make step changes in the way they do things. Of course, these upgrades are much more organic than the updates we do to our phones. They're slower, more evolutionary transitions – not sudden shifts overnight. At the same time, there's no 'restore point'. Once you've started to see yourself, the world and the people around you entirely differently, there's no putting the genie back in the bottle.

As a leader's role evolves, so too must the leader

One way of looking at these upgrades is to liken them to the transitions demanded of leaders as they progress in their careers. Peter Hawkins, Professor of Leadership at Henley Business School, offers a helpful prescription for this evolution (see below)[24].

Hawkins' transitions aren't a perfect match for the upgrades in the four capacities we're focusing on, but they are indicative.

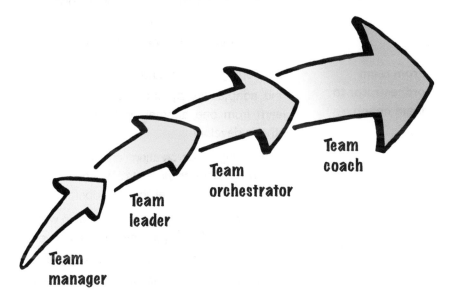

From team manager to team leader	• Less focus on managing all of the details and component parts
	• Greater focus on establishing an overarching direction that serves the collective goals of the organisation
	• Ensuring all team members understand how their individual goals and inputs support that overarching goal
From team leader to team orchestrator	• Helping team members adopt a joined-up approach to connecting with each other and with stakeholders beyond the team
	• Helping team members establish a direction of travel that is informed by their own needs and aspirations as well as those of their stakeholders and the organisation as a whole
	• Fostering trust among team members and encouraging them to take responsibility for resolving interpersonal and inter-departmental issues without their leader intervening
From team orchestrator to team coach	• Developing individual and collective resilience and adaptability by encouraging people to learn from one another and support each other's development
	• Establishing / co-creating an over-arching framework that sets the limits of freedom within which each person is at liberty to operate
	• Encouraging the team to create its own ways of working and manage itself within that over-arching framework so it is increasingly able to sustain itself as a unit without the leader's intervention[b]

You'll have a sense of where you currently fall where Hawkins' transitions are concerned. It'll serve you well as you assess the level at which you're operating in each of the four capacities.

You might also be wondering whether this means there's a correlation between people's progression through the four levels in our capacities and their progression up the organisational hierarchy. Sadly not. It's the same with Hawkins' transitions. The more senior we get, the more complex our roles become and the more important it becomes to upgrade. However, too few organisations have developed the tools to assess these capacities and help their leaders develop them. Thus, it's often the case that leaders find themselves heading up teams that include people who are operating at a higher level than them in one or more capacities. How they manage that is itself a test of their character and ability as leaders.

What's new in the 'levels' we're talking about in this book?

We've a huge amount of respect for those who laid the foundations on which we're building and it would be wrong not to name-check them here (see 'Credit where credit is due', below). Their ideas have all played a significant role and this book wouldn't exist without them.

We are building on the work they've done in a number of ways. For starters, we're translating some pretty abstract, esoteric literature into something that's easier to grasp. We've also sought to ground the research and its concepts in concrete examples and your own day-to-day experience. On top of that, by condensing an abundance of diverse ideas into a set of four separate capacities, we're creating a more manageable 'curriculum' for developing yourself and others.

---

b   Hawkins doesn't include those last two bullets in his description of the transition from team orchestrator to team coach. They're our take on his framework, based on his other work, discussions with him and some of the things we've seen leaders do once they've reached Levels 3 and 4 in our four capacities.

Credit where credit is due

Here's to the pioneers whose work informed our understanding of what it means to develop these four capacities:

Psychologist Jane Loevinger[25] opened the door to much of this with her ground-breaking work into universal stages of whole-person development (our term, not hers). Her ideas were subsequently adapted and refined by other leading lights like Susanne Cook-Greuter[26] and Terri O'Fallon[27] and then taken into a more organisational context by Bill Torbert and David Rooke[28], and Bill Joiner[29].

The following writers and researchers have been particularly influential when it comes to the development of the four individual capacities:

- **Sense-making:**   Elliot Jaques[30] and Katherine Cason[31]

- **Perspective-shifting:** Susanne Cook-Greuter[32] and
                            Terri O'Fallon[33]

- **Self-relating:**   Robert Kegan[34] and Jennifer
                            Garvey-Berger[35]

- **Opposable Thinking:**   Otto Laske[36] and Roger Martin[37]

Theirs were the most coherent, comprehensive and helpful contributions when Karen was first scouring the relevant literature. Some also had a role to play in the development of more than one capacity. They're far from the only influences, though: we're extremely grateful to a host of other people, many of whom one or both of us knows personally. So, naturally, we'll credit their contributions as we go.

We're also attempting to make it far easier for you to move deliberately from one level to the next in each capacity. The vast majority of leaders and practitioners who've encountered these ideas in the existing literature have found them incredibly insightful and thought-provoking. They've seen a world of potential open up before them, but been left wondering

'Now what?' They've been disappointed by the lack of clear answers and have moved on in search of something else.

Why is it they're struggling to work out what to *do* with those great insights? We think it's because, despite how insightful and complex much of the literature is, in one important way it can prevent us from seeing the trees for the wood![c]

We believe people find it hard to work out how to apply what they've learned about these models of adult development because the existing frameworks suggest that our *entire* operating system is upgraded in one go as we move from one OS to the next. They suggest we progress through specific and total 'stages' of meaning making or 'forms of mind', and these stages cannot be broken down further in any useful way.

For instance, according to two popular frameworks[38], at one point in your life you'll operate as an 'Expert' and sometime later you'll become an 'Achiever'. Given the right conditions, you'll eventually move through a stage one framework calls 'Individualist' and the other calls 'Redefining'. Then it's on to 'Strategist' (aka 'Transforming')[d].

The authors of those frameworks and others like them do appreciate that this is an oversimplification. They know that we evolve gradually, rather than waking up one day thinking entirely differently about the world. They also know that each of us develops aspects of ourselves at different rates – just as a child's physical, cognitive and interpersonal capabilities progress at different speeds. What's missing is a language for discussing those different aspects of ourselves in more depth – the language we're offering by introducing these four meaning-making capacities.

In our view, unless we separate out the four capacities, we're left with the developmental equivalent of a single measure of fitness. The

---

c   Yes, we did get that the right way around!

d   'Expert', 'Achiever', 'Individualist' and 'Strategist' are labels used by The Leadership Development Framework, referenced in Chapter 16. The Global Leadership Profile differs on the latter two labels, but does use Expert and Achiever. The GLP is also referenced in Chapter 16.

capacities offer the equivalent of a distinction between different kinds of fitness such as strength, speed, endurance and flexibility[39].

Imagine you visit a gym, hoping to get fitter. They run some tests and give you a single 'fitness score'. It's pretty motivating and you try out some of the machines knowing it's probably good for you. Now imagine going to a gym that gives you scores for strength, speed, endurance and flexibility. You're instantly better off because it helps you choose where to focus your training for optimal results.

Now imagine that same gym gives you a set of exercises to choose from, each tailored to one of those different kinds of fitness and each calibrated to your level of fitness in each of the four areas.

You're imagining the equivalent of this book.

If children upgrade naturally, why do I need to do it deliberately?

It's a fair challenge. While adults typically develop more slowly than children, we know that our brains show what is called 'plasticity' – we can continue to extend our mental capacities well into middle age and even the later years of our lives. Given the right conditions, you could well progress through the various levels in each of the capacities with no input at all from us or this book. After all, people have been progressing through these levels and harnessing these capacities for centuries.

There are, however, a number of reasons to consider taking a more proactive approach to your development. For example:

- Children take *years* to upgrade from one level to the next. Adults are typically slower to adapt, learn and change their habits and mind-sets. Is the world in which you live and work prepared to wait for you to evolve?

- We upgraded our childhood OSs out of necessity, to survive physically and socially. As adults, we tend to treat our existing operating system as the finished article. We respond to the challenges life throws at us by working harder, adding apps, finding workarounds and accruing the human equivalent of an exponential technology debt[40]. Is it wise to wait until that system fails completely before investing in the next upgrade?

- Whether or not they have access to formal schooling, children's development generally happens in a context that's geared towards them developing. They're expected to progress through the various stages of development at a certain pace and there are people around them, intentionally or accidentally, helping them do so[e]. To what extent does your context encourage and support your development?

- Many organisational norms and assessments assume that the peak of development is what we call 'Level 2' here – because many of the people who define the criteria for assessment are at Level 2 themselves. The more developed approaches to Sense-making, Perspective-shifting, Self-relating and Opposable Thinking are invisible within the vast majority of competency frameworks and executive training programmes. People who operate at higher levels in those capacities are just seen as more 'talented', 'mature' or having 'more potential' in some undefinable way. So, if you want to upgrade in this way at work, it's statistically unlikely that your organisational processes are designed to help you directly.

This book is designed to provide you with some of the support that might be missing – some 'scaffolding' or 'trellising'[41] you can lean on as you progress from one level to the next.

Some of that support comes in the form of the collection of practices we'll offer to help you upgrade. We'll also help you spot the 'snags, crashes and whirlpools' that can hold you back.

In the next chapter, we'll tell you where in the book to find the resources that you, specifically, need. We'll also make some suggestions as to how best to use this book and how to make the learning stick. First though, we need to answer two further questions many people have at this point.

---

e   We learn much of what we learn through observing others, rather than from what they tell us. So it's not just the formal teachers that teach us. It's the positive and negative role models in our lives.

Aren't these capacities / levels just another way of looking at personality?

No. Your capacities for Sensing-making, Perspective-shifting, Self-relating and Opposable Thinking are different from the preferences, traits, inclinations and so on that make up your personality.

Each level is a developmental step forward in your use of that capacity, an upgrade to your operating system that offers you more sophisticated ways of understanding and responding to the world around you and the people in it – including yourself.

Your personality will influence:

- The way you use the four capacities

- The way you develop these capacities

- The nature of the snags, crashes and whirlpools that are most likely to get in your way

Perhaps most importantly of all: all of the levels are open to people with any kind of personality.

If you're keen to explore this further, you'll find more on the topic in Appendix 3.

Is it always better to be operating at the next level up?

Psychologists Keith Eigel and Karl Kuhnert[42] equate progress to the next level with an artist adding another colour to his or her palette. The more colours you have on your palette – the more you progress through these levels in a given capacity – the more complete a picture you can paint of the world around you. You don't necessarily need every colour on the palette for every situation, but the more complex that world becomes the more colours you'll want at your disposal.

We agree with Eigel and Kuhnert that it is possible for "a concrete, dogmatic, egocentric person" to be *more* effective in some contexts and with some types of people[43]. However, if that way of operating is the only one that person has available to them – the only colour on their palette – then they're being driven by unconscious habit, not making conscious choices. They'll be far less adaptable and effective across a range of contexts than someone who has the ability to stick tightly to their own agenda, but *also* has the ability to see things from others' points of view and adapt their approach accordingly. Both of these people will be less effective than someone who also has the ability to read the situation, see further into the future and make a well-informed decision as to which of those two approaches will prove most effective in any given situation.

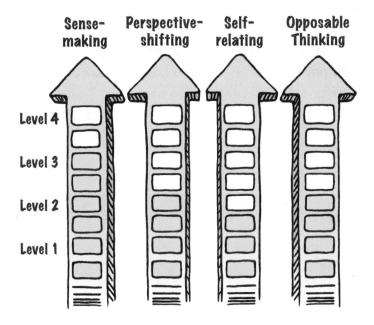

It can help to think of your profile across the four capacities like a graphic equaliser. You can dial each capacity up or down depending on the needs / complexity of the situation. However, you can only dial it *up* to the level you've reached in your own development. Thus the more you progress through the various levels, the more *range* you have open to you.

Summary

You've already upgraded multiple times in your life. As a child you went through several, commonly accepted stages of development physically, mentally and in your social skills. That development will have brought you to the first of the four levels we're focusing on in this book – the four levels at which most people in organisations are operating. In subsequent chapters, you'll assess the level at which you're currently operating. The majority of people reach Levels 1 and 2. Fewer reach Level 3 without some form of focused development. Very few make it past Level 4.

The four levels are rooted in the literature of 'adult constructivist development', which many people find too theoretical and struggle to turn to practical use. Hence this book is intended to be as accessible and immediately useful as possible.

• ● •

How best to use this book

- How the book is structured
- Where to go to get what you're looking for
- How best to turn your reading into actual learning

WE'VE FOCUSED ON making it as easy as possible for you to extract maximum value from this book. That includes bearing in mind that you could be approaching it from any one of the four levels in each of the four capacities, each of which will influence what you want from the book, how you'd like it presented and what you're willing to invest in your own development.

As you can see from the image overleaf, you're already in the final chapter of Part 1. We recommend reading Parts 2 and 3 in the order they're written, whatever your reasons for being here. However, there is an alternative approach, which we'll come to in a moment.

> "You'll never plough a field by turning it over in your mind."
>
> Proverb[44]

Part 2 takes each of the capacities in turn, using case studies to demonstrate what each of the four levels looks like and what it means to upgrade from one to the next. Each chapter ends with a summary and some 'indicators' to help you assess your own and others' current level within that capacity. There's a place to mark the level at which you think you're currently operating in each capacity. If you prefer, though, you can download a printable 'capacity profile sheet' from www.leaderspace.com/upgrade-resources, which you can then fold into the book. You'll find a range of other resources there, too.

Part 3 helps you stop and take stock. We'll provide a quick summary of the upgrades between each of the four levels within each of the four capacities – an easy reference guide you can come back to whenever you

like, which is repeated for ease of access in the Appendices at the back of the book. You'll decide where you believe you currently are and we'll help you look at your team through this lens as well. We'll share some of the things that can delay your development or drag you back to levels you thought you'd left behind. Then you'll decide what to do next.

The way you use Part 4 will depend on your self-assessment decisions at the end of Part 3. It's here that you'll find a set of practices for each upgrade in each capacity. We've called them 'practices' because they're intended not as one-off exercises, but as a means of bedding in new habits that'll serve you well in times of need. Our intention is for you to simply pick and use the practices for the upgrade(s) you want to make. Thus, at this point, you'll personally use at most a third of the content of

Part 4, perhaps less than 20%. The rest you'll find useful when you're ready for the next upgrade or seeking practices to help other people work on building these capacities.

You might feel inclined to let the learning from Parts 1 to 3 bed-in and come back for Part 4 at a later date. We'd caution against that. If you don't engage in at least a couple of practices, you risk taking on these capacities as a theoretical construct but never actually doing anything useful with them.

Alternatively, you might already be itching to get on with an upgrade. You might decide to focus on one of the capacities first, selecting the relevant chapters from Parts 2 and 4. If you take that approach, it's still advisable to read the relevant section of Chapter 8 and attend to the pointers in Chapters 9 and 10 before throwing yourself into the appropriate practices for the capacity you've chosen to tackle first. It's probably not the ideal route, as the capacities are interconnected, but it's a viable one for starters.

Part 5 helps you mine this book for even more. Chapter 15 offers hints and tips for using the practices in Chapters 11-14 to help others upgrade – whether they're colleagues, friends or people you lead. It'd be easy to assume that it's a chapter for professional coaches, trainers and facilitators. However, we've written the whole book to be accessible and useful to *anyone*. Your ability to use the practices to support others in their development will depend far less on any professional training and far more on your desire to be of use to them. Incidentally, that desire generally increases as you move up the levels in each of the four capacities.

The final chapter of the book, Chapter 16, is best read around 3 months after you read Chapter 10. It's a review of your experiences over the intervening weeks, helping you bed-in what you've learned – and what you've helped others learn. Here you'll also find ways to take your learning (and others') to the next level.

So far, we've listed Sense-making as the first capacity, but in Parts 2 and 4, we'll start with Perspective-shifting. That's because most people find it the easiest capacity to grasp and to buy into. Most of us find the hardest thing about leading and working with others is trying to understand them. So it's easy to see the value in upgrading that capacity and to anticipate what that might look like.

There's a natural flow from Perspective-shifting through Self-relating and into Opposable Thinking. Upgrading each of those capacities makes it easier for us to upgrade the next.

Why is Sense-making last? One reason is that the question at the heart of that capacity – 'What on earth is going on here?' – is so much more sophisticated once we've turned on the other three capacities than it would be without them. Thus the use of the four capacities becomes something of a cycle, with each feeding the others (as in the image below).

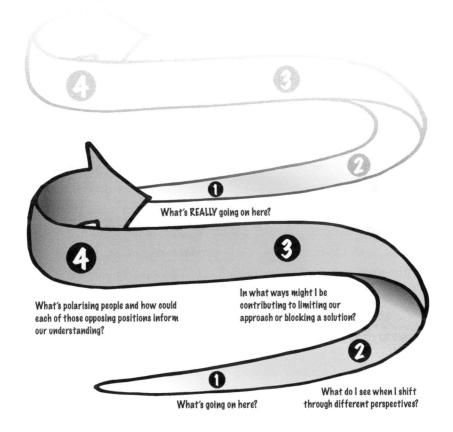

What's REALLY going on here?

4 What's polarising people and how could each of those opposing positions inform our understanding?

3 In what ways might I be contributing to limiting our approach or blocking a solution?

1 What's going on here?

2 What do I see when I shift through different perspectives?

People also tend to overrate their capacity for Sense-making if they self-assess before they've understood, assessed and worked on the other three capacities. Why is that? Well, while it may sound harsh to say it, if you're not that great at Self-relating, you're less likely to see the limitations in your current approach to making sense of the world.

Why didn't we just put Sense-making last when we first introduced the four capacities? Because the question 'What on earth is going on here?' is generally where all of us begin when entering a new situation. So it's a good entry point when first meeting the four capacities.

Can we really separate these capacities out and work on them in isolation?

Yes. The human psyche is rich in complexity and we appreciate that people operate as whole beings and everything is interconnected. We also recognise that many situations will call on all four capacities. However, in our practice, we are constantly faced with people who want to know *how* they could work on their development. Addressing the capacities separately helps clarify what each capacity is and isn't. It also helps us give you a focused 'workout' on each that will make it far easier for you to upgrade – should you choose to do so.

You'd follow a similar process if you wanted to upgrade your physical fitness ahead of some major event. You'd focus on different muscle groups in isolation, rather than trying to work on all of them at the same time. You'd separate intense cardiovascular activity from balancing exercises and strength work. Only occasionally would you pull it all together and replicate the conditions you'd be putting yourself through in the event itself.

We also recognise that the four capacities here don't cover the entire domain from which they emerged. They are, though, the most pertinent areas when it comes to responding to VUCA environments.

How does this book relate to Richard's previous books?

If you've read *ARC Leadership* or *The Boss Factor*, you may be wondering how those and the four capacities inter-relate.

ARC Leadership argues that three qualities – Authenticity, Responsibility and Courage – are required of leaders if they, their people and their organisations are to survive and thrive in a complex world. As we move up through the levels in the four capacities at the heart of *this* book, our understanding and experience of those three qualities evolves, as does our ability to manifest each of the three and manage the tensions between them.

People who are familiar with those ARC qualities have told us they've found it helpful to reflect on how their attitudes to and experience of those qualities are likely to evolve as they upgrade in each of the four capacities. We've chosen to keep this current book as focused as possible. So, if you'd like to explore that angle yourself, you'll find a short article on the topic at www.leaderspace.com/upgrade-resources. The article is designed to be as useful to readers with no prior knowledge of *ARC Leadership* as it is to those familiar with ARC.

The '10 lessons in managing up for mutual gain' in *The Boss Factor* draw on the ARC qualities and Richard's Three Core Disciplines for Leadership and Team Performance. We'll not be getting into the Three Core Disciplines in this book, but if you're familiar with them you'll notice them just beneath the surface[a].

The Boss Factor also speaks of 'habits, needs and mind-sets' and was written as the ideas for this current book were coming to the boil. You'll see common threads between *The Boss Factor*'s descriptions of different mind-sets, the notion of an underlying operating system and the levels we're focusing on here.

---

a   We did originally try to place them *on* the surface, but realised that doing so distracted people from the true meat of this book.

Is upgrading myself going to be easy?

No, but you knew that already. We *are* talking about upgrading your underlying operating system here. At certain points in this book, you might find yourself consciously or subconsciously thinking:

- "If I change how I think and do things, I'll lose what it means to be me"

- "I'll risk looking like an amateur again as I try out new ways of working"

- "I'm too busy"

- "I don't like wasting time reflecting on stuff; I just want to get on and do it"

- "It's all just too complicated for me"

Each of those thoughts plays on different fears. The fear that most gets in *your* way will be the one that's most deeply rooted in your current ways of thinking about yourself, other people and the world around you.

Facing any fear takes courage. Courage to pause when the world is rushing past us. Courage to unlearn old lessons and outdated 'truths'. Courage to go beyond applying this book to your own development in order to use it as a catalyst for developing others.

Ultimately, though, you can choose not to opt for an upgrade right now. There may be many good reasons why this feels like the best choice for you. You might already be overloaded or in need of a rest from all the complexity around you. Ironically though, it's at these times when a bit of extra inner capacity can be of most help! So if you do feel too 'full' for an upgrade, perhaps just try one or two of the practices we offer at random, using something that is stressing you as your 'case material'. We pretty much guarantee that the practice on its own will provide some insight and relief. If it does, then you may feel ready to do more.

You also have a right to refuse an upgrade entirely. We'd simply ask that you do so knowing the potential implications for you and the people around you.

Bearing all of that in mind, though, we're here to make upgrading as easy as possible.

How do I make the learning stick?

You'll increase your chances by aligning your approach to what psychology tells us accelerates learning and helps make it stick, the key headlines being:

1. **It's far easier to act your way into new ways of thinking than to think your way into new ways of behaving**

   Hence the practices in Part 4 focus on doing, not theorising or talking about doing

2. **Small, frequent doses are far more effective than large, one-off interventions**

   So we recommend repeating your chosen practices over a period of weeks and months, rather than gorging yourself all in one go

3. **True learning requires a combination of five ingredients: observation, experimentation, repetition, reflection and integration with your existing ways of doing things**

   You'll favour one or two of those ingredients over the rest, but none of us manages meaningful, sustainable development without investing sufficient time in all five

4. **If you're really working on moving from one level to the next, it'll probably trigger a certain amount of anxiety, confusion or frustration**

When that happens, remind yourself that upgrading your operating system takes you further out of your comfort zones than learning about the latest technology or developments in your areas of technical expertise

5. **Whether you're an introvert or extravert, learning with others is more effective than learning alone**

If you read and discuss this book with someone else then, even if you're at entirely different levels in one or more capacity, you'll more than double the value it brings you

6. **It's easier to move when the world around you is moving, too**

Enlist some or all of your immediate team in this work and you'll all be pulling in the same direction, making it easier for all of you to upgrade

7. **Teaching others accelerates our own learning**

Hence Part 5 is as much about bedding-in your own learning as it is about sharing the benefits with others

Finally, and perhaps most importantly: *we learn best when we apply what we're learning to actual, current challenges.*

With that in mind, we recommend you take a moment now to identify and write down two or three current challenges, problems, issues or opportunities that you're facing which have some element of complexity or VUCA to them.

....

....

....

Now, for each of the items you've just identified, make a note (above) of the capacity or capacities that'll be most useful when it comes to making progress:

Sense-making	observing, understanding and processing the complexity of a situation – e.g. getting your head around all the different interconnected topics, data, issues or causal relationships
Perspective-shifting	'zooming out' to benefit from a more realistic and multi-faceted understanding of a situation or relationship – e.g. understanding the perspectives and agendas of the various stakeholders
Self-relating	observing, understanding, regulating and transforming yourself – e.g. making sense of your own reactions, thoughts and feelings
Opposable Thinking	responding to the dilemmas and conflicting ideas that can create tensions within us and / or between us and other people – e.g. working with opposing views

You'll find it useful to bear these challenges in mind as you dig deeper into the relevant capacities in Part 2.

You'll also find you take more from this book if you embrace the various questions we offer throughout. They're an encouragement to pause, reflect and capture your thoughts. You might even use them as the focus for discussion with someone else.

We can't force you to stop and apply what you've read, of course. However, we've seen first-hand the difference it makes when people do. So, frankly, if we *could* force you then maybe we would!

Practices for groups and teams

Our first draft of this book included a number of practices to upgrade the level of discourse in groups and teams when it comes to these four capacities.

Unfortunately, they simply wouldn't fit into this book. So those practices will be available in a 'sequel' focusing on groups and teams. We've already started work on it, so if you'd like to know more, you're very welcome to get in touch.

Summary

We recommend reading Parts 1, 2 and 3 in the order they're written. In doing so, you'll work out your 'capacity profile'. You'll use this to select the appropriate practices to upgrade your chosen capacities – practices you'll find in Part 4. Upgrading won't be easy, but the practices are designed to make it as easy as possible. You'll also find your chosen upgrades are even more efficient, and sustainable, if you follow the hints and tips on page 53.

• ● •

PART 2

•●•

What each of the upgrades looks and feels like

4

Perspective-shifting: getting better at understanding other people's worlds

• ● •

- How we first develop our Perspective-shifting capacity
- More advanced ways of shifting perspective
- What it means to upgrade in this capacity
- Three slices of case study: one for each upgrade

THE INITIAL DEVELOPMENT of Perspective-shifting is the process we

touched on in Chapter 2, when we compared a baby's ability to see the world from your perspective with a toddler's ability and that of an adult.

When we talk about Perspective-shifting at Levels 1 through 4, though, we're talking about the capacity to move between four different *types* of perspective – not just taking the perspectives of different people.

Upgrading this capacity as an adult opens up two whole new ways of looking at the world. At Levels 1 and 3, we're experiencing those new ways of looking at the world as emerging abilities. At Levels 2

> "We judge ourselves by our intentions and others by their behaviours."

Stephen M.R. Covey,
The Speed of Trust[45]

and 4, each of those new ways of looking at the world has become an established way of operating.

Prior to Level 1: the first-person and second-person perspectives

Before we reach Level 1, assuming all goes well with our development as children, we've become increasingly able to see things from another person's point of view. We're able to shift from seeing things from the first-person perspective ('me' in the image below) to a second-person perspective ('you').

As we saw in Chapter 2, young children can't do this until the age of about seven. Even then, it takes time and experience to learn that others' emotions, beliefs, assumptions and expectations often differ from our own, sometimes radically.

 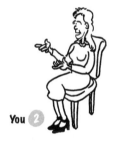

The second-person perspective enables us to understand and relate better to others. This capacity is the foundation of 'adult empathy' – empathy built on an understanding of another individual's world view rather than purely on emotional resonance.

The ability to put ourselves in someone else's shoes – to truly see the world from their perspective – is incredibly valuable. It makes us better at predicting their needs and resulting behaviour – whether they're friends, family members, colleagues, customers, the people we lead, those who lead us, or any other stakeholders. It helps us comprehend, appreciate, influence and motivate them. It helps us understand *why* they've done things that might otherwise seem illogical or malicious, which helps us respond more effectively. Most managers see this ability to take different second-person perspectives as one of the 'entry level' requirements of mature behaviour. Of course, we all fail now and again with people whose values differ wildly from our own or when we are in an emotional state – just think of the last time you had a row with a family member! However, when we're at our best we're perfectly capable of taking that second-person perspective.

Where the description of this capacity comes from

The idea of perspective shifting in all its forms comes originally from Susanne Cook-Greuter's[46] work, based on research by Jane Loevinger. Cook-Greuter was interested in 'the difference that makes the difference' in the later, 'post-conventional' stages of meaning making. This led her to focus on these shifts in perspective as a key process. Her ideas have been taken forward more recently by Terri O'Fallon[47], who was looking to create a more overarching framework to explain the 'why' of development, rather than just the 'what'. While the two authors have their differences, we find both of their approaches helpful and have drawn on both here.

The third-person Observer perspective

By the time we reach Level 1 we've already acquired the first and second person perspectives, enabling us to truly see situations from other people's points of view. What differentiates Level 1 from what came before is the ability to 'step back' from our

ongoing conversations and relationships to see things as if from a third party 'Objective observer' perspective (as shown in the image).

Here we're doing our best to be objective about the relationship and what is happening *between* us. We're lifting ourselves out of the situation at hand and taking a helicopter's eye view of the field beneath us. We're resisting privileging either party's point of view, doing our best to see things without the filters and biases that come with occupying the first- or second-person perspective.

The more able we are to shift to this third-person perspective, the better we generally become at:

- Sorting through people's advice to decide on a course of action

- Securing commitment from others

- Earning people's trust

- Resolving conflicts

- Responding to others' unusual or erratic behaviour

- Negotiating 'win-win' solutions which work for both parties

Once we have a reliable third-person perspective, we can also become good at what's often referred to as 'multiple perspective taking'. That is, we're more able to look at a particular situation through the eyes of, say, seven different people or seven different stakeholder groups – viewing points through which we're able to move at will, enriching our understanding of that situation and the needs of the various stakeholders. This can be highly effective. In understanding this capacity, though, it's important to remember that those seven different viewpoints are seven different *second-person* perspectives. Moving from one of those viewing points to the next isn't the same as moving from first person, to second, to third, and so on.

The ability to adopt the third-person perspective emerges at Level 1, but initially we are only able to take the Observer position when prompted by someone else – such as a coach or trusted colleague. We're also usually only able to do so in retrospect or on reflection. For example, if we ask a friend for some help with a difficult relationship and they suggest we try looking at the situation through the eyes of a bystander or 'outsider'.

At Level 2, we're increasingly able to adopt the third-person Observer perspective in the moment – and switch at will, in the moment, between the first- and second-person perspectives. As a result, we're able to catch potential difficulties or conflicts as they arise. We also become more and more 'neutral' and balanced in our Observer perspective – less prone to the biases and distortions which come from stereotyping, blaming or self-criticism.

The fourth-person, context-aware, Witness perspective

The next step-change in this capacity is when we become able to step back again and simultaneously look at those first three perspectives ('me', 'you' and this 'objective', non-existent Observer).

In this fourth-person perspective, we're aware of the subjective context in which the relationship is playing out. In doing so, we're able to step back and see that our 'Objective Observer' perspective isn't actually objective at all. After all, it is still 'me' looking at the world from *my own* perspective, with all the history, experiences and biases I carry within me. My Observer's view of the world is still filtered through decades of baked-in beliefs, assumptions and expectations. Its 'objectivity' is still, in truth, subjective – and it always will be.

From this fourth-person 'Witness' perspective, we're able to see the dirt, smudges and distortions on (and in) the lenses we (and others) previously trusted to give us an objective, helicopter view of the world. This makes it an invaluable perspective to be able to adopt, whatever the situation. The more complex and ambiguous the situation, though, the more essential this capacity becomes.

At Level 3, our ability to adopt the fourth-person perspective is just emerging. We've realised we need to be far more interested in our own (and other people's) *subjective* experience of our shared world. We've recognised that if we genuinely want to collaborate or negotiate good outcomes for everyone, we can no longer rely on finding an 'objective' right answer, only a 'best fit for all of us'.

At Level 4, the fourth-person perspective becomes more established. We're clear that all readings of a situation are, themselves, context-dependent – shaped by our collective norms, belief systems and ways of making meaning of the world. We're also able to step back and look at things at a global level, becoming much more sensitive to the impact of national cultures, life-experiences and social contexts on our organisational practices and systems.

The third- and fourth-person perspective in action

By way of example, one of us was coaching Claire, a relatively senior manager who was by all accounts very effective when it came to solving complicated problems and managing large projects under considerable pressure.

The coach paused the second coaching session halfway through and asked Claire what she noticed about the nature of the conversation.

It took Claire a while to adopt the third-person Observer perspective required to answer the question.

"I'm jumping around a lot, not focusing," she said, her tone and body language full of disappointment. "I'm wasting time talking in lots of detail about stuff that's actually pretty trivial. We're way behind where I thought we'd be when I sent you the agenda for this session."

"What does that remind you of?" the coach asked. The intention here was to help Claire broaden her third-person Observer perspective in order to see this situation in the context of *other* situations.

Claire really struggled. She needed help to see that the behaviour she was displaying in this session was another example of a pattern she displayed in her day-to-day work and leadership. In fact, it was one of the patterns that had prompted her to seek coaching in the first place.

Once they'd explored that observation, the coach took another tack and asked, "What do you notice about the way you responded to my original question – when I asked what you noticed about the nature of our conversation?"

Here the coach was inviting Claire to move to the fourth-person perspective – requiring Claire to comment on her own supposedly-objective observations of the conversation she'd been having with her coach.

Claire's facial expression said it all: her coach was asking her to adopt a far more complex perspective than she usually took when thinking about her interactions with others.

When the coach helped her access that fourth-person Witness perspective, though, Claire realised she had instantly slipped into looking for what was wrong with the conversation. Not once had she thought to mention (or even look for) the things that were going well in the conversation. Instead, she'd focused on herself as the cause of the 'problem' when in fact there were two people in the conversation. Following her long-established pattern, she realised, she had once again deferred to the coach as the expert and assumed her own responses would be less true and less insightful. Her lack of confidence had clouded her judgement.

What lies beyond the fourth-person perspective?

There are perspectives beyond the fourth-person which take us into ideas about how historical and societal perspective shifts play out and how we can become aware of their effects on our personal meaning making. If you're keen to know more, check out the aforementioned work by Susanne Cook-Greuter[48] and Terri O'Fallon[49].

What it looks like to upgrade this capacity

Claire's conversation with her coach is a snapshot of her in time. To bring the *development* of this capacity to life, we offer the following evolving case study.

From Level 1 to Level 2: stepping out and looking in

Mark is a successful sales rep working for a company that manufactures medical instruments. For the past six months, his relationship with Tina in the accounts department has been growing increasingly tense. Mark's boss Anna has been hoping he'll resolve the issue but has decided that's unlikely to happen without some kind of intervention. So she asks Mark about it over coffee.

Anna: "What do you think it's going to take to make some progress with Tina?"	Anna's question is deliberately open. She's testing whether Mark is willing to consider his own part in this issue or will try to lay the blame on Tina.

Mark, shaking his head: "She's going to need to understand that penalising my clients for late payments is going to push them away – straight to our competitors."	Mark immediately jumps to his view of what Tina is doing 'wrong' – a first-person perspective of her behaviour. He may or may not be correct in his assessment.
Mark, continuing: "It's typical Finance, really: just chasing the cash, not worrying about the relationship with the client or thinking about the need to invest for the longer term."	Here Mark makes generalisations and leans on stereotypes, which is quite common at Level 1. We all do it from time to time, of course, but it becomes increasingly less likely at Level 2 and beyond.
Anna: "I can understand why that would worry you. I know Kirsten and Rakesh have the same problem with some of their clients, too. How's Tina's relationship with them?"	Anna is trying to get Mark to adopt the third-person Observer perspective to compare his relationship with Tina with other people's relationships with her. Kirsten and Rakesh are two of his three peers in the sales team. The fourth is Geoff.
Mark: "She seems fine with them, particularly Kirsten."	
Anna: "Why do you think that is?"	

Mark, after a sigh and long pause. "I hate to play the gender card, Anna, but they are both women."	Mark is reluctant to consider more nuanced reasons for Kirsten and Tina's better relationship and again falls back into a stereotyping response. Rather than looking for clues in how Tina or Kirsten handle the relationship, he assumes it is a simple biological factor that makes them get on better.
Anna: "I guess that common ground might help. You said Rakesh has a good relationship with her, though. What's his secret?"	Anna shows she's open to gender being a factor but is curious about other factors, too.
Mark: "I don't know. They just seem to get on. She even agreed to extend the payment terms with WelCare."	WelCare is Rakesh's largest client. This statement shows Mark is adopting neither the third-person Observer position nor the second-person perspective. In second-person, he'd imagine the situation from Tina or Rakesh's point of view. In third, he'd step back to look at the situation more objectively.

Anna: "Permanently?"

Mark, shaking head: "For the rest of this financial year."

Anna: "So what does that say about her?"

Mark, shrugging: "I guess that she can be flexible..."

Anna: "Within clear limits."

Mark: "With the right sweet-talking."

Anna: "Is that how Rakesh did it?"

Anna is continuing to try to draw out Mark's Observer. He does eventually respond but does so dismissively by referring to 'sweet-talking'.

Mark confesses that he's no idea how Rakesh did it, but commits to asking. When he does, Rakesh tells him he told Tina that WelCare is having some cashflow issues as the company has been investing heavily in a new building that's being part-financed by the government. However, that next instalment of public funding is already guaranteed.

This is a great experiment for Anna to suggest. Mark is struggling to imagine how other people are thinking, so she's encouraging him to inquire openly into their positions and strategies.

Rakesh: "We agreed that it'd be really good for the relationship if we showed we were on WelCare's side as it's looking to grow."	Rakesh is giving Mark a window into a third-person perspective, explaining how he and Tina changed the way they were relating to each other by both taking the same side in relation to WelCare.
Mark: "But Finance never goes for that kind of argument. Why was she so flexible for you?"	
Rakesh: "I guess it helps that both of us knows the other is trying to do their job to the best of their ability and that we have different objectives – and that our bosses expect different things from us. Mine wants good sales figures. Hers wants a steady, reliable income stream."	Rakesh offers Mark insights into his own (first-person) perspective and shares what he's learned about Tina's. This gives Mark more to go on when forming his own second-person perspective. It also role-models Perspective-shifting.
Rakesh, continuing: "I've always asked that she ask me to follow up on late payments, rather than doing it herself, as that makes her life easier and helps me manage my relationship with the client."	Rakesh shows how his own use of the second-person perspective enables him to understand what makes Tina's life easier. Then he takes action to capitalise on that understanding for everyone's benefit.

Mark: "That's a good idea.
I hate it when she hassles my
clients. We know they'll pay."

Rakesh: "Until they don't.
Tina was burned a couple of
times in her previous job by
sales people overpromising.
One client even went bankrupt
owing her previous firm so
much money they had to make
people redundant. Anyway, on
this occasion, when she asked
me to chase them, I told her
about the cashflow issues they
were facing, the government
contract and all that. I said
I knew we still needed to
manage our own cashflow and
I asked what creative approach
we could take to make sure our
books balanced while showing
support for a profitable client
going through a difficult few
months. That's when she came
up with the idea of making it
predictable by extending the
terms but upping the penalty
for any payments that went
beyond that extended period.
Her boss was happy with that,
as long as it didn't go beyond
this financial year, and the
client was happy to sign up to
it, too. Really grateful, in fact."

Rakesh has taken further steps
to understand the situation from
Tina's perspective, seeking
to understand the reasons for
her reaction to late payments,
rather than assuming she's
wrong or irrational.

As we upgrade from Level 1 to Level 2 we become increasingly convinced of the value of gaining understanding about others' needs in order to create a joint solution to what we are trying to do.

If Mark simply copies Rakesh's approach with Tina, or applies that approach to other members of the Finance team, he'll be accessing Level 2 Perspective-shifting but he won't yet be *owning* it.

That could be enough to achieve his objectives, at least for now. However, the move to Level 2 requires that he become able to spontaneously and consistently 'step out of himself' to look at relationships from that neutral, third-person Observer perspective – to better and more objectively understand other people as individuals, as Anna and Rakesh did.

Critically, once he's operating at Level 2, Mark will see *positions* not just people: thus he'll see that his position is different from Tina's and not just that they are different people. This might seem like a petty distinction to make, but it's key to being able to step back and properly take that third-person perspective. Only when I see my own views as just one of many positions can I start to examine my views objectively.

Finding someone frustrating?

To access this 'third-person perspective', think of all of the possible backstories to that other person's situation that, if true, would make their behaviour make sense.

Include stories in which you are the villain of the piece – not a pantomime villain but one that is demonstrating exactly the same behaviours as you are but for all the wrong reasons.

Then look for the truth in each of those possible backstories.

What changes can you make to your own approach to create the necessary shift in this relationship?

From Level 2 to Level 3: noticing how I notice myself and shifting perspectives at will

Mark's boss Anna is driving home, reflecting on the conversation with Mark earlier that day. It's a 40-minute drive and she's been silent for some time when her passenger, Helen, finally asks what she's thinking about. Helen works for the same company but in a different department, and lives near Anna. Most days they take it in turns to drive each other to the office.

Anna: "I'm trying to work out if I should have done things differently with Mark."	
Helen: "How do you mean?"	
Anna: "Well, his relationship with Tina's been stuck for ages and I think we made some progress today, but I'm wondering if handing him off to Rakesh for advice was the best way to approach it. Maybe I should have closed that loop myself."	Anna adopts the third-person Observer perspective to examine the actions she took earlier that day.
Helen: "What would you have done differently?"	Helen encourages Anna to stay in the third-person perspective by asking her to consider what else she could have done.

Anna: "Maybe I'd have given him clear feedback on his own behaviour, told him how I think he's contributing to the problems he's having with Tina."

Doing so would have given Mark some data to help him take a third-person perspective on his handling of the situation with Tina, instead of staying stuck in his own first-person perspective. Anna is acting as an Observer to the relationship between Mark and Tina here, even though she has her own first-person experience of the situation too.

Helen: "What stopped you?"

Anna, after pausing to change lanes: "I was trying to be less directive, trying to use questions instead so he'd come to his own conclusions."

Helen's question prompts Anna to embrace this third-person perspective more deeply. She's now *thinking about her thinking*, rather than just the actions themselves.

Anna, continuing: "I know that's partly because he's older than me and that makes me more reluctant to tell him what to do, but I am trying to help him get better at seeing these things for himself. So I'm reasonably confident it's more about that than the age thing. I guess I was trying to get him to step back, empathise with Tina a little... to understand the impact he has on other people sometimes and... well, just grow up a little. But I'm very aware that I am bringing my own biases about Mark in here."

Anna is now starting to feel the pull towards the fourth-person Witness perspective. She is noticing a pattern of action that is triggered by dealing with someone older than her. As she speaks, she's testing whether it was this pattern that drove her decision in that earlier conversation with Mark.

Helen: "What do you mean?"

Anna, biting her bottom lip: "That whole thing about wanting Mark to grow up. That's a thing. I can hear my mother saying it to my older brother. He was successful, too, just like Mark is, but I was always seen as the mature one. I wonder if I'm expecting more of Mark purely because he's older and more experienced, and I wonder if that meant I was starting with the assumption that he's the real cause of the issues with Tina, rather than considering the possibility that it could be entirely down to her. I mean, it's possible isn't it?"

Anna is now trying out one aspect of that fourth-person Witness perspective. She is using an understanding of her own personal patterns and history to test for biases in her own interpretation of the issue between Mark and Tina.

Helen: "I guess so."

Anna: "Mark's numbers are really good. His clients love him. He can't have achieved all that without being pretty skilled in managing relationships. Plus he is a nice guy. Really nice, actually. He can be tough when he needs to be, but day-to-day pretty much everyone likes him."

Having visited the fourth-person Witness perspective, Anna is now able to adopt the Observer perspective more objectively. This allows her to recognise Mark's considerable strengths. These now form a counterbalance to her assessment of his role in the relationship issues with Tina.

Helen: "So how come you found it so easy to judge him and take Tina's side?"

Anna, frowning: "I wonder if the trigger was Mark suggesting Kirsten got on better with Tina because she was a woman. It felt like a sexist thing to say, but I felt I managed that. I felt I genuinely accepted that it could be a factor – some common ground between Kirsten and Tina. Now that I look back on it, though, I think I still allowed it to skew my thinking. I reckon it nudged me even further away from considering the possibility that Tina was the main cause of the issues."

What perspective(s) do you think Anna is adopting at this point in the conversation?

Helen: "You don't think you could be overthinking this?"

Anna: "Can you ever over-think this stuff? You said it yourself, once: people are like onions. Layer after layer after layer."

In the conversation above, we're seeing how Anna is moving from Level 2 Perspective-shifting to Level 3 with Helen's help. She's already very comfortable adopting the third-person, Observer perspective. As the conversation unfolds, she's increasingly able to move between the Observer perspective and the fourth-person Witness perspective. As a result, she's increasingly able to:

- Explore how her own ways of thinking, feeling and responding might have affected her approach to the situation with Mark

- Proactively seek feedback from a trusted colleague in order to improve her approach

- Question the objectivity with which she's doing that third-person 'stepping out and looking in'

Where the latter is concerned, she's noticing how her 'objectivity' is skewed by the various unconscious or subconscious patterns she's picked up over the years – her mother's attitude towards her older brother, her identity as a woman and so on. As she settles into Level 3, Anna will become increasingly aware of these patterns and increasingly curious as to their origins and the extent of their hold on her.

Importantly, though, she's still only able to step into the fourth-person, Witness perspective *retrospectively*. It's only at Level 4 that we're able to make full, controlled use of it *in the moment*.

From Level 3 to Level 4: establishing an almost-always-on[a] 'Witness' of my own and others' subjective experience

Initially, Anna will operate at Level 3 only with conscious effort. With time and practice, she'll find that activating that fourth-person Witness perspective gets easier and takes up less of her mental 'bandwidth'.

It's a bit like learning to drive a car: the more practiced she becomes, the easier it is to multi-task, making fourth-person observations of her own and other people's subjective realities without it distracting her from everything else she's doing. We call this 'double channelling' in our work with clients. It's the ability to be both *in* the action, fully paying attention

---

a   As we'll see in Chapter 9, we can still lose this perspective from time to time.

to what is going on and simultaneously *outside* the action, watching the dynamics with a more detached eye.

It's a few months later, then, that we find Anna in the car again with Helen. This time, Helen's at the wheel and they're on their way to the office. In the conversation that follows, Helen helps Anna access her fourth-person Witness perspective to address a new, trickier interpersonal challenge she's encountered at work – this time involving her boss, Bob.

You'll see that Anna's become more practiced at accessing her Witness, but she can still struggle to do so when something presses her buttons – at least until Helen gives her a prompt to step back and reflect.

Helen: "I heard you and Bob had a bit of a head-to-head yesterday. You didn't mention it last night on the way home but you seemed pretty fired up."

Anna: "He wouldn't let me change Rakesh's appraisal score. It's yet another example of how biased the whole appraisal process is. We talk about valuing and rewarding difference; we put pictures of women and ethnic minority people on our job ads, intranet and notice boards; we run courses in unconscious bias... But the reality is: it's all just noise. If your face doesn't fit here you'll be penalised come year end."

Anna's frustration has caused her to lose her usual objectivity. She's exaggerating, generalising and globalising more than we might expect from someone at Level 3. She's been 'snagged'[b] by an experience that has dragged her back to a level of Perspective-shifting she thought she'd left behind.

---

b   More on 'snags' in Chapter 9.

Helen: "I heard you made a pretty strong accusation."

Anna: "You spoke to him?"

Helen: "I am one of our diversity champions, Anna. And Bob and I have known each other for years."

Anna (her voice toughening significantly): "So you're on his side in this."

Again, Anna has been triggered into an assumption about Helen's likely reaction, despite their long-standing trusting relationship. She has temporarily lost her ability to adopt a second-person perspective to predict how Helen is *really* likely to respond.

Helen: "You know me, Anna. I always do my best not to take sides. I like you both a lot, I'm loyal to a fault at times and I'm as passionate about fairness as I am about diversity. I also have my blind-spots and my preconceptions and I do my best to manage them. Right now, I can see you're upset and I know Bob's upset, too – and I don't think it's just because you accused him of racism. If I can do anything to help you guys work through this, I will. If that helps move us forward on the diversity front, all the better."

Helen's compassionate response is rooted in her own well-developed fourth-person perspective and her ability to genuinely step into the other person's experience while not denying her own. She knows Anna is upset, so she's willing to give her some leeway rather than react in kind. At the same time, to calm the tone and bring greater objectivity back in, she references her own track record of fairness and her intention to help Anna and Bob work this through.

Anna: "None of that changes the fact that Rakesh is a four."

Helen: "What do you notice when you say that, and when you say it in that way?"	Helen is encouraging Anna to use her fourth-person Witness in the moment, in this conversation so that she can build the muscle in a safe place.

Anna: "I'm being defensive."

Helen: "Which is understandable. For starters, I'm wondering if that defensiveness tells us you're not 100% confident that Rakesh does deserve a four. He's your direct report. You like him, you want him to be successful and – I know you – you'll feel like you're letting him down if he doesn't do well. But this is me you're talking to, not Bob."	Helen is trying to help Anna adopt the third-person perspective she's lost, so she can more objectively assess the facts of the matter.

Anna, sighing: "He had a bad start to the year. He was eager to please – me, the firm, his clients – and he gave too much away to secure contracts and rescue an account he thought we might be losing. But he's ended the year well."	Helen's approach works. Anna has now become more realistic in her assessment and dropped some of her reactive defence of Rakesh's position.

Helen: "So, if you were being truly objective with no fear of letting him down – maybe even if we lived in a world where he'd never even know the score – what rating would you give him if he'd maintained the same performance throughout the year?"

Anna: "I'd give him a two. But with the same reasoning, I'd give him a four for his performance in the final quarter... I know what you're thinking, Helen."

Helen: "Actually, I'm thinking about Bob. I'm wondering what other reasons he might have for debating the rating you'd given Rakesh. Other than being an out-and-out racist, that is."

In asking Anna for a less biased appraisal of Bob's actual worldview, Helen is encouraging her to use the fourth-person perspective to filter out her own assumptions and emotions so she can better understand Bob's experience of the situation.

Anna: "Well, I know Bob's bonus pot is tight this year. He's going to be looking for reasons to push scores down so there's enough in the pot to ensure the highest performers feel their share was worth the effort."

Anna's immediate response is to jump to an unflattering judgement rather than consider Bob in a more rounded way.

Helen: "What do you notice in the way you say that?"	Helen is asking Anna to observe herself, using the fourth-person perspective in the moment, to assess what she's just said about Bob.
Anna, groaning: "I'm judging him. It might be true that the bonus pot is tight, but I'm making assumptions about his response to that, rather than seeing it from his perspective and trusting that he'll be trying to do the best with what he has."	Anna sees what she's done. She is yet to adopt the fourth-person-perspective in her assessment of Bob. However, she is at least aware that she's not being fair and that she needs to make more effort to understand his reality.
Helen: "Which he may or may not be."	
Anna, echoing Helen: "Which he may or may not be."	
Helen encourages Anna to think of other reasons Bob might have for seeking a lower rating for Rakesh. Anna comes up with three, each better than the last, including that Bob might feel she's overly lenient towards the younger people in her team – he also challenged her rating for Geoff, who's a year younger than Rakesh, making him the youngest member of her team.	Helen is asking Anna to exercise the fourth-person Witness perspective in a very effective way. Imagining a variety of possible interpretations of another person's motives and experiences helps us develop a far better, deeper understanding of them.

Helen, seizing on those hypotheses: "So Bob might think you're unfairly penalising Kirsten and Mark – expecting more of them for being older...?"

Anna: "I think that's what made me angry. I hate being accused of favouritism... Hang on... It's happened again, hasn't it? That business with me and my brother. Just like in that conversation with Mark about Tina. Bob accuses me of favouring the younger 'siblings' in my team, so I get defensive – probably because there's some truth in it as I do expect more of the older ones. So when that button's pressed, I start judging Bob, just like I judged Mark, rather than stepping back and looking at what might really be going on in the conversation. Which is where that accusation came from..."

Here Anna has spontaneously accessed her fourth-person Witness perspective in the moment. She's spotted her pattern, noticing how it's been triggered by this specific experience with Bob and spotting its roots in her own history. Thus she's able to see, from that fourth-person perspective, why she's found it so hard to maintain a more neutral Observer perspective in this situation.

Helen: "And your accusation might have been a fair one, but it might not have been."

Anna: "True, it's not exactly fact-based, is it, that accusation? It doesn't factor in the alternative explanations for Bob pushing back on my rating. Plus I've fallen into the same pattern of judging him here. Winding back a little, though: you said the accusation could be a fair one. You know Lorna got a three?"

Helen: "I heard."

Anna: "She's had a similar year to Rakesh: a bad start and a good ending, and for similar reasons. Her boss gave her a three and Bob agreed."

Helen: "So what can you do with that?"

Anna, smiling. "Well, I can start by resisting the temptation to fall back into judging him for being biased. I'm going to get some time with Bob as soon as possible today. I'm going to apologise unreservedly and I'm going to ask to have the conversation again.

I'm going to work through Rakesh's year with him, just like you and I have done, and I'm going to ask – as neutrally as possible – if we can compare his year with Lorna's, if only so I can have a robust explanation for Rakesh in the event that we do settle on a two, or even a three. And I'm going to manage my hot buttons better this time. I'm going to do my best to genuinely listen to what he's saying, rather than looking for evidence that he's making these decisions for the wrong reasons."

Anna is using her fourth-person perspective to develop a strategy for dealing with the situation. That strategy includes recognising her own part in the problem and owning and tackling the biased thinking that caused her to accuse Bob of racism.

In the conversation above, Helen is helping Anna access a more sophisticated third-person Observer perspective than she typically does spontaneously, particularly in these kinds of situations.

Together, they're also honing Anna's emerging fourth-person Witness perspective. With Helen as a catalyst, Anna sees how her own historical patterns and current beliefs affect her ability to neutrally observe what has happened with Bob. She's Witnessing:

- The recurring patterns in her tendency to judge others when she herself feels judged – whether that's by Bob, Mark or even Helen

- A tendency to become defensive and reactive in situations that seem to echo the dynamics between her, her mother and her brother

- The need to improve her ability to develop a more nuanced, complex understanding of other people's perspectives and the reasons for them, especially when emotions are running high

- The need to weave that complexity into a 'good enough truth' to take action without being suckered into thinking it's the *absolute* truth

- The need for that action to serve not just her own needs or beliefs, but the needs of the wider system

Thus, Helen is helping Anna 'clear her filters' and improve her self-witnessing so that she can approach the next conversation with Bob in a much more neutral and open way. In that future interaction, she'll be far more open to his subjective experience of the issue and less focused on blindly promoting her own point of view.

In helping Anna upgrade to Level 4 in this capacity, Helen's enabling her to become more flexible, empathetic, inclusive and calmly authoritative. With practice, Anna will earn a reputation for being able to gather the seemingly conflicting views of others and find a way forward that is clear and decisive and weaves those perspectives together into something greater – neither a binary decision that favours one side or the other, nor a simple compromise that leaves everybody wanting.

On the following pages, we'll offer a summary of each of the four levels and the upgrades between them. Then we'll ask you to decide where on that continuum you believe you're currently operating.

Summary and self-assessment

> You're relying on Perspective-shifting whenever you're trying to understand the subjective perspectives of others, to examine what is going on in a relationship and to notice how alternative ways of viewing a problem can generate new ideas and solutions. Perspective-shifting is essential when negotiating, collaborating, attempting to empathise or building rapport. It's also key to maintaining healthy, vibrant and developmental relationships.

Our individual and collective capacity for Perspective-shifting is rooted in our ability to move quickly, consciously and effectively between four types of perspective:

1. Our own view of the world – the first-person perspective

2. The views of others – the second-person perspective

3. A third-person Observer perspective which attempts to be objective and neutral

4. A fourth-person Witness perspective which recognises the subjectivity that lies underneath all attempts at objectivity

That Witness perspective enables us to see how our own deep-rooted beliefs, assumptions and expectations distort the lens through which our supposedly 'objective' Observer views the world.

We've summarised the four levels and the upgrades between them below. Throughout, we've used the word 'I' not 'you'. You'll find this makes it easier to be honest with yourself and to use this chapter to help others gauge the level at which they're currently operating.

We suggest you read through the following descriptions, ticking the statements that apply to you. Then decide and record the level at which you believe you are currently operating. Many people are tempted to over-rate themselves, so we'd encourage you to be as honest as possible. Two things can help here. Firstly, remembering that the point of this book is to help you upgrade. Secondly, recognising that – for reasons we'll cover in Chapter 9 – you might currently be operating at a lower level than you've reached in your development to date.

Your rating here will obviously be your view on you. Some people prefer a more 'robust' assessment of their current operating system. There *are* tools out there that can help on that front, with some additional interpretation, and we've been developing our own focusing specifically on these four capacities. We'll return to that topic in Chapter 10 and you're welcome to get in touch if you'd like to know more.

For now, though, we suggest that if you're keen to go beyond your own self-perceptions, you seek feedback from others to help you gauge where you're at. We'd also recommend talking to someone about two relationships you have: one relationship that's been really enjoyable and one that's been more challenging and less rewarding. Afterwards, use the descriptions below to gauge the level at which you've been operating with regard to each of those two relationships. You'll find it's even more effective if you can record that conversation about those two relationships, so you can hear first hand how you're operating.

Prior to Level 1, I have been learning to...

☐ Form my own view of the world, i.e. my first-person perspective

☐ Articulate that first-person perspective and state what I want from a given situation

☐ Take a second-person perspective, seeing things from another person's point of view and imagining what they might want, which helps me negotiate and agree with others how best to proceed – although I may still struggle to understand people I don't particularly like or whose values differ from my own

At Level 1, I...

☐ Recognise that people have different needs and points of view and that I need to work to understand them

☐ Start taking an Observer position in relation to my own relationships

☐ Talk about the quality of the relationship, not just each person's position

☐ Tend to either over-advocate my own viewpoint or to give in too easily to the opinions of others, and find myself locked into a 'win / lose' style of negotiating, especially about things that matter

☐ (If I'm brutally honest with myself) tend to stereotype groups or types of people

As I upgrade from Level 1 to Level 2, I'm getting better at...

☐ Stepping out and looking in at the situation from the perspective of a neutral Observer

☐ Relating to people as three-dimensional individuals rather than two-dimensional stereotypes

☐ Recognising that people are complex and have multiple reasons for behaving the way they do

At Level 2, I...

☐ Invest in more in-depth attempts to see things from the other person's point of view, especially when there are strong differences and / or when that person matters to me

☐ Encourage others to take their own third-person Observer perspective to solve relationship problems

☐ Do a pretty good job of analysing most of my relationships, but am prone to biases and unrecognised distortions in particularly close or emotive relationships

☐ Inquire openly about other people's thoughts and feelings, but tend to stay just beneath the surface and only ask about these things when the stakes aren't too high

☐ Usually seek win-win solutions as the most sustainable option

As I upgrade from Level 2 to Level 3, I'm getting better at...

☐ Stepping outside my strongly held biases and beliefs to look at a person or situation from a more neutral point of view (especially if those people are very different from me)

☐ Noticing the biases in my ways of objectively observing the world, and the sources of those biases

☐ Understanding the world as seen from the perspective of others, without needing to take a side when those perspectives appear to conflict

At Level 3, I...

☐ Really try to get under the skin of the subjective experiences of others, even those I find difficult or unappealing – although I still struggle when there's a clash of values

☐ Opt for considerable depth of inquiry into what's going on for people, even when emotions are high

☐ Find it easy to step back and notice what's going on in the moment

☐ Frequently draw on that ability to step back in order to mediate, negotiate or facilitate

☐ Am starting to access the fourth-person Witness perspective to observe myself, others and interpersonal interactions during the action, although I tend to lose my grip on that perspective if the situation is heated or the stakes are high

As I upgrade from Level 3 to Level 4, I'm getting better at...

☐ Managing my own 'hot buttons', 'psychological baggage' and unhelpful patterns of thinking, feeling and reacting – or at least noticing them as they happen and taking prompt corrective action

☐ Finding or creating ways in each moment to understand others' habits, needs and mind-sets – their beliefs, assumptions and expectations about themselves and the world around them

☐ Accurately appreciating, with minimal judgement, what other people's lives actually feel like for them and how they came to develop their own habits, needs and mind-sets

At Level 4, I...

☐ Have a fully-baked muscle-memory for Perspective-shifting, meaning I can quickly and accurately shift back and forth between my own view and those of a wide variety of people, enabling me to predict how others are likely to experience the situation

☐ Have my Observer perspective switched on almost all of the time, so I can stand back from the action easily, even at difficult moments

☐ Have a well-established Witness perspective, which means I quickly notice the quality of my own attention – spotting my own biases, rigidity and prejudice in the moment

☐ Often 'meta-commentate' on the perspectives in the room (including my own) and encourage others to do the same

☐ Understand on an *intellectual level* that, however much I try to take an objective perspective, my viewing point will always be subjective and distorted by my most rigidly held assumptions – and that everyone's lenses have been shaped by the full span of human history. However, I still struggle to put that knowledge to any real, practical use

Mark (on the arrow on the right) the level at which you believe you're currently operating. There's space for each level and a space between each for you to use if you feel you're in transition between one level and the next.

You'll see there's also a box for you to tick if you believe you're currently developing *towards* Level 1 in the Perspective-shifting capacity. It's perfectly possible that, if you're brutally honest with yourself, you'll find yourself there in one or more capacities.

If you do rate yourself as presently operating at one of the lower levels in this capacity, it could be a temporary dip (as we'll see in Chapter 9). It may also have taken some courage to admit it. Indeed, few people operating at the lower levels in a given capacity *would* admit it. If you're that honest with yourself, then the chances are you'll be at a much higher level when it comes to Self-relating. Plus, in the long run, that honesty will serve you well.

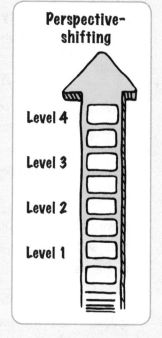

Perspective-shifting

Level 4

Level 3

Level 2

Level 1

Thinking about your key responsibilities with regard to leading / working with other people, what are the implications of continuing to operate at this level?

....

....

....

An experiment to test this out

You'll find it helpful, too, to use this lens to examine an upcoming meeting or conversation involving at least four other people. It needs to be a discussion where you'll have sufficient time and bandwidth to slip into an observer role for five to ten minutes.

In that meeting, listen to the ways people talk *to* each other and the ways they talk *about* people who aren't present in the meeting.

Which of the perspectives do you think were in play (first, second, third, fourth)? What gives you that impression? What level would you use to describe the Perspective-shifting in that discussion?

....

....

....

....

....

Self-relating: getting better at understanding and managing ourselves

• ● •

- What 'relating to yourself' really means
- From being 'had by' to 'having' our inner experience
- What it means to upgrade in this capacity
- One person's journey through all three upgrades

THE BETTER WE UNDERSTAND our 'inner landscape' and are

able to manage our responses to the world, the more effectively we can operate in *any* context – no matter how complex, VUCA or simple it is.

We've called this capacity 'Self-relating' to emphasise that it is an ongoing activity. It's not a quality (like self-awareness) or an objective (like self-knowledge). It summarises our ability to relate directly to aspects of our inner experience – our thoughts, emotional responses, beliefs, gut-feels, historical patterns and habits-of-mind. These things play out continuously in the internal theatre of our brains and bodies, influencing our

> "If you can keep your head when all about you are losing theirs and blaming it on you..."
>
> Rudyard Kipling, *If*[50]

actions and decisions whether we are aware of them or not.

Thus our capacity for Self-relating plays a pivotal role when it comes to interpreting and operating in this world. The more we understand the source of our habits, decisions and choices, the less we are at the mercy of unconscious forces and rules-of-thumb that bias our thinking and can keep us stuck in unhelpful patterns of behaviour, thought and emotional response.

We each focus differently and with different amounts of energy when it comes to consciously examining and managing our ways of making sense of the world. The very notion of Self-relating stirs up a range of reactions in different people, some positive, some negative. The most common are:

- ☐ Introspection feels like self-indulgent navel-gazing

- ☐ Digging deep can stir up pain and too much self-awareness is a crippling thing

- ☐ If you don't understand yourself, you can't make conscious choices, and if you're not making conscious choices you're just a beast in a suit

- ☐ Seeing your unhelpful patterns just causes frustration if you can't change them anyway

- ☐ How can you lead others if you can't even lead yourself?

- ☐ You can only be authentic if you really know yourself

- ☐ Self-exploration is an ever-present quest

- ☐ There is no 'true self' to relate to

They're all understandable reactions. However, as we upgrade in this capacity, we're enhancing our ability to:

- ● Overcome our limiting patterns of thinking and behaving

- ● Observe ourselves in the moment

- Understand ourselves and our internal processes with increasing complexity and nuance

- Notice the changes within us over time

- Take responsibility for choosing our own direction and crafting our own identities

- Initiate increasingly difficult, complex and profound change in ourselves – including updating our own internal operating system

We're also more able to consciously switch our Self-relating capacity on and off, rather than letting it dominate our attention and distract us from using the other capacities.

There are clear links between this capacity and what's happening to us as we reach Levels 3 and 4 in Perspective-shifting. When we adopt the third-person Observer perspective, we're trying to look at ourselves more objectively. When we move to that fourth-person Witness perspective, we're taking a further step back from ourselves. We're observing our thoughts, feelings and behaviours in a way that's more ongoing, understanding how they are shifting in real time. At the same time, that examination takes us far deeper and reaches further back in time, looking at the roots of those thoughts, feelings and behaviours. So it inevitably changes the ways we relate to ourselves.

Where the description of this capacity comes from

When initially defining this capacity, Karen drew most heavily on the work of Robert Kegan[51] and Jennifer Garvey Berger[52].

Kegan describes adults' natural progression as being from the 'socialised' mind, through 'self-authoring' to 'self-transforming'. You'll see aspects of that in our descriptions of the four levels and in the case study we use in this chapter.

The essence of the upgrades in this capacity: 'having' our inner experiences, rather than being 'had by' them

One of Robert Kegan's masterstrokes where this capacity is concerned was to draw attention to different ways of *relating*[a] to our inner experiences[b]. There are those that we're 'subject to' and those we can 'hold as object'. Colloquially, Kegan talks about being 'had by' a belief when it is like the water we swim in or the paper we are written on. We cannot question it, view it objectively or 'get outside it' to see how useful it is in our current circumstances. For example, if I am 'had by' a belief that 'a good person is loyal to their team', I might find it almost impossible to stop defending a team member to one of my peers, even if that team member has repeatedly failed to deliver on an important milestone. However, if I'm able to step back, reflect and notice that I 'have' this belief, then I can effectively place the belief on the table in front of me and examine it. This enables me to decide whether it should apply in this situation or whether I need a more nuanced set of criteria to decide when loyalty is really due.

When we were younger, many of our thoughts, beliefs and emotional responses were based on the way we were brought up. We were 'had by' our families' patterns of thinking and feeling. Then we shifted our interest towards peer groups outside our homes and took on the beliefs and norms of those groups wholesale.

When most of us entered early adulthood, that's where we were at when it comes to Self-relating. We'd reached the start of Level 1, adopting what Kegan calls the 'socialised form of mind'[c]. Later, at Level 2, if all

---

a   'Relating' is our word for it, rather than Kegan's, and it's the reason for the name we've given to this capacity.

b   Thoughts, emotions, beliefs, assumptions, values, psychological patterns, etc.

c   Kegan's different 'forms of mind' are basically qualitatively different ways of making meaning, in our heads, out of all the things that go on in and around us – the data that comes in through our senses, as well as our thoughts, feelings, actions, etc.

goes well, we become more focused on aspects of our own individuality, starting to differentiate ourselves from the ways our background and society have shaped us. In Kegan's terms, we're starting to shift into the 'self-authoring form of mind'.

If and when we progress to Level 3, our attention shifts from fitting in with the expectations of others towards working out what it means to be 'truly ourselves'. We seek opportunities to develop ourselves and create our own way of life on our own terms – becoming what Kegan now calls 'fully self-authored'. Level 4 comes if and when we've pursued this project of self-understanding for long enough and start to adopt what Kegan calls a 'self-transforming form-of-mind'. Where previously we've been building a version of ourselves that's wholly ours and designed to last, we're now more interested in constantly evolving and in understanding what that might mean for us, our work and our relationships.

As you'll see in the case study below, with each upgrade, a different cluster of inner experiences shifts from being something we're 'had by' to something we 'have'. With each upgrade, we're able to extract and place on the table an even more complex, deep-rooted set of habits, needs, values, feelings and beliefs. Thus, developing this capacity for Self-relating enables us to be 'had by' fewer and fewer potentially unhelpful aspects of that inner world. Each upgrade makes us progressively more choiceful, autonomous, adaptable and resilient. We hope you'd agree that that's definitely something worth aiming for.

What it looks like to upgrade in this capacity

Our case study for Self-relating is Jean-Paul ('JP' for short). He's a nurse in a specialist stroke unit in a wholly-government-owned hospital on the outskirts of one of the country's biggest cities.

The case study spans a number of years. When we first meet him, JP has recently been promoted to Deputy Manager. This has put him in charge of the day-to-day running of the unit where the nursing staff are concerned. It's the first role he's had that sees him clearly in the managerial hierarchy. With previous promotions, he was still always considered one of the nurses.

Over the past twelve months, several departments in the hospital have consistently missed central government targets, prompting an investigation by one of the health sector's 'arm's-length' bodies. JP's unit missed its own targets just twice in those twelve months – under what the hospital's management considered extenuating circumstances. Nevertheless, his department has also been included in the investigation.

A lot of the work we do when we're Self-relating happens in our heads, so we'll need to share less dialogue and more of JP's inner monologue in this case study than we offered in Chapter 4.

From Level 1 to Level 2: balancing social norms with self-determination

It's Friday night and JP and three colleagues are in a bar near the hospital. Ros and Ingrid are nurses. Elise is Deputy Manager of the special care baby unit. Hers is one of the units that have been consistently missing their targets.

Elise has just told the others that her boss, Dean, has been encouraging the other managers to take strike action to protest against the upcoming investigation.

Elise says she's inclined to agree with Dean that the investigation is a witch hunt and believes that striking will only be effective if other units join in, too. Ros agrees and asks JP what he thinks.

JP considers his response carefully. Both of the hospitals he's worked in have a strong union ethos, as has the college where he qualified. At the same time, he prides himself on his diligence, work ethic and the attachments he forms with the patients in his care.

"I'm not sure a strike's going to help matters," he says, pausing to gauge their reactions. "I just think... well... we're a hospital. We're here to save lives."

Ros responds with "Just because we do important work doesn't mean we should be held to ransom over it. Surely it's the *fact* that we save lives that means we should be treated fairly, and with some respect."

Elise repeats her boss's description of the investigation as a witch-hunt. "If we don't stand together, they'll come for us one by one," she says. "You've got problems in your unit, too, JP. They'll be looking for someone to

Commentary / analysis

JP is noticing a conflict between the way the rest of the group sees the situation and his own personal values. He's deciding whether to go along with their views or take a stand by sharing his own opinion.

This is a classic challenge for someone moving towards Level 2. As we start to become what Kegan calls 'self-authoring', we form opinions of our own. At some point, those opinions are sufficiently different from other people's that they're in conflict. We might air that conflict openly or just feel it within. Either way, we're forced to choose between our sense of what is right and our desire to maintain important relationships (e.g. with friends, family, close colleagues, mentors and other significant senior figures).

blame and your unit's only stopped meeting its targets since you became Deputy Manager."

JP feels himself tense. *Maybe she's right*, he thinks. *Maybe we do need to stick together. Maybe I'll get blamed for the dip in performance and maybe my boss [Selene] and the rest of the team won't back me up if I've refused to go along with the strike.*

He's about to agree with Elise when he realises that his temptation to do so is rooted in the anxiety her comments have provoked in him.

He stops for a moment and considers the reasons his unit failed to meet its targets in those two months.

As far as he's concerned, they're straightforward supply-and-demand issues: more stroke patients were admitted than the unit could handle. The records actually show that the unit's efficiency *increased* during those periods, as people worked harder and smarter to cope with the added pressure.

In noticing his anxious reaction, rather than allowing it to define his next move, JP is accessing Level 2.

It's Level 2 that enables him to pause and calm himself down. From there he's able to reflect on what has been said and decide how he really wants to respond. Thus he 'has' that anxious reaction but is less 'had by' it than he would have been at Level 1.

He decides that, on this occasion, it's more important to hold to his own viewpoint than to go along with the mood of the group. So, instead of agreeing, he says "I'm not so sure, Elise. Surely, if the watchdog finds ways to improve our efficiency, that helps us all. I think my unit's been performing well, so I'm not worried that they'll find anything that'll make us look bad. Either way, though, if we decide to strike it would feel to me like we're trying to dodge our responsibilities. It would feel like we're focusing on ourselves at the expense of our patients."

He can tell Elise is annoyed but Ros defuses the situation with an attempt to respect both points of view. The conversation eventually drifts onto less contentious topics.

As he makes his way home at the end of the night, JP reflects on the fact that he almost fell into agreement with Elise purely because of the emotions she provoked in him. While he's pleased he didn't succumb, he realises she'd inadvertently prodded a tendency he has when things go wrong: blaming himself or worrying that others will blame him.

One thing's for sure: he knows the debate isn't over and will only grow more heated and urgent as the investigation approaches. He knows that, sometime soon, he'll have to choose between his loyalty to his friends and the core values that make him who he is.

At Level 2, we begin to notice the patterns in the ways we think about and act towards ourselves. However, we're usually only able to do this with hindsight and we've yet to really explore how those patterns were first created.

When it comes to JP's ultimate decision as to whether or not to support strike action, if he's operating at Level 2 the choice will probably remain a binary one: he'll be in or out, and will then do what he can to deal with the consequences of that decision.

While he stays at Level 2, he'll bring a sense of 'choosing his battles' to this decision and others like it. Sometimes he'll stick to his guns; sometimes he'll follow the general consensus.

In JP we see the essence of an upgrade from Level 1 to Level 2. In early adulthood and right through Level 1, our ways of looking at the world are borrowed from the people and contexts around us – family rules, cultural norms, social practices, political and religious beliefs, and so on. We ingest and adapt the beliefs, assumptions and expectations of others regarding what's ethically right and wrong, what's factually correct and what's logical.

Even when we rebel and oppose a family belief, our identity is still being shaped by that opposition. Consider, for example, the teenager who chooses a socialist political stance simply as a reaction to her mother's active support of the nation's most conservative party.

At Level 1, we learn to step back from our thoughts and emotions and examine them as objects in their own right – like they're on the table in front of us, as in the image below. However, we're not yet truly distinguishing our beliefs and reactions from those of the groups to which we belong. Those distinctions, behind us in the image, are out of view but still affecting how we operate.

Level 1

Also out of view are our less socially acceptable emotional reactions to things – the darker emotions we feel, which others might frown upon or fail to understand. Those come into the foreground – onto the table – as we reach Level 2.

As we've seen, Level 2 heralds the emergence of increasingly independent thought and the tensions that brings with it. I am starting to separate out my own beliefs from those of my peers and significant others. What I can't yet examine in the moment are the processes I'm using to form those beliefs, and the underlying patterns of thinking, feeling and behaving.

Level 2

From Level 2 to Level 3: working to
create myself as the person I really want to be,
rather than the person others expect me to be

We return to JP two years later, in the middle of his next upgrade where Self-relating is concerned. He's six weeks from taking on his boss Selene's role. JP was an obvious successor and beat eight other shortlisted candidates. However, now that the thrill of outperforming his competitors has passed, he's beginning to doubt whether he and the hospital have made the right decision.

To help him prepare, he's been sent on a management development programme. It's Day Two. Last night, JP and his fellow participants completed a questionnaire to help them identify their core values, the intention being to deepen their understanding of what it means to be authentic. While some of his colleagues are openly or whisperingly sceptical, JP finds the work has tapped into something that's been bothering him for quite some time.

One of the tutors on the programme, Suzanne, asks where he thinks his top five values came from.

He looks again at the words he's chosen:

- Responsibility

- Humility

- Self-discipline

- Helping others

- Independence

"Humility definitely comes from my mother," he says. "She's done so much with her life – had an amazing impact on other people and worked all over the world. But she's always more interested in hearing about other people's experiences and achievements than talking about her own. Helping others: that's her, too. It's there in everything she does."

The transition from Level 2 to Level 3 is equipping JP with a fairly good understanding of the ways in which his values and opinions were shaped by his upbringing, and by his parents in particular. He can describe how he has been 'authored' by his life experience.

"Sounds like she takes a lot of responsibility," Suzanne observes.

"She does, for sure, and I guess part of my sense of responsibility comes from her. The word itself, though, that's my father. It's the same with self-discipline. There's an ease with which my mother goes about things. With Dad, it's all about pushing, striving to be better... to do more, to make more of a difference in the world."

"I notice you're tensing up as you say that."

"I am. I feel like I'm letting him down. He's pleased that I got the promotion, but I can tell he's still disappointed that I've not done something else with my life."

"And your mother?" Suzanne asks. "What do you think she thinks of what you've chosen to do with your life?"

JP half-laughs. "She's happy as long as I'm happy. Which means I'm letting her down, too."

"You're not happy?"

"Mum's always happy with whatever she has. Dad's achieved what he has by never being content with what he's already got. I feel like I'm some weird, paralysing blend of the two of them: unable to feel satisfied with where I am but also afraid of developing my father's insatiable appetite for achievement."

"How's that tension affecting you now, as you think about your aspirations for yourself and the people you lead?"

"It's making me doubt myself," JP says. "I think I know what I want to do, but I keep wondering whether that's what I want to do or what they hope I'll do. And with one of the things I *really* want to do, I'm worried my father wouldn't approve."

"And what is it that you really want to do?"

"I've been looking at studying social policy."

"What draws you to that?"

The more he settles into Level 3 Self-relating, the more aware JP becomes of the internal tensions *between* his values / beliefs, and the more aware he is of the effect those tensions are having on him.

He's seeing these tensions because he's had time overnight to reflect on them. At Level 3, though, it's still unlikely that he would notice those tensions in the moment when he's caught up in them.

Like many people upgrading to Level 3, JP is very aware of the struggle he is having between defining himself on his own terms and the need for his father's approval.

As the conversation progresses, he starts to make clear choices about which values and beliefs he wants to incorporate as part of his identity and which may need to be questioned or amended.

"The desire to make a bigger difference. I guess it's a sense of responsibility playing out again. I feel we're responsible for the people in our care day-to-day, but our hands are pretty tied when it comes to making the big decisions. Everything we do is dictated by policies set by people we never even get to speak to. I'm thinking if I can somehow find a way into that world, then I'll be able to influence how those policies are shaped."

"So why would your father object to that?"

JP rolls his eyes. "Because, as far as he's concerned, social policy is left-wing nonsense. If I'm going to go down that route, I might as well start wearing polo necks and leather patches on my elbows and stick a poster of Lenin on my living room wall."

"So, on the one hand you have a career path that feels authentic and embraces a responsibility you feel to the wider world. On the other hand you have your sense of responsibility to your father's aspirations for you."

That identity was shaped by his parents' beliefs, assumptions, aspirations and expectations. So, in seeking to 'edit' it, he'll be stirring up real or imagined conflict with his parents and their core beliefs. Increasingly, at Level 3, he'll feel prepared to face into that conflict – while also recognising the potential cost to his relationship with them.

Here Suzanne helps JP by restating and clarifying the internal conflict he's feeling so he can stand outside it. This helps him 'have' the tension rather than being 'had by' it. Until he gets beyond Level 3, it'll be hard for JP to do this himself, especially with regard to relationships or matters of identity that are particularly important to him.

Like many people upgrading to Level 3, JP is noticing the forces around him that might make it harder to fulfil his own aspirations. He's wondering if the only way to be the person he wants to be is to free himself from those inhibiting influences – either by distancing himself from those people or by cutting the ties completely.

To return to our images from earlier, he's able to examine the ways his thoughts and feelings are changing from moment to moment. He's also bringing onto the table the drivers behind those thoughts and feelings.

JP is also open to Suzanne's feedback regarding the ways in which the *combination* of his values creates potential problems for him. At Level 3, he's still less able to spot those interactions himself – the underlying patterns of thinking, feeling and behaving are out of view, except when someone else helps him shine a light on them. He's also still treating that list of five values as though they're *his own* values, despite knowing where they come from.

Thus, like most people operating at Level 3, JP is focusing on managing and mitigating the impact of 'being wired the way he is', rather than questioning the validity or rigidity of the wiring. It's only when he starts upgrading to Level 4 that he'll entertain the possibility of discarding or radically changing that wiring.

From Level 3 to Level 4: recognising that the self I have created can be re-created in many different ways, depending on what is required by the situation

When we check in on JP five years later, he has completed his Masters degree in social policy. He works three shifts a week at the hospital and spends two days working with an 'arms-length body', running a nationwide best-practice review of stroke prevention, prediction and care.

His previous boss Selene was a keen advocate for him when he negotiated the arrangement with the hospital. His colleague Ros has been an enormous help, too, having stepped in very proactively as his deputy. Their relationship still has its tensions – rooted in the strike action a few years back – but for the most part JP has been able to manage his own reactions when emotions might otherwise have flared.

A prime example of this is the day it emerges that Ros had made a mistake affecting their inventory. The error itself was small – just a single slip in an equation in a spreadsheet. Nevertheless, the impact was significant: their supplies of a critical drug have run dangerously low and they've been forced to order an urgent delivery at considerable cost.

The moment JP hears they're low on the drug, some of his less-sophisticated instincts kick in. A little voice in the back of his mind points out that this is his unit and he is ultimately responsible – whether it was truly his fault or not. He's the one who'll be punished. Finding out how it happened is standard practice, of course, but he's already hoping the evidence will point in someone else's direction.

That initial emotional response takes mere seconds to play out, but JP is able to notice it happening in the moment. He feels the emotions just as acutely, but instead of being consumed by them he's able to step back and recognise them as evidence of an old, familiar pattern.

Previously, like many of us, he would have allowed those emotions to become a filter through which he would then appraise the situation – skewing the data on which he would then make his decisions. Today, though, he's able use the emotions as a signal to remind him to step back and consider things more objectively.

In doing so, he sees that once again his core value around responsibility is showing its dark side. He also notices the role his value of 'helping people' is playing in this process: he's afraid he might have been responsible for a sequence of events that he considers the opposite of helping the patients in his unit – or that his superiors will think he's let them or the patients down. Not only that, he is well aware that this is a pattern laid down when he was a child. It's a pattern of worrying about getting the blame, because with blame comes the shame of not being good enough – 'good' meaning 'clever' in his father's eyes and 'kind' in his mother's.

He smiles rather ruefully at the familiarity of those patterns and lets the tension they provoke dissipate. Then he writes a mental list of the immediate assumptions he's making about the situation, its causes and its potential implications.

Now that he's accessing Level 4, JP can notice his emotional responses in the moment and use them as important information. At Level 3, he learned to pause before reacting. Now, at Level 4, he's treating the emotions he's feeling as a signal that draws his attention to the patterns driving his response to the situation. Those emotions no longer trigger an automatic response.

At Level 4, he can also notice how his emotional response might be affecting his thinking – the ways he's making meaning of the situation. This means he's using Self-relating to understand how his thoughts and feelings might be skewing his use of the other three capacities. As a result, he can set to one side his overactive sense of responsibility, fear of blame and not being good enough. In doing so, he doesn't stop 'having' those patterns but he's no longer 'had by' them, meaning he's able to investigate the matter at hand more objectively and effectively.

He spends some time engaging his *Perspective-shifting* capacity then goes to see Ros and works up a plan of action with her. When they find the source of the error, he notes his internal, emotional reaction: relief that the mistake wasn't his and anger that her lack of attention to detail put patients at risk and made the whole unit look incompetent.

Rather than letting that internal reaction consume him, he lets it pass. It doesn't affect his posture, the tone of his voice or the things he says about the outcome to Ros and others.

Prior to Level 4, that internal reaction could have caused JP to respond by:

- Shouldering responsibility that was not his to bear

- Blaming Ros, to avoid being blamed himself

- Feeling paralysed into inaction because of his sense of not being 'good enough'

What follows is a fair and emotionally honest interaction in which he challenges Ros appropriately while maintaining the relationship and helping her learn from her mistake.

To return to our images from earlier, JP has demonstrated one of the key ingredients in the shift from Level 3 to Level 4. He's able to place his underlying patterns of thinking, feeling and behaving onto the table and examine those patterns and how they are playing out in the current moment.

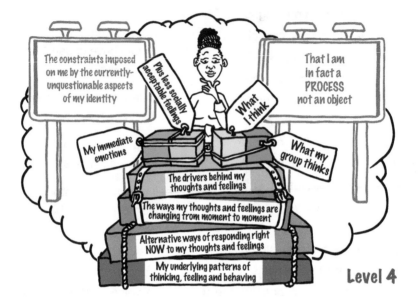

Like anyone at Level 4, he'll still have another layer of subconscious or unconscious 'stuff' that he finds hard to bring to the foreground and examine. These will likely be aspects of his identity that he considers core, immutable and unquestionable. Perhaps, for JP it's 'I'm a nice person. I help people. That's just who I am.'

People who move *beyond* Level 4 in this capacity begin to recognise that even their identity and sense of self are just constructs. As such, they're open to unceasing inquiry and change. If this sounds a little tiring, it is!

Summary and self-assessment

You're relying on Self-relating when you're managing, in the moment, the influence on your behaviour of your habitual ways of thinking, feeling and responding. It's this capacity that helps you identify, question and adapt your own beliefs, assumptions and expectations. It's this capacity that's core to your wellbeing, resilience and ongoing development.

Progression within this capacity helps us consciously examine, master and work on increasingly deep-rooted aspects of ourselves, such as our:

● Immediate emotions

● Beliefs and assumptions

● Needs and motivations

● Patterns of thinking, feeling and behaving

● Values and core identity

As before, we've summarised the four levels and the upgrades between them below. Again, the intention is that you read these descriptions, then indicate which level best describes your current capacity for Self-relating.

Before you do, though, take a moment to note (in the space below) your initial reactions to what we've covered so far on Self-relating. If you do so without censoring that thinking, the things you write here will offer you further insights that will inform your assessment of the level at which you're operating in this capacity.

....

....

....

Prior to Level 1, I have been learning to...

☐ Manage my immediate impulses rather than acting on them (e.g. resisting the pull towards road rage when someone steals 'my' parking space)

☐ Balance immediate gratification against what is best for me in the longer term (e.g. choosing the salad rather than those tasty-looking doughnuts)

☐ Articulate my thoughts and feelings regarding important topics and specific situations – although this is typically after the event, when prompted, rather than in the moment

At Level 1, I...

☐ Start to notice my own personality traits, preferences and emotional state

☐ Notice some of my 'difficult' feelings or 'problematic' thoughts, although I may not yet be able to discuss them openly with others

☐ Tend to blame or criticise myself or others when things go wrong

☐ Deny some of my more extreme emotional states (e.g. anger, depression) despite other people being able to clearly see those emotions in the way I'm behaving

☐ Struggle with conflict and tend to either deny it or blow it out of proportion

As I upgrade from Level 1 to Level 2, I'm getting better at...

☐ Identifying my own personal values and beliefs, separate from those of the people around me – perhaps even from the social norms of the environment in which I grew up – and choosing when to take an independent stand, despite the risk of alienating myself from people whose approval is important to me

☐ Noticing some of my thoughts and feelings as they happen and using techniques to change them in the moment

☐ Noticing how I interact with myself (e.g. seeing the worst in myself) and making conscious choices about the ways I want to treat myself

At Level 2, I...

☐ Demonstrate a sound understanding of my core beliefs and values and can articulate them in a way that feels congruent with my self-image

☐ Attend to my own resilience, including getting better at noticing and regulating my emotions – although I still tend to put work or the needs of others first[d]

☐ Am very aware of my 'inner critic' and I'm interested in psychological models more generally

---

d   Notice your reaction to this one. This isn't about which priority is right or wrong. It's purely what people at this level tend to prioritise.

☐ Find it easier to deal with external conflicts, but pay little attention to the conflicts *within* me

☐ Am still pretty sure I created my own identity and that it is 'the real me' – so I'm reluctant to change the thoughts, feelings and behaviours that are simply 'me'[e] (or believe it's impossible to)

As I upgrade from Level 2 to Level 3, I'm getting better at...

☐ Using reflection and hindsight to recognise how my counterproductive patterns of thinking, feeling and behaving may have played out, and to notice whether I could have done something different

☐ Accepting feedback and challenge from others regarding my limiting / counterproductive beliefs, assumptions and expectations

☐ Realising I am 'had by' a huge range of limiting beliefs and habitual behaviours that my younger self absorbed from the family and culture I grew up in – thus, if necessary, I may be able to decide to distance myself from people whose influence makes it hard to swap my existing patterns for healthier ones

At Level 3, I...

☐ Can notice changes in my thoughts and feelings as they happen, rather than after the fact

☐ Am very interested in my own unique experience of situations, and in my personal psychological patterns and how they have arisen

---

e   Of, if you prefer a more technical description: 'those beliefs, emotions and behaviours that seem rooted in my personality and sense of identity'

☐ Feel acutely (sometimes painfully) aware of my own internal contradictions and tensions, including things I really don't like seeing in myself (e.g. prejudices and hypocrisies)

☐ Can become consumed with or overwhelmed by the endless opportunities for self-examination as I discover layers of intertwined complexity within myself

☐ Still struggle to genuinely step outside and question those aspects of my identity which still feel core to who I am (e.g. believing 'I just *am* a very kind person and there is no way I want to change that')

As I upgrade from Level 3 to Level 4, I'm getting better at...

☐ Quickly spotting *in the moment* when I am caught in one of my personal patterns – then doing what I can to get myself out of it

☐ Seeing how my various patterns of thoughts and emotions interact with each other, and choosing which to prioritise changing and which to leave untouched for the time being

☐ Adopting and maintaining practices that help me explore and untangle myself from my unhelpful habits, needs and mind-sets (e.g. mindfulness, coaching, therapy, peer learning groups)

At Level 4, I...

☐ Can 'double channel', being simultaneously fully present in the moment and attending to my internal world – to the extent that I can, *if it's helpful*, commentate on my current thought processes and emotions

☐ Understand and accept most of my personal patterns of thinking, feeling and behaving, although the most 'unacceptable' ones may still be somewhat hidden from me

☐ Acknowledge my internal 'shadows' and weaknesses, and accept that these are part of the human condition (in a more relaxed way than I could manage at Level 3)

☐ Am adjusting my life to bring it increasingly in line with my principles and preferences – and coping with the tension that arises when I'm not (or not currently) able to make some of the life adjustments I'd like to make

☐ Have yet to fully open myself up to the possibility of my identity being constantly transformed, even by those experiences which feel distasteful or very painful – I understand this intellectually, but I'm still clinging to those parts of my independent, self-created identity that are most dear to me without realising they're also often the things that most inhibit me

Mark on the right the level at which you believe you're currently operating. What makes you think that?

Self-relating

Level 4

Level 3

Level 2

Level 1

. . . .

. . . .

. . . .

. . . .

. . . .

How do you feel about being at that level? What does *that reaction itself* say about the level you're at?

....

....

....

An experiment to test this out

Now, to bed in your appreciation of the four levels, seek out an opportunity to have an informal conversation with two or three different people about an aspect of their personal (rather than professional) development[f]. They could be colleagues or people you lead.

In that conversation, ask them:

a. What they think they're good at

b. What they think they need to develop, and

c. How they think they should approach that development

What do you notice about their focus in each of those three areas? Which level does it suggest they're operating from when it comes to Self-relating?

....

....

....

• ● •

---

f   The intention here is not to devalue professional development but to avoid this conversation following the same patterns as an appraisal or professional development review.

6

Opposable Thinking: getting better at handling polarities and dilemmas

• ● •

- The ubiquity and 'business critical' nature of dilemmas and conflicting positions
- The value of 'Opposable Thinking' in critical or transformative thought
- What it looks like to upgrade in this capacity
- How a team of people at different levels approaches the same dilemma

THE TERM 'Opposable Thinking'[53] was coined by Canadian business leader, author and academic Roger Martin. He describes it as our capacity "to hold two conflicting ideas in constructive tension"[54].

Like the opposable thumbs that have been instrumental in our success as a species, Opposable Thinking provides "an intellectually advantageous evolutionary leap through which

"The test of a first-rate intelligence is the ability to hold two opposed ideas in mind at the same time and still retain the ability to function."

F. Scott Fitzgerald, author[55]

decision-makers can synthesize 'new and superior ideas.'"[56] It's a claim that's based on Martin's own research into key factors underpinning success in business. It's also highly consistent with our own observations of individuals, teams and organisations attempting to survive and thrive – whether that's in VUCA worlds or not.

Failing to develop this capacity is associated with impairments in people's ability to critique their own thought processes[57]. It's a capacity that's essential when it comes to developing and honing sound judgement and transformative thinking. It also underpins our ability to exercise our Sense-making, Perspective-shifting and Self-relating capacities to best effect.

There's an awful lot to be said about this capacity and related concepts like dialectical thinking (see below). For the sake of this book, though, we'll focus on what's most relevant to most managers: upgrading our ability to deal with external dilemmas and polarising ideas.

Where the description of this capacity comes from

There's a lot of complex thought available on this topic. One of the most original thinkers in the field is Otto Laske[58], whose work is also influenced by Robert Kegan, as well as by psychologist Lawrence Kohlberg and philosophers Roy Bhaskar and Georg Hegel.

If you want to go deeper on this topic and become more transformational in your own thinking, we'd recommend looking into Laske's work and the realm of 'dialectical thinking', a way of thinking that goes beyond logic. Laske builds on Bhaskar's work to offer four types of thought process, each more sophisticated than the last. Each renders us better able to examine our own concepts as they arise. Each makes for a deeper level of listening and a richer form of dialogue with the people around us. While there is considerably more depth in Laske's work, we have drawn on aspects of this progression when developing our four levels of Opposable Thinking.

Understanding polarities

You'll have been relying on Opposable Thinking most whenever you've been faced with a dilemma with no obvious answer, or when the people around you have become polarised into seemingly intractable positions on a contentious issue.

At the heart of many of these situations lies a 'polarity', described by David Dinwoodie at the US Center for Creative Leadership as:

"...a pair of interdependent opposites – if you focus on one of those to the neglect or exclusion of the other, at some point in time you dip into negative unintended consequences."[59]

Barry Johnson, psychologist and pioneer of 'polarity management', offers 'attitudes to sharing' as a very simple example of a polarity[60]. Sharing involves two right answers:

1. Looking after our own needs

2. Looking after the needs of someone else

If we focus purely on achieving 1, the outcome won't be satisfactory for the other person. If we focus purely on 2, we'll be left unsatisfied ourselves. However, if we want to maintain a positive relationship with that other person in the long term, we need to look after our own needs *while* we're looking after the other person's needs, and vice versa! Thus, the two poles are interdependent: we need to find a way of balancing our own needs and those of the other person so that we also meet the need of maintaining the overall relationship.

Common polarities in organisations include:

- Centralised control vs Decentralised autonomy (see box below)
- Offering a variety of products or services vs 'Sticking to the knitting'
- Customisation vs Operational efficiency

- Focusing on personal performance vs Individual development

Polarities many societies face include:

- Justice vs Mercy
- Order vs Liberty
- High quality public services vs Low taxation
- Supporting the vulnerable vs Promoting individual enterprise

Centralise! No, decentralise!

If you've been in an organisation long enough to view at least one cycle of 'Centralisation vs Decentralisation' then you'll have seen this polarisation first hand. As the move to centralise takes hold, those nearer the 'coal face' start to see their colleagues at 'HQ' as controlling, power-crazed and too distant from the action. Meanwhile, those working in the centralised functions experience business unit leaders as resistant, (also) power-crazed, overly parochial or worried about their own fiefdoms.

Eventually, a new decentralising orthodoxy takes hold, often coinciding with the arrival of a new person or people at the top of the organisation. The positions get reversed with predictable results. We don't know about you, but we'd love to see a robust analysis of the amount of time that's been spent worldwide on this particular back-and-forth in large corporates.

Polarities many of us face as individuals include:

- Professionalism vs Transparency
- Head vs Heart
- Intimacy / Belonging vs Separation / Freedom
- Tact vs Honesty

As the examples above suggest, sometimes the struggle over a polarity happens within us, between competing beliefs, priorities or motivations. Often the dilemma is one we're facing collectively – as a group, team or organisation.

When the dilemma is a collective one, it's common for different people or business units to each have their own beliefs and assumptions regarding the problem and their own proposals when it comes to deciding on the best course of action. This, in turn, can cause a perfectly valid polarity to become a polarising force in the organisation as people take sides, join their tribe and dismiss those with the opposing view for 'not having the best interests of the organisation or its stakeholders at heart'.

Some polarities are fairly innocuous; others have far greater impact in (or on) our organisations or at a societal level. These dualities can create distinctly different ways of comprehending reality – radically different beliefs about fundamental things. Things like our sense of what's morally right and wrong, what's true and what's not.

Sounding familiar?

In arguing for the importance of Opposable Thinking[61], Johnson cites two best-selling management books, *In Search of Excellence*[62] and *Built to Last*[63]. Both are rooted in research into the distinguishing features of organisations that significantly outperformed their competitors.

The companies in *Built to Last* that outperformed the market by a factor of 15 or more were particularly good at "tapping the power of polarities"[64] – not just *managing* them.

Similarly, of the 43 companies singled out as 'excellent' in *In Search of Excellence*, the 14 that retained that title five years on were primarily distinguished by their ability to manage seven important polarities[65].

What it looks like to upgrade our capacity for Opposable Thinking

As in the previous chapters, we'll show the four levels in action through a case study. First, it's helpful to give you a sense of what to look out for.

Why do we encounter so many polarities?

We've embedded polarities in many of our languages, particularly in the so-called Western World. Many of our most basic concepts can only be understood with reference to something they oppose. You can't grasp what 'up' means without understanding the meaning of 'down'.

Those linguistic polarities are probably derived from the fact that our bodies – and particularly our eyes – are wired to focus on contrast, the borders between one stimulus and another.

Polarities also thrive in one of the most ancient forms of collective problem-solving: the debate – a process that necessitates 'for' and 'against'. Debating is so ingrained in many cultures that it's also the primary means of deciding whether someone is innocent or guilty of a crime, hence the predictably polarising outcomes and perceptions of injustice.

Thus – particularly in the West and increasingly in other cultures – we're constantly bombarded with physical, linguistic and cultural messages that encourage us to divide the world into pairs of opposites. No wonder these binary ways of thinking are baked in so deeply to our personal operating systems.

Level 1

When we meet a polarity with Level 1 Opposable Thinking, we see only one right answer. It's binary, black or white, and we're committed to upholding our side of the debate. We don't even  see how our position might be connected to (or even created by) the opposing position. For instance, if we take the 'centralise-decentralise' debate, at Level 1 we're unaware that our demand for more autonomy is a response to the need elsewhere in the organisation for more central control, and vice versa.

Level 2

At Level 2, we view the two poles as options among others, but still don't see the connection between them. We'll choose to either promote our preference or argue for some form of compromise. If

we opt for the latter, we may truly accept the compromise or we might still favour our preferred option, either openly, surreptitiously or passive-aggressively. Another option that's open to us at Level 2 is 'agreeing to disagree'. Importantly, though, it still means we favour our position. We're not truly putting ourselves in the place of those holding that opposing view.

As we evolve our thinking within Level 2, we start to also notice 'shades of grey' between the black and the white and to accept that an 'either/or' solution may be too simplistic or unacceptable to some parties. We become better at negotiating and finding ways to allow both sides to win.

Level 3

At Level 3, we switch from seeing the two poles as separate alter-natives to automatically noticing the underlying polarity *and* the conflicts associated with taking either position. We've moved

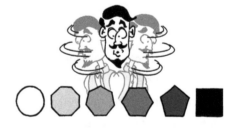

from Level 2's sense of there being shades of grey to noticing the inherent tensions in our thinking. We also realise that it's impossible to resolve dilemmas without addressing the contextual factors that created or maintain those dilemmas.

Level 3 also shows us that the two poles are concepts that relate to each other and shift over time depending on how we look at them. Thus, when dealing with dilemmas in the world around us, we often find ourselves mediating between positions while others polarise into them. Sometimes, though, we oscillate between our own preferred alternatives, tolerating the resulting tension but frustrated by the difficulty of finding a way forward that truly respects the complexity of the issues.

Level 4

The transition to Level 4 is characterised by us developing a range of strategies for responding to polarities. All involve stepping back from the dilemma to look at it from the outside – holding both ideas as valid and acceptable at the same time (as F. Scott Fitzgerald so aptly noted in the quote at the start of this chapter).

Once we've taken this step back, new ways of responding open up to us. We begin to see dilemmas and polarities as *opportunities for improving our thinking about a situation*, rather than problems to be resolved. Importantly, from a leadership perspective, this realisation drives a new set of behaviours. We start to actively seek out polarising or contrary viewpoints as a way of enhancing our thinking. Previously, if we're honest with ourselves, we'd have been seeking to influence or exclude those views because they over-complicate things or mean people are simply 'not-on-the-bus'.

The images below show three different ways of approaching a polarity we've spotted to find a better way forward than we would have done if we'd compromised, generalised or chosen one end of the polarity at the expense of the other. The three – which we've called 'tacking', 'including' and 'inhabiting' – are options we have available to us at Level 4. None is better than the other and there will be other approaches, too. The three can be a little difficult to get one's head around – that's the nature of Level 4, really. So we've fleshed them out with examples.

With **'tacking'**, we recognise that there is no single, enduring 'right answer' so we'll need to consciously move back and forth between the two poles over time, choosing the point on the continuum that's most appropriate given the circumstances in which we find ourselves. We also look for ways to weave together different features from various points on the continuum, creating new combinations that serve an overarching purpose.

Level 4: tacking

For example: imagine you're managing someone who's very talented, inexperienced and craves autonomy. At Level 4 you'd see it as a one-to-two-year project that will hopefully culminate in both of you knowing when your input is required and when it isn't. In the interim, you'll inevitably oscillate between over-checking and under-checking, occasionally making mistakes and hopefully learning from experience. At Level 3, you'd feel a great deal more angst over the need to get the 'tightrope walking' right every time.

When **'including'**, we notice that within each of the poles exists the seed of the other. We then seek to explore the ways in which the two poles inform and interconnect with each other so we don't get caught by a 'flip' between polarities.

For instance: imagine you're a very nurturing leader spending a great deal of time and energy supporting your people. At previous levels in this capacity, you'd

Level 4: including

eventually exhaust yourself then flip to the opposite, non-nurturing pole (withdrawing or lashing out). At Level 4, you'll see the risk of over-caring that's inherent in your nurturing style. You'll also accept that there's likely a selfish, punitive part of you buried somewhere within all that nurturing.

When **'inhabiting'**, we accept that the polarity is an ever-shifting, ever-present tension in meaning making which is created (within and between us), by the thought processes which generate it. We then fully immerse ourselves in the dilemma for a period of time so we can examine the underlying assumptions that have given rise to it.

Level 4: inhabiting

By way of example, consider the polarity created in many organisations by the ideas of meritocracy vs inclusion. On one hand is the desire to include people from all backgrounds. On the other is the need to select those who are most likely to do the best job. Many well-meaning conversations about 'working with Millennials' or 'maximising Asian talent' are riddled with assumptions. For instance, that Millennials are a homogenous group; that popular comparisons between the generations are based on actual data; that the things today's older generations are saying about Millennials are much different to the things these elders' own elders said about *them* when they were that age. Sadly, the conversations that characterise organisations' struggles with this polarity might be doomed to failure and compromise if we stick with the hierarchical, individualistic cultures that prevail in most Western corporates. Ultimately, meaningful, sustained progress with regard to this polarity will probably require a very significant shift in the usual Western corporate *context* that created and sustains the dilemma.

Opposable Thinking in action: meet the team

Rather than share case studies for each of the three upgrades, we'll focus on one conversation that shows how challenging it can be when different people are applying different levels of Opposable Thinking to the same problem.

Thus the characters you'll meet here aren't in transition. Each is looking at the situation from a particular level when it comes to Opposable Thinking. As the conversation unfolds, we'll explore how each team member's contribution reflects the level at which they're operating.

MacraSet is a publicly listed company with around 5000 employees that has been trading for 25 years. The company was founded in their garage by brothers Geoff and Paul Hughes using a fairly generous redundancy pay-out when Paul opted to leave his previous employer of 20 years. Geoff and Paul are now non-voting shareholders, maintaining an interest but taking no active role in the way the business is run. That responsibility falls to MacraSet's five executive directors under the watchful eyes of the Board – led by the chairwoman, Lisa Hamilton, who is supported by three other non-executive directors.

MacraSet has experienced a sudden dip in sales since a new competitor entered the market. The five executive directors have been actively disagreeing for three months about what to do, during which time the position has worsened month on month. This quarter's results

> **"We look for lessons in the actions of great leaders when we should be looking at what is going on in their heads – particularly the way they creatively build on the tensions between conflicting ideas."**
>
> Roger Martin, Dean, the University of Toronto's Rotman School of Management[66]

are about to be announced and they're expecting a significant impact on share price to add to the company's troubles.

The executive directors' names and roles are shown below, as is the level at which each is operating in this conversation.

Team member	Role	Level
Adam	Sales Director	Level 1
Beth	Finance Director	Level 2
Bill	Commercial Director	Level 2
Charles	Managing Director	Level 3
Davina	Operations Director	Level 4

We join the team as tempers have begun to fray. They've thirty minutes left before the time they've allocated for the discussion comes to an end, and they're due to meet with the Board in the morning. The day after that, they'll be in front of MacraSet's investors.

It's your choice whether you read the whole dialogue before the commentary or absorb both simultaneously. Either way, we strongly recommend that, as you go, you note down each dilemma or polarity the group is grappling with. There are at least 7, so it'll be good practice to see how many you can find.

Team member	Dialogue	Commentary / analysis
Charles (MD, Level 3)	Please, guys: we need to get to a consensus on this so we can show the Board a united front. They need to know we've got a handle on this and we all need to feel we're well set for the investors' meeting.	Looking at the situation from Level 3, Charles recognises the need to find a way forward that reconciles the various conflicting ideas and beliefs at play. However, as we'll see, he's yet to develop the capacity to marshal or integrate those differences.
Davina (Operations, Level 4)	I'm not so sure, Charles. I think we should open up to the Board about the dilemmas we're facing and how different our views are. They know us and they trust us, and we'll get much better feedback from them if we're honest about our conflicting opinions.	From Davina's Level 4 point of view, the conflict of opinion is a positive thing and closing it down too soon would be to the organisation's disadvantage. She feels that, by taking their differences to the Board, the team remains more open to whatever the Board might contribute to the decision-making process.
Adam (Sales, Level 1)	I couldn't disagree more, Davina. Charles, if we can't go to them with a single, coherent vision – a clear way forward – they will think we've totally lost control of the business. All we're missing is the proper research into what's happening in the market and with our own sales processes. Once we have that, we can make a good, solid recommendation.	Adam's Level 1 approach prioritises generating one, single 'correct' answer based on robust analysis of the facts. From his point of view, any other approach would be illogical and suboptimal.

Team member	Dialogue	Commentary / analysis
Beth (Finance, Level 2)	And meanwhile, the clock is ticking and the numbers are going South... I agreed with Davina's recommendation at our last meeting and it's even more urgent now. I think we should start a set of small experiments across the whole range of channels to get some data about why this has hit us so hard. None of our other competitors seems to be feeling the heat as much as we are.	Beth prioritises an expedient approach that has the greatest positive impact given the time and resources available. Like many people at Level 2, she's open to borrowing ideas from elsewhere – particularly from people who are more developed in this capacity. In this case, it's Davina's proposal to experiment.
Bill (Commercial, Level 2)	I just can't see what we'll gain by 'experimenting'. We'll look like we have no idea what to do and that'll undermine our reputation in the market even more. We need to keep it simple and come up with a process to gather more information using the channels we already have.	Bill and Beth may both be coming at this situation with a Level 2 lens, but that doesn't mean he agrees with her. They're merely operating at the same level of complexity when assessing the options in this situation. Like Beth, Bill is looking for the most expedient course of action. Like her, his opinion as to which option is most expedient is based on the beliefs, assumptions and concepts to which he has become attached through prior experience and the requirements of his role in the organisation.

Team member	Dialogue	Commentary / analysis
Davina (Operations, Level 4)	There are two conversations going on here: one about how we handle the Board and one about what we do to actually understand what's going on. I suggest we focus on one at a time.	Operating at Level 4 in this capacity enables Davina to step back and notice the two different dilemmas the team has with regard to this problem. She separates them out so that each can be tackled separately.
Charles (MD, Level 3)	I think the Board issue is the most important one. We *have* to work out what we are going to say tomorrow!	Charles is recognising here that he doesn't yet know how to resolve the dilemmas facing them unless he can first manage the anxiety that it creates in him. So he responds by focusing on what he *can* manage – i.e. their approach to the meeting tomorrow.
Beth (Finance, Level 2)	Well, I know it's urgent, but if we could settle on an approach to understanding the problem, *that* would give us the coherent message we're looking for. So we'd come across far better in the meeting, too!	Again, Beth is focusing on the approach that will get the best result for the smallest investment. While we may agree that she's chosen wisely, she's still choosing one of two options. She's not seeking to understand the opposing views, integrate them with each other or explore other options.
Charles (MD, Level 3)	Sorry, Beth. You're absolutely right. Lisa [the Chairwoman] can be pretty unforgiving at times and I was letting my anxiety about tomorrow get the better of me. Davina, can you talk us through this experiment idea again?	Here, Charles shares the insights offered by operating at Level 3 in the *Self-relating* capacity. This helps him articulate his reasons for favouring one option over the other, which enables him to then instantly align with the opposing option. While this

Team member	Dialogue	Commentary / analysis
		has its benefits, it is also evidence of one of the common challenges at Level 3. At Level 3, we're often so willing to invest in understanding everyone else's opinions that we align and realign too easily, agreeing with whoever spoke last or most convincingly.
Davina (Operations, Level 4)	I can, but I'm pretty wedded to it as I'm convinced it's our only option. Perhaps, rather than me continuing to push that approach, someone else should suggest an alternative? Just because I can't think of one myself doesn't mean there isn't one.	Earlier, Charles noticed how his anxiety was affecting his preference for one option over another. However, he did so in response to a challenge from Beth. When Davina calls out her own bias towards the experimentation option, she's noticing and naming a far subtler internal process – biases simply don't generate the same overt physiological warning signs as anxieties do. Davina is also noticing this bias spontaneously, without any external force bringing it to her attention. As before, Davina doesn't just notice that inner process playing out in the moment. She intervenes to create a less biased route forward in the pursuit of an optimal collective decision – one that factors in the various perspectives *and* the complexity of the situation.

Team member	Dialogue	Commentary / analysis
Bill (Commercial, Level 2)	We've run customer surveys in the past. I can't see any reason why that wouldn't work. Plus, it's far less risky.	Again, Bill is aligning with one option based on his assessment of the likely return versus the effort and risk associated with adopting the other option currently on the table.
Beth (Finance, Level 2)	I can see the merits in a survey approach, Bill, but we won't know what questions to ask. Consumers can rarely tell us exactly why their preferences have suddenly changed. Even if they can, it won't necessarily tell us what we should do next. If we take Davina's route and experiment with things like price, packaging and small promotions, it'll give us some direct, tangible data to show us what – if anything – will help us claw back some market share.	Beth's response to Bill's argument is similarly expedient. She acknowledges his point of view, but – like him – takes no steps to better understand it. She sets out the two elements of the dilemma: 'seek more quantitative information by running a traditional customer survey' vs 'run a series of small experiments to understand why preferences are changing'. However, she doesn't explicitly state that it *is* a dilemma. She then goes on to advocate for one position (experimentation) in opposition to the other (Bill's preference for a survey approach).
Davina (Operations, Level 4)	Hang on, Beth. I think we should let Bill put some more flesh on the bones of his idea before we decide whether or not it's workable. Tell us more, Bill.	Again, Davina uses Level 4 Opposable Thinking to better understand the merits of Bill's alternative, rather than siding too soon with one option – even the option she herself suggested. This enables them to harvest any benefits from Bill's suggestion and integrate them into whatever solution they choose. In doing so, she's

Team member	Dialogue	Commentary / analysis
		demonstrating an interest in 'tacking' (one of the three Level 4 approaches we covered on page 128).
Bill (Commercial, Level 2)	Well, I am not sure there's much more I can say, really. Adam, how long would it take to generate a quick-and-dirty survey? I imagine that's better for you and your teams than for them to have to work out how best to support a whole range of temporary fixes – even if we do sell them to your teams and the rest of the organisation as 'experiments'.	Here, Bill is focused on expediency but clearly shows his ability to see that Adam and his team also have reasons to support this option. Interestingly, that ability to empathise is still very much in service of making a decision that favours his preferred option. That decision, he hopes, will enable the team and the organisation to move forward with a tried-and-tested course of action.
Adam (Sales, Level 1)	I think the term 'quick-and-dirty' says it all, Bill. If we don't do it properly, the data we get back could take us down the wrong path entirely. The data simply won't be sufficiently valid and reliable for us to base any decisions on it. Look everyone: I know you all have your views, but this is a sales problem, pure and simple. I've already got my best team on it and we've hired a business school professor who's at the cutting edge where the post-digital sales cycle is concerned. We'll have a recommended course of action at the end of the month.	Adam is operating at Level 1 when it comes to Opposable Thinking. From there, he views expediency as a threat to accuracy and treats it very much as a binary trade-off. He's not closed to others' perspectives, though: he has hired someone with even greater expertise than him. Like most people operating at Level 1, he'll adapt his way of doing things if that business school professor sells him a better approach.

Team member	Dialogue	Commentary / analysis
Davina (Operations, Level 4)	I hear you, Adam, and getting an outsider's views could stimulate some genuinely new thinking. At the same time, this problem is much more complex than that and it affects the whole organisation. I wonder if we focused your professor more on offering a number of different perspectives on the nature of the problem, rather than a single solution, that might actually be more helpful as it'll feed more effectively into our thinking. We can all see the market shifting faster than ever before. We need to evolve at least as quickly as *it* does, ideally even faster. If we're going to do that – and if we're to have any chance of fixing things before the drop in sales hits our next quarter, too – we need every part of the business, everyone in this room, to be bringing their brains and different perspectives to the table.	Davina is acknowledging Adam's position with regard to this particular polarity, partly in order to avoid encouraging him to polarise against her and dig his heels in further. For the same reasons, she's also trying to be inclusive and (somewhat) tentative with her proposal. In making her suggestion about the professor's input, she's opening up the opportunity to use another, external perspective to see if the group can reframe the problem itself. This is an attempt at further 'inhabiting' the dilemma to help the team examine the underlying thought processes which may be keeping them stuck – 'inhabiting' being another of the three Level 4 approaches to polarities we covered earlier in this chapter.
Charles (MD, Level 3)	I have to confess, I am at a bit of a loss here. You've all got good ideas and each of you makes a really good case. Maybe we should just try all of them – throw everything we've got at the	Charles's Level 3 Opposable Thinking helps him clearly see the dilemma and the complexity of the situation. He understands the merits and underlying 'truths' in each of the proposed solutions.

Team member	Dialogue	Commentary / analysis
	problem. You said yourself, Davina: we need to move at least as quickly as the changing market. So, can I ask you to scope out some possible experiments? And, Adam: work up a short customer survey and keep your teams focused on coming up with those recommendations – although I'd rather we had them well before the end of the month. Beth can help with any financial data any of you need. This way we can tell the Board we have a whole range of strategies in play.	However, without access to Level 4, he's still struggling to marshal and integrate the opposing options. Until he upgrades to that next level, he'll continue to struggle to find a suitable way forward in situations like these. He'll find his lack of clarity and the pressure to be seen to be doing something spur him into moving forward with all of the possible options at once.
Beth (Finance, Level 2)	Oh Charles, I'm all in favour of compromise when it's the only option, but trying to do everything will just spread us way too thin. I say *you* choose one of the options and we go with that. We're all adults here and ultimately you're the boss. I vote for experimenting. What do the rest of you think?	Here we see Beth's expedient Level 2 approach seeming far more decisive – and thus *appearing* more productive – than Charles's Level 3 approach to the situation. Again, she states a position on the options as well as a position on the process the team should follow now to make a decision. It's notable that she then seeks views from the rest of the team. However, our experience with teams tells us that the way she's done so is unlikely to resolve the dilemma in a way that secures everyone's commitment to a single, collective direction. It's more

Team member	Dialogue	Commentary / analysis
		likely that one option will 'win' without those who support the alternatives feeling sufficiently heard that they will truly fully commit. Not only that, but if the team follows Beth's guidance, the solution they settle on probably won't draw on the strengths of the discarded alternatives.

Whether or not you have a similar mix of levels operating in your team, we're hoping MacraSet's attempts to resolve their dilemmas has given you a clear picture of how people working from each of these four levels approach challenges that require Opposable Thinking.

We suspect you'll have recognised many of the patterns at play in that conversation. Perhaps the circling; the lost conversational threads; the difficulties the team had following an argument; how they struggled to reach consensus. In our experience – and perhaps yours – this is typical of group conversations where a series of dilemmas are at play but have yet to be properly surfaced.

The polarities within

Given the nature of the MacraSet case study, it would be easy to assume Opposable Thinking applies only to dilemmas and polarities *between* people. In reality, life throws many dilemmas at us and plenty of those play out inside a single individual, creating tensions and unresolved conflicts within our inner world. As you'll have noticed when we explored Self-relating, each upgrade to our Opposable Thinking capacity increases our awareness of the polarities within us. There's a risk of that generating significant internal conflict. So, thankfully, those upgrades also enhance our ability to respond to those emerging polarities.

How many polarities did you spot at MacraSet?

We said at the outset that we're aware of at least seven dilemmas the team faced in the course of that one conversation:

- [ ] Open the conversation out to the board vs Show a united front

- [ ] Openly inquire into the underlying causes vs Ensure we appear 'in control'

- [ ] Use a traditional data gathering approach vs Experiment to gather information

- [ ] Go quick and dirty vs Follow best practice

- [ ] Prioritise speed of response vs Prioritise maximum data-gathering

- [ ] Open the conversation out vs Use a small group of experts

- [ ] Seek consensus as a group vs Ask the leader to decide

Which of those seven did you spot, and what others did you find that we've missed?

Once we reach Level 4 in Opposable Thinking, particularly if we've *also* reached Level 4 in Self-relating, we're able to make more conscious choices regarding our engagement with our internal conflicts and dilemmas. We need to do so because, while we're far better at polarity management than we were at other levels, it still takes up a fair amount of bandwidth. So we'll invest in the polarities that matter most to us and give ourselves a break on the rest. Giving ourselves that break means learning to accept that we will always contain a multitude of unresolved tensions. It's part of the rich fabric of human existence.

Summary and self-assessment

You're relying on Opposable Thinking when you're attempting to examine your own thinking – to notice when your beliefs are keeping you stuck, when you are 'disagreeing with yourself' internally or when you find yourself in conflict with others. It is essential for working with organisational dilemmas or with your own competing values and beliefs. It's a capacity that's key to the creation of options and decision making in complex situations, and in generating change when things get stuck.

As we upgrade through the levels with regard to this capacity, we're increasingly able to step back from polarities, understand both poles and the space between, and use our insights to craft a way forward.

To ground your self-assessment in a current reality, we suggest you pick a dilemma that you and your colleagues (or your wider organisation) are currently facing. It needs to be something in which different people have different beliefs about the best way forward.

If nothing immediately springs to mind, look for some of these common symptoms of an underlying polarity:

- A stalled decision – everyone knows a difficult decision needs to be made but the conversations go around in circles as different options are repeatedly asserted without resolution

- Overt conflict – between individuals or departments, based on disagreements about the best way to operate

- Avoidance of an issue – opposition to a planned course of action is not voiced but 'goes underground' so that direct conflict does not get triggered

Then think back over the days, weeks or months that this dilemma has continued unresolved. What are the polarities involved?

....

....

....

Bear those polarities in mind as you read through the following summaries. Then, as with the other capacities, indicate the level at which you believe you're currently operating.

Prior to Level 1, I have been learning to...

☐ Articulate a complex position, albeit in quite a categorical, one-sided way

☐ Play with my ideas and imagine other possible interpretations of what is going on

☐ Hone my logical thinking as the foundation of my day-to-day decision-making

At Level 1, I...

☐ Focus on upholding my own position when there are conflicting views

☐ Find myself quickly polarising against people who hold opposing opinions or who have interpreted the situation differently

☐ Tend towards binary, black or white thinking, missing possible shades of grey

☐ Consider compromise to be an inferior outcome

Find reasons (when under pressure) to avoid exploring possible options or the wider context, considering them 'irrelevant', 'distracting' or 'time-wasting'

As I upgrade from Level 1 to Level 2, I'm getting better at...

Seeing the shades of grey and context-dependencies inherent in what previously felt like global, tightly held black or white truths (e.g. the belief that 'I must always make sure I finish my work according to the client's initial brief' might become 'Sometimes it is best to leave some questions open so the client can add more nuance later')

Noticing evidence that suggests that my long-and-dearly-held belief or assumption could be wrong – although I still tend to ignore or absorb the contra-indications rather than overhauling my belief system

Accepting that I might not have all the answers, even if I'm supposedly the expert

At Level 2, I...

Can see strengths and weaknesses in opposing positions and am starting to see some shades of grey between the extremes

Am developing an appetite for techniques that help me and my colleagues explore opposing ideas (e.g. the polarity-manage-ment practices we'll share in Part 4)

Am keen to find negotiated solutions or compromises

Am starting to genuinely value others' feedback and positions on situations, even when those points of view differ markedly from my own – thus I'm becoming open to the possibility of co-creation and genuinely collaborative action

☐ Am beginning to notice *how* these polarities play out in my organisation, once they have been pointed out to me

As I upgrade from Level 2 to Level 3, I'm getting better at...

☐ Doubting any position or stance that claims to be 'right' or 'better than the alternatives'

☐ Understanding and inquiring about the deeper reasons for people taking the position they have with regard to a given polarity

☐ Noticing conflicts and contradictions between my own stated beliefs and actions (e.g. that I say I believe in autonomy and empowerment, but constantly wade in and solve my people's problems for them)

At Level 3, I...

☐ Am more aware of the dilemmas at play in my work environment – and of the polarising effects on people and groups of adhering too rigidly to opposing views

☐ Am eager to surface, explore and work through dilemmas – and I use a variety of techniques to do so in an open and engaging way

☐ Am noticing some of my own internal conflicts – and starting to see how they connect with (and play out in) my conversations and relationships with other people

☐ Find that my awareness of polarities and shades of grey sometimes traps me in a loop, leaving me struggling to make a decision or feeling torn between different people's conflicting advice

☐ Find it harder to resolve dilemmas in which people who are important to me seem to hold the opposing view to mine – a situation that triggers an additional polarity within me (between my need to maintain the relationship and my desire to be true to myself)

As I upgrade from Level 3 to Level 4, I'm getting better at...

☐ Overcoming my predisposition towards compromise and a sufficiently harmonious 'third way' – and, in doing so, I push our thinking forward using a decision-making process that's as fair, creative, robust and inclusive as we can make it

☐ Finding a way forward that none of us would have foreseen at the outset but which surfaces and pulls together all of the threads, perspectives, differences, biases, assumptions and choice-points, without seeming judgemental or taking sides

☐ Discriminating between the momentary dilemmas and long-standing internal conflicts that are part of the way I experience the world (and probably always have been)

At Level 4, I...

☐ Accept dilemmas and conflicting values or beliefs as inherent in the way people think, feel and interact with each other

☐ Actively seek opposing and contradictory views to stretch and improve my own thinking

☐ Consider all positions as potentially offering valuable contributions, as long as they can be backed up by data or sound logic

☐ Can articulate in considerable detail my own current 'dilemmas-in-action' and how they're playing out in my life

☐ Challenge my own hypocrisies and polarised thinking *in the moment* (e.g. by arguing against myself; imagining data or contexts that would render my beliefs invalid; asking people with radically opposing views to play devil's advocate and genuinely embracing their attempts to persuade me)

☐ Still find it hard to objectively critique the most deeply held beliefs and values that make me 'me', or to experiment with truly adopting a view that radically opposes my own – while I can do so on an intellectual level, it generally triggers emotions in me that lock me even more rigidly into my existing world view

Bearing in mind the dilemma you chose (on page 142) to act as the backdrop to your self-assessment, at which level do you believe you're currently operating? What makes you think that?

Opposable Thinking

Level 4

Level 3

Level 2

Level 1

What do you notice about your own approach to the polarities involved in this particular dilemma? If the level at which you're operating in that situation is different to the level at which you *normally* operate, why do you think that is?

....

....

....

....

....

....

An experiment to test this out

Now, to deepen your appreciation of the four levels of Opposable Thinking, use the table below to zoom in on three or four of the other key players in the dilemma you chose above.

These needn't be the people who are most attached to a given position. You'll learn as much from those who are less committed and anyone who's attempting to reconcile other people's differences.

Identify each person's position in relation to this dilemma and its polarities. Then consider the way they've approached their own positions and those of others. On reflection, at which of the four levels does their approach suggest they're operating[a]?

---

a As we'll see in Chapter 9, the level at which they're currently operating in this situation could be different to the level at which they're *capable* of operating.

Name	Position in relation to the polarities	Approach	Level of Opposable Thinking

7

Sense-making: getting better at handling complexity

● ● ●

- How Sense-making helps us handle all things VUCA
- The links between Sense-making and IQ
- What it means to upgrade in this capacity
- How people at each of the levels approach the same problem

HERE'S THE BAD NEWS: your IQ will have peaked somewhere between the age of 18 and 21. Since then, you've either been maintaining that level of IQ or failing to maintain it.

Oh, and those 'brain-training' games? Unfortunately, the balance of evidence is that the only thing they help you get better at is... brain-training games.

Most of us make up for that by accumulating experience. The more we know, the less reliant we are on raw IQ. Thus, we can usually summon up tried-and-tested solutions quicker than someone whose brain is faster but lacks our extensive knowledge.

Eventually, though, if we don't also upgrade our capacity for Sense-making, our growing

> "A child has no stronger desire than to make sense of the world..."
>
> John Holt, teacher and school reformer[67]

stockpile of knowledge and prior experience delivers diminishing returns. This is particularly true when we're faced with situations or environments that are volatile, uncertain, complex and/or ambiguous.

Of the four capacities, Sense-making is the most purely 'cognitive'. Imagine all the information within you and coming at you is flowing through a network of pipes inside your head. You can push and push that system, pump more and more data through it, but eventually you'll go too far. You'll clog the pipes and the flow will slow and eventually stop. You'll have exceeded your capacity for processing all that data. You'll have to stop and wait for the pipes to clear before you can take anything else in.

When we upgrade this capacity, we're widening the pipes. Processing the same amount of data – the same levels of volatility, uncertainty, complexity and ambiguity – now uses far less of our total 'bandwidth' than it did previously.

Upgrades to this capacity enable us to improve our thinking in a number of areas, including:

- Diagnosing situations over longer timeframes, looking further into the past and the future

- Drawing on broader and more diverse data-sets

- Gathering masses of data into increasingly sophisticated 'chunks'

- Seeing more and more layers and interdependencies as we move to a more systemic understanding of the issues we face

- Becoming increasingly comfortable processing all of that messiness and turning our understanding into a coherent and adaptable way forward

Getting better at these things makes it easier to assess what's happening around us in a VUCA world and decide the best course of action. After all, the political, economic, socio-demographic and technological landscape is moving at what feels like an exponential rate. We see competitors emerging from unexpected places. Your external stakeholders' expectations of you are evolving and escalating, whether you call them customers, clients, service users, beneficiaries or something else. At the same time, their opinions of your organisation are influenced by always-on, globally distributed news, fake news and fickle hashtags.

All of this makes it harder and harder to work out the best route to our chosen destination. It makes it harder to sell that journey to the people we need to take with us. Not only that, it makes it increasingly difficult to know with any certainty that our chosen *destination* is itself the right place to be headed.

Sense-making can help with that, particularly when it's used in combination with the other three capacities.

The really good news is this: unlike IQ, you can continue upgrading this capacity well into your forties, fifties, sixties and even beyond.

What does it mean to upgrade in this capacity?

Initially, up to and at Level 1, we borrow tools and processes for identifying, analysing and solving problems from the people around us – experts, teachers, parents, siblings, colleagues, mentors and so on. We think in a 'step-by-step' way, one task or sub-goal at a time. Hence, we can get lost in the detail of each step, losing sight of the whole process as we go.

As we progress through Level 2, we begin to create tools and processes of our own, especially in relation to the things that most interest us – whether that's innovation, sales or accounting processes, manufacturing improvements, capability frameworks, marketing models or something else.

We're generally proud and excited to be doing so, which can cause us to cling too tightly to those tools and processes, privileging our new inventions over others and assuming they're better than what came before.

We're also thinking in a way that is more end-goal directed than at Level 1. We'll take our objectives and map out a whole trajectory for reaching them. This might include various potential obstacles and contingency plans to overcome or circumnavigate them. However, once we're underway, we can get blind-sided when our carefully designed processes and programmes hit an unexpected snag. So we often resort to simply pushing harder, rather than stepping back and seeking an alternative path or altering the destination to better suit evolving conditions.

Where the description of this capacity comes from

This capacity draws on a rich, fertile and sometimes impenetrable field of research and ideas, which includes mind-bending concepts crafted by some immensely conceptual thinkers[68].

Karen's greatest influences in her initial work in this area were Eliot Jaques and Katherine Cason, whose ideas are neatly summarised in their book *Human Capability*[69].

Jaques and Cason interviewed a range of leaders and analysed the cognitive complexity of their answers to broad and potentially contentious social questions. There were clear differences in people's ability to construct a coherent and convincing argument. Some people focused on a single viewpoint or type of data. Others brought in a wide range of different opinions and arguments, considering the far-future consequences of social choices and using their own perspective as just one data point.

Jaques' subsequent organisational work[70] produced a framework that aligns well with the stages of adult development that have informed our approach to differentiating between the four levels in each capacity.

Once we hit Level 3, we start to notice that there are many acceptable (or good enough) ways of reaching a given objective. As a result, we become less attached to the tools and ideas we lovingly crafted at Level 2. We're more willing to improve them, discard them or use them interchangeably with other tools to suit the situation in which we find ourselves. We're not just able to identify different paths to a given objective, we're also starting to question the objectives themselves. It's only when we reach Level 3 that we're creating alternative *ways of reasoning* about a situation or issue – rather than just different arguments within the same way of thinking. We also start to compare the usefulness of those different ways of reasoning, and each approach's fit with our values.

Level 4 is a water-shed in our ability to handle complexity. We suddenly develop new ways of thinking about the multiplicity of possible pathways and desired outcomes which hit us at Level 3. We start to develop our own overall models and frameworks for thinking about the situations or professional domains we've been mastering. We're able to gather up a hugely diverse set of ideas and influences into a single map of 'what's going on around here', then use that map to choose strategies, drive decisions and establish what is negotiable and what isn't.

In Chapter 2, we observed that progress through the four levels in these capacities is rarely correlated with ascent through the organisational hierarchy. This is particularly so when it comes to Sense-making. We believe this is because so few assessment processes recognise the crucial role that an individual's complexity of thought plays in their ability to lead effectively. Hence, it's not uncommon for teams to include people who are operating at a higher level than their leader when it comes to Sense-making – sometimes two or more levels higher.

That can be absolutely fine. It can also be a nightmare. Which way it goes depends heavily on the dynamics in that team. In part, that's about the relationships between the leader and the team, and between the various members of the team – which brings in questions of trust and ego, which Richard has explored in *The Boss Factor*. In part, it's down to the processes the team members use to harness the diversity of approach and perspective they have available to them. All of that relies on the other three capacities: Perspective-shifting, Self-relating and Opposable Thinking.

Warning: be wary of your own IQ

Your intelligence is a fantastic asset. It also has its downsides. Having a high IQ can make it easier to grasp this capacity – and the levels within it – on an intellectual level. However, somewhat paradoxically, it can also make it harder to progress from one level to the next.

The cleverer we are, the quicker we tend to reach our own conclusions; the more effectively we can argue that our existing ways of thinking, feeling and behaving are right and others' ways are wrong. The easier we find it to pump large swathes of data through our mental 'pipes', the more likely it is we'll have been able to get away without upgrading in this capacity.

If you're blessed with an especially high IQ, be very careful when assessing your own current level in this capacity. You're probably accustomed to being at the top of the class in things, so it'll be tempting to assume you must be at Level 3 or 4. Statistically, you're no more likely to be there than anyone else. That's no reflection on your IQ or on your value as a human being. It's just a reflection of the fact we'll generally only *naturally* develop this capacity to the higher levels if we're repeatedly exposed to certain kinds of complexity or extremes of innovative thinking.

How four people at different levels approach the same problem

For this case study, we'll focus on the Strategy team at Panagen, a successful general insurance company looking to expand into the health sector.

Panagen is led by an ambitious team of directors who are keen to pursue a new direction that capitalises on emerging opportunities in a growing and evolving market. The new Managing Director, who operates at Level 4 in this and some of the other capacities, is keen to encourage people to develop in the jobs they're already doing. She has asked the Strategy Director and the Director of Organisational Design and Development to come up with a process that will be 'deliberately developmental'[71] for a group of managers in the Strategy team and, potentially, for the wider group of directors.

The work itself isn't especially urgent, so the Strategy Director nominates his four most promising young managers Andrea, Brandon, Colin and Dominique – each of whom is currently operating at a different level when it comes to Sense-making.

They're all given the same task: dedicate one day a week, for three months, to coming up with a strategy for this new sector. They have access to a small budget, which can be used for anything reasonable. Each manager is also allowed four hours access to each of the Board Directors as well as unlimited support (within reason) from the in-house data analytics team.

The approaches they take demonstrate the clear differences between the four levels in this capacity.

Andrea (Level 1): using tried-and-tested rules and processes

Andrea assumes the best approach is to use the well-established strategic planning process that the Strategy Director brought with him when he joined the company five years ago. This leads her to take the following steps:

1. Undertake exhaustive desk research into the health insurance market as a whole, seeking guidance on general trends, Panagen's competitors and best practice in the industry

2. Commission a substantial analysis of Panagen's customer database,

focused on identifying the characteristics that determine which customers will be most open to the company cross-selling them other products

3. Conduct two-hour interviews with each of the Directors, sharing the information she's gathered and asking how they think their division might cope with a shift into delivering a different set of products

4. Invest the following month in making sense of all of the opinions and information she has gathered

She then calls a two-hour meeting with the team of directors to share her recommendations. In that meeting, some of the team notice contradictions in the industry data and in the opinions of the various commentators and contributors. They also have different interpretations and opinions of their own regarding what Andrea has brought to the table. For example:

- One director believes the market is consolidating, so Panagen should opt for a partnership or joint venture with an existing player

- Another believes the market is wide open, offering opportunities as yet untapped by anyone else, so the company should be bullish and go it alone

However, Andrea encourages the group to move on to the 'option assessment' phase of the strategic planning process on which she's based her approach. This involves her working up three potential models through which Panagen could enter healthcare, each brought to life with an existing example of that model working well for one of the company's competitors.

As per the agreed process, Andrea works with the Finance team to evaluate each model against four criteria:

1. The level of investment required

2. The potential returns over the next five, ten and twenty years

3. The model's risk profile

4. The degree of fit with existing processes, infrastructure, staffing and culture

The most compelling option is to invest in building three state-of-the-art private hospitals. It's a model that has worked well for one of Panagen's closest competitors, a Chinese company called Zhŭshén. Andrea makes her final recommendation to the Board based on this 'copycat' option, which would create a foothold into the European market at the premium end of the private healthcare spectrum.

Like Andrea, those of us who are most successful while operating at Level 1 have honed our ability to craft logical, rational arguments based on past experience and the prevailing wisdom in our chosen discipline.

As with any well-developed muscle, though, we tend to rely too heavily on it.

When tackling VUCA challenges from Level 1, we can generally see that there are lots of variables. We respond to them by 'bracketing off' whatever seems irrelevant so that we can attend to what's manageable.

If anyone else tries to force all of that added complexity back onto the table, we'll probably get frustrated with them. Whether we voice that frustration or not, we'll feel they're over-complicating things or being overly philosophical. In doing so, we're treating those VUCA challenges as complicated, technical puzzles that can be tackled with linear solutions.

If we're a team operating at Level 1, we do that 'bracketing off' partly by breaking the problem into chunks and allocating each chunk to different people or business units according to their expertise. Each of those independent units then works on their chunk of the problem, usually in isolation from the others. Then they share their solutions with whoever divvied up the work – or present them to the collective, one after the other.

Then comes the challenge of weaving it all together. If we're all stuck at Level 1 that will generally prove pretty difficult, because we are all still finding it difficult to make connections between different *types* of idea.

Whether it's with a group or on our own, when it comes to establishing direction, Level 1 Sense-making generally looks like the image on the right. When we're operating at Level 1, we assume that the next step in a sequence of events will be 'the one in the existing project plan'. Progress is generally from our current position to the next logical position. Thus, each move is a reaction to the context in which we find ourselves at the time – or to the advice of people whose opinions we respect. Hence, we might expect Andrea to change her plans based

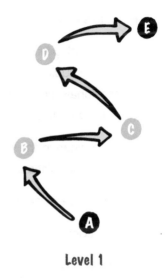

Level 1

on the advice of the Finance Director, then again when she speaks to the Sales Director – bouncing off them like in the image above. Each time, she's absorbing that person's views in their entirety, rather than stepping back from them and critiquing them as part of a larger whole. Thus, at Level 1, while we may *appear* to be adapting to changes in the situation, we're not really making conscious, informed choices based on an integrated appraisal of the complexities of that situation.

Brandon (Level 2): prioritising goal-focused action over adherence to inherited rules and processes

Brandon's approach is similar to Andrea's in some ways but significantly different in others. Like her, he spends considerable time understanding the market, sizing the opportunity and analysing Panagen's existing capacity and unique selling points.

When it comes to generating options, though, rather than asking what other organisations in insurance and healthcare are doing, Brandon looks at other industries in search of inspiration.

"How would Uber approach what we're trying to achieve?" he asks. "What would Airbnb, Apple or Facebook do?"

From this emerges a wealth of ideas, including:

- An app that connects patients directly with relevant health professionals, including a system whereby users rate or 'like' those health professionals so other users can make an informed choice when deciding who to see about their current ailment

- A setup wherein the health professionals are all self-employed with their own premises and Panagen works as a broker

- A mobile healthcare service that treats patients in their own homes

- Secure consultations by video conference

- A wearable device that monitors key indices of health and transmits those to a central hub that gives the user advance warning of impending illnesses

Like Andrea, Brandon convenes a meeting of the Directors and takes them through a process where they evaluate each of the different strategic options.

In doing so, they're using criteria Brandon has chosen to cover a wider range of domains: cultural fit, shift in the overall value of the company brand, level of innovation in the market, etc. As a result, the group selects a route that's riskier in the short term but has greater potential to transform the market.

Andrea's recommendation was essentially a carbon copy of an approach that had proven successful for one of Panagen's competitors. The option the Board favours following Brandon's session is one drawn from beyond Panagen's own industry and transported wholesale into the world of healthcare. In this case, it's to mimic Uber.

Once the initial choice is made, Brandon moves swiftly to work up a draft strategy that includes a target operating model and key milestones articulated in terms of customer numbers, revenue, profitability and geographical coverage.

He then sets up a steering group consisting of one member of each director's team. Within a week, the group puts forward a proposed four-year implementation plan. It's an adaptation of Uber's implementation over the same timescale, reworked to account for the differences between Panagen's and Uber's organisations. Those adaptations also factor in the practical and legal implications of the differences between Uber's offerings and Panagen's.

The plan acknowledges that the journey could be fraught with challenges. However, it doesn't factor in the possibility that the shape of the organisation will continue to change over the next four years, or the fact that the market itself will have moved on by the time Panagen reaches the final stop on the group's impressively extensive roadmap.

The steering group's roadmap is a classic example of Level 2 Sense-making. When we upgrade from Level 1, we start doing what's technically referred to as 'serial processing'. We start creating our own 'if this, then that' logics, where previously we borrowed them from others. This enables us to build more intricate plans for action – action being a key focus at this level.

When it comes to deciding how to respond to the situations around us, it's very much about establishing a goal, objective or solution and pre-determining a programmatic series of steps that will lead us towards it.

Like Brandon's roadmap, the plan for getting from 'where we are now' to 'where we want to be' can be highly sophisticated. Just as he adapted Uber's approach, so we – at Level 2 – will probably *start* the planning using someone else's template but then craft content that is very clearly something new, tailored to this specific situation. It'll often build backwards from the end goal and might include a sequence of steps or critical paths that stretch far into the future.

At Level 2, we're better at coming up with multiple routes to our chosen destination and choosing between them. We're also increasingly adept at noticing and predicting things that could interfere with the journey (from

A to F in the image on the right) – technical issues, efficiency challenges, fluctuating resource constraints, other people's conflicting goals, etc.

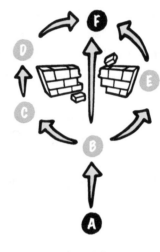

Level 2

We get better at managing and mitigating those risks, too, particularly if we've developed our capacities for Perspective-shifting and Opposable Thinking. Unfortunately, that's also the kind of thinking that causes us to treat anything that gets in the way of that journey from A to F as a problem. It's much harder for us to treat that obstacle as useful data or the seed from which new opportunities might emerge.

The wall at the centre of the image above shows another, related phenomenon that's common when we're operating at Level 2. While we may plan for potential obstacles and can be good at finding ways around them when they arise, we can also become so focused on the objective that we overinvest in 'smashing through' the obstacles in our way, sacrificing ourselves (and potentially others) on the altar of achievement.

So, at Level 2, we get better and better at getting from A to F. We've also learned a different approach to 'bracketing off' those VUCA things we consider obstructive or distracting. We create distinct places or teams where those slices of complexity can be allowed to 'do their thing'. For example, we create 'incubators', 'skunk works' and 'innovation teams' to give the 'disruptors' in our midst a home away from 'business as usual'. Thus they're able to make their contribution to the journey from A to F without disturbing or being overly constrained by their more conventional colleagues.

What could we do instead? Perhaps treat the positions of 'disruptive' and 'business as usual' as a polarity...?

What we're much less likely to do at Level 2 is question whether F is the right destination. That comes at Level 3. We also typically define F in quite narrow, inflexible terms. This happens whether F is a goal, objective, vision, mission statement or some other form of desired destination. Consider these two, for example:

- "We'll put an end to ovarian cancer by 2050"

- "We'll double our revenue in the next three years"

It's tempting to say one is somehow better than the other, but when it comes to Sense-making, they're at the same *level* in terms of complexity. Both are the kinds of goals we tend to create (or choose to sign up to) when we're operating at Level 2.

Let's take a look at what happens when we upgrade to Level 3.

Colin (Level 3): questioning the model of 'pathways and goals' and exploring a multitude of potential ways forward

Colin has a sense that, if Panagen is going to move into a whole new domain, the existing 'realities' of the organisation might need to change dramatically – including its overall strategy and approach to workforce planning, perhaps even aspects of the company's culture. Even if they don't ultimately *need* to change, he believes working within those existing constraints is a poor guide to what is possible. So, too, is working only with views that originate inside the organisation.

With this in mind, Colin starts his exploration by interviewing a very wide range of colleagues, customers, suppliers, etc., sourced through his own network and others'. He asks each of them "How would you imagine a new future for healthcare?" Throughout, he keeps the question broad, gathering a very wide range of opinions and as many creative suggestions as he can.

For his next step, he chooses not to use up his time with the directors through interviews and formal meetings. Instead, he collates the stories and ideas he's collected then calls a half-day creative workshop for the whole team, which he facilitates himself.

He presents the data in a variety of unusual ways, including storyboards, graphical maps and video clips of patients and professionals. The session sparks a number of new ideas, delighting the directors and resulting in seven wholly new and radically different schemes. All of these schemes emerge in a co-created way from the discussion. All fit with the company's core purpose and values. All seem financially viable and each has a highly enthusiastic sponsor on the leadership team as well as every other member's full endorsement.

Colin then works up 'safe-to-fail' prototype plans for each of the seven ideas. He presents these to the Board at a second meeting. During that meeting, it dawns on everyone present that, despite the energy and creativity it generated, the previous half-day workshop and Colin's work since then *haven't* produced two important ingredients:

1. Clear and agreed criteria by which to assess the extent to which each of the initiatives has been a 'success'

2. A process for evolving those seven initiatives as they unfold

Colin watches as the directors' energy wanes. Someone wonders out loud whether the approach is too scattergun and counter-cultural. It's a notion that's sufficiently infectious to prompt others to raise the issue of the potential impact on the morale and motivation of the teams assigned to those initiatives.

Like most people at Level 3, Colin has developed a hunger for uncertainty, complexity and ambiguity. While someone at Level 2 might relish the adrenaline rush of adapting to survive in a VUCA environment, Colin's more interested in exploring all that messiness and connecting what he finds in it.

Like Colin, at Level 3, we're combining ideas from eclectic sources and splicing together different processes to create genuinely new ways of doing things. As we settle into this way of looking at the world, we get better at processing whole chains of thought or consequence in parallel. Previously we were handling one chain at a time, although that chain might have been very long and complicated.

At Level 3, we respond to situations by imagining multiple unfolding scenarios. This opens up a wide range of potential ways forward and causes us to question not just the route to an established 'destination' but the destination itself. Hence, with regard to a particular situation, we'll see not just multiple ways to fulfil one objective, but multiple possible objectives (the F, K and P in the image below). Each of those objectives could be consistent, interdependent or in tension with any or all of the others.

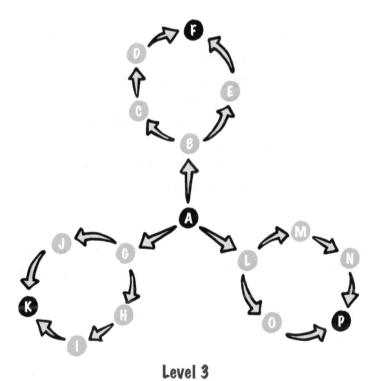

Level 3

Arguably, there's also a subtle but fundamental difference in how the term 'objective' is interpreted. At Level 2, it's a place to be reached, an interpretation of 'objective' that has an inbuilt singularity to it. At Level 3, an 'objective' is seen more as a requirement to fulfil, opening up the possibility of multiple, negotiable and potentially contradictory requirements within a single endeavour. Thus, at Level 3, there's less of a rigid attachment to a single pre-established goal and greater openness to a number of different possible outcomes or end points. Hence, at Level 3 we start to prefer the term 'outcome' to 'objective', and we tend to only use the latter when consciously speaking the language of people for whom 'objectives' are still popular currency.

There's a lot more "Let's see what happens" at Level 3, which (as we'll see) can be a source of tension for others. Similarly, many people, teams and organisations operating at Level 3 respond by moving forward in many different directions at once without choosing between the various options. Thus, where Level 2 corporate objectives resemble something like "We'll double our revenue in three years", those at Level 3 are more like:

"We've a hugely talented team of people with diverse interests and our clients have complex needs, so we'll leverage both to provide support in six core areas: strategy, technology, human resources, M&A, outsourcing and liquidation services."

While the wording might get tidied up into something snappier for internal and external marketing purposes, the underlying objective retains that underlying Level 3 complexity.

If Level 3 sounds overwhelming, it can be. The upgrade from Level 2 to Level 3 is one of the hardest transitions we make in our capacity to make sense of the world around us.

This upgrade can be difficult for the people around us, too. The challenges we see most frequently are:

1. **We're honing the skills required to notice and understand complexity but we've yet to develop the ability to discuss that complexity with people at Levels 1 and 2**

   As a result, it can seem like we're massively overcomplicating things and have our heads in the clouds, which conflicts with others' desires for a simple explanation or a clear plan of action

2. **We're increasingly aware of the unhelpful patterns in our organisation, department or team, as well as the contradictions between our espoused direction / values and 'how things are actually done around here'**

   While sharing those insights *can* earn us respect and potentially catalyse change, it's also a potential source of conflict, particularly if we're clumsy in the way we communicate (which is more likely if less developed in any of the other three capacities)

3. **Most organisations prioritise fast, decisive action over the more considered, more expansive decision-making processes characteristic of Level 3**

   Given enough time and attention, the Level 3 approach should yield a more effective, more adaptive way forward. After all, we're trying to consider all contributing factors, options and possible futures. However, from the outside it can look like dithering and it can lead to paralysis by analysis – in part because it's not until we hit Level 4 that we're able to consistently weave the various data points together into a clear, coherent way forward

4. **People waiting for a decision can become anxious or frustrated because of what they see as a lack of clarity, expediency, confidence or competence, or a failure to appreciate the gravity of the situation**   If this happens and goes unchecked, people's trust in a Level 3 decision-maker can falter, affecting commitment and morale. Ultimately, it can stir up resentment, disillusionment and quiet or open rebellion

If you're at Level 3 and finding it challenging, the good news is this: the combination of the frustrations you might be feeling and the momentum you've accrued should make it easier to upgrade to Level 4.

Dominique (Level 4): weaving multiple, intricate and complex threads into a coherent, holistic map

Dominique takes a different approach again. She calls the directors together right at the start. She shares her intention to establish a frame for what she calls a 'strategic inquiry process'.

The frame they come up with together is a single, broad question: "How might insurance act to improve health?"

Dominique commits to using that question to shape her approach going forward. Then she helps the directors develop a model that clarifies their risk appetite with regard to this project and whatever it produces. These boundaries include the ratios of investment-to-return they'd accept and a range of more subjective criteria against which they'd evaluate whatever she comes up with.

She then spends two weeks 'walking the floor' at Panagen, involving a diverse range of colleagues in putting together a long list of people who might have an interest in the possible answers to that single, framing question. The list includes employees from all levels throughout the company, but also outsiders representing customers, intermediaries and

Panagen's entire supply chain.

Importantly, whereas Colin brought likely allies and interest groups into the conversation, Dominique actively seeks out potential provocateurs and voices of dissent – people who'll challenge the prevailing wisdom in the business or across the industry as a whole.

She speaks to stakeholders she believes will oppose Panagen's entry into the healthcare market entirely, not just on commercial or legal grounds but for reasons rooted in their own personal values. Dominique knows that this approach is crucial if Panagen is to avoid the groupthink that could emerge if she only involves like-minded people with aligned agendas – like Colin did.

Dissenters aren't the only 'outsiders' Dominique includes, though. She uses her professional and personal networks to involve hyper-healthy pensioners and people who make little or no use of health professionals. She wants to understand what ageing, health and healthcare mean to them. She is keen to hear from the non-customers, too – not purely in the hope of converting them but in the interests of better understanding the market and its possible futures.

She invites all of these people to a single, two-day workshop aimed at anyone interested in that initial framing question "How might insurance act to improve health?" Sixty people accept the invitation. All but two show up.

She asks the directors to attend as much or as little of the workshop as they choose. Most turn up on the morning of the second day and decide to stay until the end, enjoying working as peers with a hugely diverse collection of people on a question that matters to all of them – albeit for different reasons.

Dominique has done her research on two fronts. Firstly, she's gathered the quantitative and qualitative data the attendees will need to make good decisions. Secondly, she's designed the event to enable these sixty, very different people to work together in an engaging, creative and effective way, with everyone contributing and learning from the experience.

At the end of the event, the directors are surprised and delighted to find that a number of attendees are keen to turn the mass of ideas into a suite of small, fast-fail experiments. Some will be run as simulations by Panagen's data analytics team; others can be turned into shadow products to be tested by Marketing.

Some of the directors are disappointed that there's no single recommended strategy. However, they have a real sense of a broad direction of travel developing and they can see how these different starting points could weave together into a coherent whole.

Sensing their need to leave with a clear focus that they can share with the Board and other stakeholders, Dominique persuades the directors to spend an impromptu hour together at the end of the day. In it, they co-create:

- An overall narrative that includes the most viable possibilities that have emerged

- The choice points and dilemmas ahead

- The 'known unknowns' that necessitate further research

If it sounds like Dominique has a lot going on, it's because she has. The thing we need to remember is that she's operating at Level 4. Those metaphorical pipes in her brain are wider than they were when she was operating at Level 3. So the cognitive load involved in managing all that complexity feels lighter for her than it would for Colin, Brandon or Andrea – even though she is deliberately working at the edge of her understanding throughout.

At Level 4, our ability to process multiple paths in parallel builds and builds into a more connected system of ideas. We see our organisation and its operating environment as a complex system comprised itself of complex inter-related systems. We find it easier to hold in our heads how a set of actions taken by Marketing will impact customers, people in the Finance department and specific suppliers. We can see, too, the potential chain reactions and the ping-back effect on the folk in Marketing whose actions started it all.

Our capacity for pattern recognition has taken another leap with this upgrade. The appetite we developed for complexity as we moved into Level 3 becomes a passion for reframing or re-organising that complexity. We go from pulling on the multitude of strings and creating a mess towards weaving those strings together into thick, strong ropes – ropes we can then use to move things forward.

Psychologically, the transition from Level 3 to 4 is similar to the transition from 1 to 2. We're taking isolated elements and forming them into coherent wholes that we can then use to make decisions and move things forward.

It's similar to the way chess grandmasters are able to remember the position of all of the pieces on a chessboard, having had just a few seconds to look at it. Less experienced players try to remember the locations of all 32 different pieces on an 8 x 8 board; the grandmaster sees the overall pattern and unpacks the individual locations from that[72].

The key difference between the upgrade to Level 2 and upgrade to Level 4 is the nature of those constituent chunks. When we move to Level 2, we're pulling together separate pieces of information and decision-making processes from a single domain or area of specialism. The upgrade to Level 4 sees us aggregating information, observations and ideas from a wide range of sources to form our own clear, practical views on broad domains of thinking. We've used the image of a bellows to show how the concepts from these different domains are drawn together and combined to create something new and fully integrated.

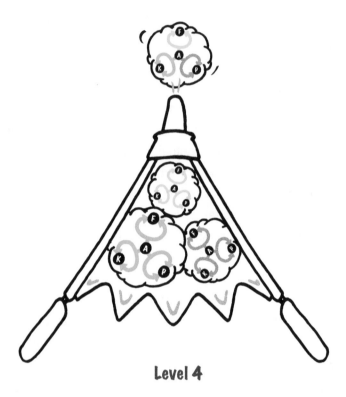

Level 4

An example of this would be the middle-manager who develops her own set of ideas on the topic of organisational culture. In doing so, she draws on different disciplines like organisational design, social psychology, anthropology, sociology, history, zoology and her own first-hand experiences in the school of hard knocks.

Another example is the head of a maturing start-up who's able to simultaneously attend to the realms of financial health and talent, bearing all of the factors in each of those realms in mind when making judgements and decisions. At Level 3, she'd have focused on one realm at a time, exploring different ways to create the right approach to HR, then attending to financial sustainability and periodically flicking back and forth between the two.

The shift to Level 4 is like the shift from standard two-dimensional chess, to playing the game in three dimensions. We're thinking in terms of trade-offs between different domains, looking at which board needs a move right now and accepting that there will be temporary contradictions between what's happening on one board and what's happening on another. We're able to maintain multiple chains of thought while being clear in our minds how each of those chains links to the others.

In playing chess in three dimensions, we might decide to take a financial hit for two years to increase diversity in the organisation, based on a belief that in five years that additional diversity will mean the organisation is more innovative and successful than it would have been. Otherwise, we'll also be taking that decision understanding the implications for union relations, morale in some parts of the organisation, and so on.

When it comes to establishing the way forward, the approach Dominique demonstrated is typical of Level 4.

At Level 2, the goals we set have the ring of "Double our current revenue in three years' time".

At Level 3, as we've seen, it's something like "We've a hugely talented team of people with diverse interests and our clients have complex needs, so we'll leverage both to provide support in six core areas: strategy, technology, human resources, M&A, outsourcing and liquidation services." Essentially, it's a 'shopping list' approach.

At Level 4, we're willing to work within enabling constraints but *unwilling* to set or adhere to constraints that will disable us, unnecessarily inhibit us or leave us more vulnerable in VUCA environments. Thus we're more likely to establish direction through statements and imagery that speak to questions of identity, such as:

"We're an organisation with significant expertise and logistical capability, with people who care passionately about sustainability, continuous development and delighting everyone who travels on our trains. We'll apply that expertise and passion to reduce this country's overall energy consumption in the Netherlands."

It's a statement of intent, not just an objective for the company we run or work for. It makes no reference to being a market leader, as pursuing that goal could potentially limit our creativity when it comes to the organisation's overall intent.

At Level 4, we see the kind of direction-setting that describes the domain and parameters within which we're operating – without precluding a variety of different, emergent ways forward. Those parameters provide clear boundaries that tell us what we *won't* do as a team or organisation, rather than making statements about what we *will* do. This give us freedom to manoeuvre as the changing context requires.

As the image above suggests, Level 4 brings new focus to the expansive thinking of Level 3. It combines the ability to see multiple paths to multiple possible goals with the ability to prioritise between those goals

Chasing bunnies

There's a saying: "If you chase two rabbits, you won't catch either of them."

At Level 2, we'd be compelled to choose one, ignore the other and start chasing.

At Level 3, we'd agonise over the merits of one rabbit over the other, the implications of failing to catch both and the ethical implications of chasing rabbits in the first place.

At Level 4, we'd step back and ask: "What's the intention behind chasing these rabbits?" We'd do some quick research, discover one is female and the other male, and that there's no huge urgency on the food front. Then we'd come up with a plan to get the rabbits to corral themselves together. They'd settle down to produce enough baby rabbits to keep us fed for years to come, while we use those Level 3 factors to work out how best to manage the rabbit farm.

and paths – and potentially combine aspects of each to create something greater. The result is a broader remit than Level 2 offers, allowing the organisation and its people to adapt and grow in response to the world in which it operates. At the same time, when we operate at Level 4 we're painting a broad brush picture of the direction in which we're headed – doing away with *unnecessary or disabling* uncertainty and ambiguity, but not tying ourselves into a single possible future.

So, in one sense, Level 4 direction-setting is like a Russian doll that contains the approaches taken by Levels 1, 2 and 3. Perhaps it's no surprise, then, that leaders operating at Level 4 generally find it easier to communicate their ideas *across* levels than do people at Levels 1, 2 and 3. There's some common language there that doesn't exist in quite the same way until we reach Level 4.

Another reason, though, is that when we reach Level 4 we're not just more able to *form* a coherent view from what was previously an overwhelming amount of complexity, we're better at strategising adaptively. Gone are the huge edifices of enduring strategies that take years to come to fruition. In their place is an evolving sense of purpose that both captures the imagination and moves with our changing reality.

We're also better at *articulating* that view clearly and in a straight-forward, understandable way.

At Level 4 we're better at *consciously choosing* whether or not to unpack the ideas we've formed to reveal the layers of thought, experience and experimentation that went into creating them. In contrast, at Level 3 we found it harder to resist unpacking that complexity, causing us to lose or confuse some people, and leave them behind.

When we're engaging in Level 4 Sense-making, we also construct and make greater use of pictures, maps, stories and metaphors to help create a shared understanding of:

- The complexity itself – as well as the associated volatility, uncertainty and ambiguity

- The meaning we've found (individually or collectively) in all that VUCA messiness

- The options for moving forward

- The mechanisms for deciding between those options.

This, in part, is why we're better able to speak the language of people operating at Levels 1, 2 and 3. It helps us bridge the gaps that often open between them. How effectively we do so, of course, will depend on the level at which we're operating in the other three capacities.

Summary and self-assessment

You're relying on Sense-making when you're attempting to solve complex problems, particularly when those problems are also laced with volatility, uncertainty or ambiguity. It's the capacity we depend on most to help us understand unfamiliar contexts, like a new role, organisation or area of responsibility. Our capacity for Sense-making also underpins our ability to be usefully creative and to design (or redesign) processes for getting things done.

Progressing through the levels in this capacity requires us to increasingly 'helicopter up' cognitively and become more and more flexible and insightful in the way we look at the world around us. We shift from diagnosing *complicated* problems using tried-and-tested methods through to seeing the interconnectedness of *complex* situations. Once we're at Level 4, we're able reframe that complexity, weaving the disparate threads into a single, coherent way forward.

As with the previous chapters, we recommend that you bear in mind a particular situation when reviewing the summaries that follow. In this case, we suggest either observing or recalling a recent discussion in which you and others were trying to make a decision when faced with a complex problem or opportunity.

Depending on your grasp of the other capacities, you might want to keep things simple by avoiding choosing a discussion that centred on a polarity. While most complex issues require us to use more than one of the four capacities, our purpose at this point is to help you gauge your current level when it comes to Sense-making – not Opposable Thinking.

You might also find it helpful to discuss that conversation with someone who was also present at the time, but that's entirely up to you.

If it helps, make a brief note of the conversation here:

....

....

....

Now take a look at the following summaries. Then indicate the level at which you believe you're currently operating.

Prior to Level 1, I have been learning to...

☐ Use a wide range of cognitive skills to work with the physical world (e.g. building dens, riding bikes, playing sports, cooking dinner)

☐ Absorb the abstract ideas that enable me to learn new languages, grasp mathematics and understand the various sciences

☐ Follow instructions and processes, play with the ideas I've been given and articulate my interpretation of a situation

At Level 1, I...

☐ Typically specialise in a particular professional field or area of interest

☐ Prefer to handle and hone one idea at a time

☐ Tend to focus on the finer details, precedents, best practice and excellence

☐ Use respected models and tools that I've accumulated through my professional training and practice

☐ Prefer quantifiable data – I'm suspicious of qualitative or subjective data as it's too intangible and involves too many confounding variables

As I upgrade from Level 1 to Level 2, I'm getting better at...

☐ Adapting existing processes to accommodate new data and 'exceptions to the rule' in pursuit of a clear goal (or at least a sense of tangible progress)

☐ Assessing progress against goals – and responding to any shortfalls by changing direction or closing any gaps between what we have and what we need to succeed

☐ Identifying commonalities and incompatibilities between my own goals and others', and negotiating where necessary

At Level 2, I...

☐ Am pulling existing ideas together to form processes, plans, programmes and strategies – I'm not yet *truly* creating entirely new processes from scratch

☐ Use structured approaches to problem-solving that draw on a wider variety of 'management thinking' tools than I used previously

☐ Consistently consider the impact of one factor on another across different domains (e.g. the potential impact on employees' morale of imposing a new quality framework)

☐ Am interested in qualitative feedback, as long as it's backed by a rigorous methodology for gathering data

☐ Assess actions and processes based on the likelihood that they'll help achieve the stated goal – I'm not yet comparing potential routes based on other criteria (like values), nor comparing alternative goals

As I upgrade from Level 2 to Level 3, I'm getting better at...

☐ Not just challenging perceived wisdom, but generating novel, creative alternatives

☐ Noticing contradictions and paradoxes (e.g. "Our espoused values are at odds with our actual behaviours"; "Our cut-throat approach to the competition undermines our people's belief that we're a caring, socially-responsible organisation")

☐ Questioning whether the things I'm striving for (the goals themselves) are actually the things I want (or *we need*), and identifying any necessary change in direction

At Level 3, I...

☐ Want to understand connections between ideas, between new initiatives and the status quo, and between concepts from different domains (e.g. "How could design-thinking inform our HR processes?"_

☐ Introduce left-field, creative problem-solving techniques (e.g. hackathons, storytelling, use of different media)

☐ Find myself increasingly interested in subjective data, starting to wonder if 'how things feel' could be just as important as formal logic

☐ Find it hard to evaluate and prioritise between competing goals, options or possible futures

☐ Can come across as contrary, impractical, lost in the clouds, indecisive or like I'm overcomplicating things – because I've yet to develop the ability to describe the complexity I'm seeing in terms that appeal to people at Level 1 and 2 (i.e. in ways that are clear, evidenced and actionable)

As I upgrade from Level 3 to Level 4, I'm getting better at...

☐ Quickly digesting large quantities of diverse, novel and conflicting data (including the empty spaces where there is no data) and deciding a course of action

☐ Investing in understanding other people's thinking and how it can support my own emerging models of how things work

☐ Noticing inconsistencies and incoherence in my own and others' thinking – and seamlessly changing direction when the disconnect is between the outcomes I'm getting and the ones I was hoping for

At Level 4, I...

☐ Use a wide variety of collaborative techniques for working with problems and strategising, helping me become genuinely adept at *co*-creating new ways forward

☐ Supplement traditional analytic information with a very wide range of different data (e.g. stories, big data, 'weak signals' and intuitions)

☐ Begin to create overall theories of how my professional domain 'works' by integrating data and ideas from diverse sources and even across different domains (e.g. new frameworks, guiding concepts or reframes of existing thinking)

☐ Rarely notice *in the moment* how my most strongly-valued conceptual frameworks limit the attention I pay to contradictory data and anything beyond my existing boundaries

☐ Still find it hard to truly appreciate that the processes and fundamental assumptions on which my frameworks are built both distort those frameworks *and* reduce their relevance to very different contexts and people coming from very different starting points

Bearing in mind the conversation you chose on page 177, at which level do you believe you're currently operating in this capacity? What makes you think that?

Sense-making

Level 4

Level 3

Level 2

Level 1

....

....

....

....

Which other levels do you think were also present in the conversation, and what are your reasons for thinking that?

....

....

....

....

Which of the four levels do you believe *dominated* the discussion? How did that affect the outcome?

....

....

....

....

• ● •

PART 3

•••

Where you're at and what to do next

Recap and
self-assessment

- The essence of each capacity
- The core focus of each level and the upgrades between them
- Your current capacity profile
- Gauging the profiles of colleagues and the people you lead

IN THIS CHAPTER, we'll weave the various strands of Parts 1 and 2 into a quick summary

that will help you crystallise your understanding of the four capacities and
serve as a reference point whenever you
need a quick reminder.

Your understanding of your 'capacity
profile' will probably have evolved since
you read the first couple of chapters in
Part 2. So you'll reassess where you're at
in terms of the levels within each capacity.
We'll also offer further help with gauging
the capacity profiles of others. You'll find
this helps on many fronts, especially when
it comes to helping them develop.

> "Whoever acquires knowledge but does not practice it is as one who ploughs but does not sow."
>
> Saadi Shirazi,
> philosopher and poet[73]

The essence of the four capacities and the levels within them

The next few pages are the antithesis of the rich detail and case studies in Part 2. Here, we've distilled the essence of each capacity into a single image. That does mean we've shed a lot of the nuance and that we've had to strip out certain things for the sake of clarity, simplicity and ease of use. So please bear that in mind.

For each capacity, we've included:

- A single question intended to sum up the kinds of question that capacity helps answer

- A single-word description of the key focus at each level

- A description of the transition from each level to the next

Those transitions are characterised by two things:

- The ways of operating that we're waving goodbye to as we leave one level behind, and

- The ways of thinking, feeling and behaving that we're embracing or 'saying hello to' as we settle into the next level

As we'll see in Chapter 9, those goodbyes aren't permanent: there are a number of things in life that can cause us to drop back temporarily to previous levels.

As you review these descriptions, we'd encourage you to either circle your current level in each capacity on the page itself, or mark out your capacity profile on the page that follows.

Sense-making

What on earth is going on here?

Re-framing

GOODBYE: uncertainty about how to handle a myriad of complex options
HELLO: weaving disparate threads into a single, coherent, co-created and adaptable set of strategies

Connecting

GOODBYE: pursuing single, pre-set goals
HELLO: spotting numerous, interconnected ways forward and possible valuable outcomes

Diagnosing

GOODBYE: relying on tried-and-tested rules and processes when seeking to understand and respond to the situation
HELLO: focusing on action, incremental improvement and results

Analysing

Perspective-shifting

What more can I see when I step back and back and back from my own, first-person perspective?

Co-Creating

GOODBYE: having my objectivity hijacked by my own 'baggage' and 'hot buttons'
HELLO: finding creative ways to step back from my own and others' viewing points to see how our subjective realities affect each other

Inquiring

GOODBYE: inadvertently filtering my 'objectivity' through deeply held beliefs and biases
HELLO: noticing how and why my beliefs and biases affect my attempts to see the world through others' eyes

Co-operating

GOODBYE: seeing other people in terms of simple categorisations that are, I now realise, really just stereotypes
HELLO: recognising that people are complex and have multiple reasons for doing what they do

Acknowledging

Self-relating

How could I best 'show up' here?

Self-determining

GOODBYE: being hijacked by my own 'hot buttons', limiting beliefs and unhelpful patterns of behaviour

HELLO: aligning my life with my principles / preferences; managing the tension if I can't; genuinely reinventing myself to be what my context demands

Experimenting

GOODBYE: treating my identity as a single, stable, logically-coherent thing

HELLO: being increasingly aware of my unhelpful patterns of thinking and feeling, and increasingly able to shift those patterns over time

Balancing

GOODBYE: typically only noticing afterwards when I've been hijacked by my emotions, or by my most rigidly-held values and beliefs

HELLO: striking a balance between meeting others' expectations and living up to my own, individual values and beliefs

Noticing

Opposable Thinking

How do I best respond to dilemmas and conflicting views regarding the nature of the problem and how to proceed?

Integrating

GOODBYE: feeling discouraged by the absence of any objective 'truth' and the reality that some dilemmas are simply unresolvable

HELLO: integrating both poles' underlying 'truths' into a mutually attractive way forward; challenging my own internal polarities in the moment

Mediating

GOODBYE: treating polarities as 'either/or' debates

HELLO: finding polarities everywhere, including in my own thinking; noticing their causes and divisive effects; finding creative ways beyond mere compromise

Negotiating

GOODBYE: believing in one correct, black or white answer

HELLO: starting to see shades of grey and believing the 'best answer' can vary depending on context

Upholding

You'll also find these summaries right at the back of the book in Appendix 4, so you can flick back to them whenever you like.

Your capacity profile

We recommend using the following table to mark out your current capacity profile. Depending on how quickly you've worked through the previous chapters, it may be a simple case of transferring your data from pages 92, 118, 147 and 182. Bear in mind that we've put Sense-making first again in the image below, rather than last, reflecting the order in which we first introduced these capacities, back in Part 1 – which is the order in which they're most typically applied in life.

You might decide to recalibrate – either because you feel you've shifted since you read some of those chapters, or because you've a deeper understanding now of what it takes to be at each level in each of the four capacities.

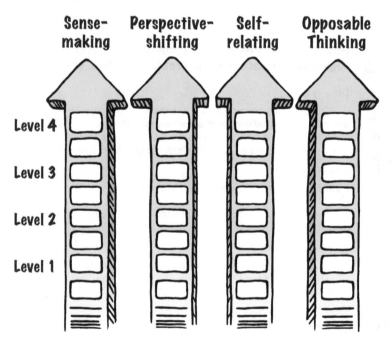

Looking at your capacity profile through a different lens

Many readers have found it helpful to explore their development of the four capacities in this book through the lens of the three qualities at the heart of Richard's book *ARC Leadership*[74]. As each of us moves through the levels in the four capacities, it changes what it means to us to be Authentic, Responsible and Courageous. It also changes the nature of the challenges we face when trying to embody those three qualities.

As we mentioned in Chapter 3, if you'd like to explore your capacity profile through that 'ARC' lens, you'll find a short article in the 'Upgrade resources' section at www.leaderspace.com. You won't need any prior knowledge to find it useful.

Your learning edge

Given what's happening in your working world right now, and what you see coming in the next few weeks and months, which capacities are you most keen to develop? In which order should you attend to each of them to ensure you're best placed to rise to your biggest or most urgent challenges?

....

....

....

....

....

....

How are these capacities playing out across your team?

Another way of seeing the capacities at play in your working life is to look at how they play out in the conversations and dynamics within and across teams. Gauging the level of that 'discourse' helps you see the levels in others, but also sharpens your attention to your own current operating system. So try observing a forthcoming meeting and considering the following questions:

- **Sense-making:** How are the various different members of the group handling the complexity of the situation?

- **Perspective-shifting:** To what degree is each person able to step back from their own position to observe what's going on or witness their own thinking and reactions to the situation?

- **Self-relating:** What is each person able to recognise and acknowledge about their own way of relating to the issue?

- **Opposable Thinking:** What do you notice about the flexibility of each person's beliefs and opinions?

- **Any or all capacities:** What do you notice about any alliances (or attempts at alliances) forming between members of the group?

We've found it's more helpful if you focus less on individuals and more on gauging the level of *discourse between* them. It's also easier than watching everyone individually, once you get the hang of it.

We lean on different capacities depending on the topic we're working on. So, to dig deeper in your analysis of this team's current OS, use the following pages to identify which capacity (or capacities) are most relevant to the topic discussed in that meeting. Then work out the level at which the group as a whole was operating.

Sense-making: observing, understanding and processing the complexity of a situation

Applies to:	◯ 'Wicked' or complex problem-solving ◯ Strategic direction-setting
Level 1 (Analysing):	◯ Handling one component of the issue at a time (e.g. financial, marketing, product design) ◯ Having few models or tools for examining new situations, leaving the group relying on general conversation or debate ◯ Excluding non-quantifiable data ◯ Presenting quantifiable data in traditional and unchanging ways
Level 2 (Diagnosing):	◯ Using formal, structured (and typically well-known) tools for solving problems and making decisions ◯ Considering the impact of one factor on another (e.g. how various different approaches to customer service might impact feedback from consumers) ◯ Including pre-analysed qualitative feedback (e.g. surveys) in discussions ◯ Engaging in creative analysis of quantifiable data
Level 3 (Connecting):	◯ Introducing more creative problem-solving techniques (e.g. design thinking, tools for lateral thinking and innovation) ◯ Consciously taking different roles in relation to the problem in order to 'represent' different inputs and stakeholders (e.g. customers, shareholders, employees) ◯ Taking a less structured approach to conversations, which may lead to the group becoming lost in detail or heading down cul de sacs or rabbit holes in pursuit of 'shiny' ideas
Level 4 (Re-framing):	◯ Making significant efforts to frame the conversation to make sure it stays on a broad but consistent track ◯ Employing many different techniques for understanding and responding to problems ◯ Bringing external voices into the room, whether directly or via research ahead of the discussion ◯ Making good use of 'big data' gathered by specialists but not pre-analysed

Perspective-shifting: 'zooming out' to benefit from a more realistic and multi-faceted understanding of a situation or relationship

Applies to:	☐ Conversations about stakeholders or employees ☐ Conflicts within the group or team
Level 1 (Acknow-ledging):	☐ Spending the majority of the time and energy advocating or opposing one view with another ☐ Tending to simply state one's own opinion or 'stick up for' one interest group ☐ Speculating about other people's motives and intentions without seeking the data required to validate that speculation ☐ Engaging in generalised stereotyping of other groups (e.g. 'sales people', 'Finance', 'politicians')
Level 2 (Co-operating):	☐ Making effective use of techniques like 'persona identification' or stakeholder stories[a] ☐ Trying harder to see things 'from the other person's point of view' ☐ Engaging in open inquiry into each other's positions, but usually at quite a surface level (e.g. focusing on each other's beliefs rather than the motives or values driving those beliefs) ☐ 'Agreeing to differ' (and maybe even shaking hands on it)
Level 3 (Inquiring):	☐ Engaging in far greater levels of inquiry, both with each other and regarding outsiders' views and experiences ☐ Using techniques that help people voice difficult or conflicting viewpoints, enabling the group to 'get under the skin' of underlying differences ☐ Bringing voices into the room and including them in conversation; sometimes becoming lost in the differences and struggling to find a way through the variety of possible interpretations
Level 4 (Co-creating):	☐ Most members engaging in fluid Perspective-shifting, including moving between one's own view, inquiring into each other's views and sharing evidence of the views of people outside the room ☐ Members noticing when they are locked into their own view and why ☐ Using effective group practices that allow people to share contentious opinions or emotions without interruption, enabling the group to co-create a new way forward

a   'Persona identification' is a term used in sales, branding and marketing. It involves identifying types of customer and seeing the world from their perspective by imagining oneself in their position.

Self-relating: observing, understanding, regulating and transforming yourself

Applies to:	☐ Discussions of individual / collective performance
	☐ Any 'high stakes' or conflict situation
Level 1 (Noticing):	☐ Very rarely disclosing personal feelings or thoughts that others might find 'difficult'
	☐ Blaming others outside the meeting for performance issues
	☐ Avoiding conflict / blowing small issues out of proportion due to unresolved interpersonal tensions
	☐ Relying on 'the leader' to mediate differences between members
Level 2 (Balancing):	☐ Engaging in more objective analysis of team issues or performance problems, often using a tool or model for assessing the health of the team
	☐ Using personality frameworks or psychological models to discover and discuss difference
	☐ Drawing on informal protocols for surfacing difference but keeping the 'temperature' of those discussions low to avoid any underlying conflicts
Level 3 (Experimenting):	☐ Disclosing a great deal of personal, internal thoughts and feelings
	☐ Developing group / team 'rituals' or habits for checking in with each other and understanding members' individual subjective experiences
	☐ Fluently describing one's own viewpoints and responses
	☐ Overtly tolerating different ideas, while sometimes getting stuck due to a desire to achieve 'consensus' on topics like the values and purpose of the group
Level 4 (Self-determining):	☐ Moving fluidly back and forth between the task of the moment, personal disclosure and in-the-moment reflections
	☐ Using a variety of techniques for quickly checking in to understand the 'temperature' of the conversation and understand 'where people are at'
	☐ Treating conflict as healthy and creative, surfacing it easily within an atmosphere of trust

Opposable Thinking: responding to the dilemmas and conflicting ideas that can create tensions within us and / or between us and other people

Applies to:	☐ Decision-making in complex, uncertain or ambiguous situations
	☐ Exploring dilemmas or conflicting views / positions
Level 1 (Upholding):	☐ Tending to polarise between opposing solutions or readings of the situation, sometimes with one or two 'minority' members being closed down if / when they stand against the orthodoxy
	☐ Typically generating or discussing only one or two options for resolving a given issue
	☐ Tending to engage in group-think in difficult situations, allowing the group / key individuals to regain a sense of control
	☐ Excluding other possible ideas as 'irrelevant to the matter at hand'
Level 2 (Negotiating):	☐ Having one or two techniques for working with opposing ideas (e.g. group line-ups[75])
	☐ Noticing how positions can become polarised, then attempting to understand the shades of grey and negotiate solutions or compromises
	☐ Perhaps succumbing even more readily to group-think than at Level 1, due to people's desire to be 'team players' and show that they are 'on the bus'
Level 3 (Mediating):	☐ Using a variety of approaches to surface and work with dilemmas and opposing views – *during* meetings, rather than 'offline' / outside the room
	☐ Showing interest in the origins and basis for each of the opposing views – *if* the values underpinning that view are consistent with the group's
	☐ Spotting the potential for group-think and taking steps to avoid it – although still clinging to some sacred cows and taboos
Level 4 (Integrating):	☐ Actively seeking opposing, contrary and controversial views with the intention of stretching and improving the group's thinking
	☐ Using well-practised techniques for understanding dilemmas and managing polarities
	☐ Seeing all positions as potentially valid, as long as they can be backed up by argument or data
	☐ Using a variety of different but well-coordinated approaches to 'test to destruction' any prevailing group view or orthodoxy

Returning to the group or team you were thinking about earlier and their approach to a specific topic, mark the level at which you think you are collectively operating in the relevant capacity or capacities.

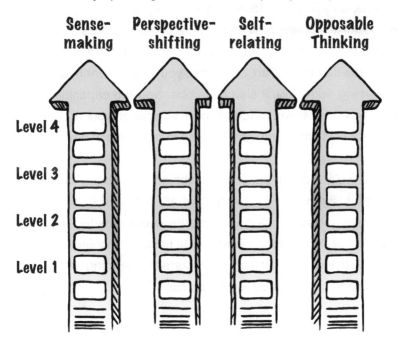

How are you reacting to the approach the group is taking?

. . . .

. . . .

From your own current level in the relevant capacities, how might you intervene to help the group approach the situation in a more fruitful way?

. . . .

. . . .

. . . .

In summary

In this chapter you'll have found the antithesis of Part 2. It's a one-stop checklist showing how each upgrade gives access to ever-more-effective ways of tackling the challenges of a VUCA world. Bringing the threads of Part 2 together, you'll have identified your own learning edge. You'll also have observed the capacities at work in a group or team, which will have sharpened your ability to spot the level at which you and others are operating in any given moment.

Next, we'll look at the journey behind and ahead of you, giving you insights into the things that will help and hinder you going forward. You'll find those insights useful whether you're upgrading from your current level to the next, developing others or simply trying to maintain your current operating level in situations that might cause you to regress.

●●●

The journey behind and ahead of you

• • •

- Why upgrading yourself (or others) is slower and messier than upgrading your phone
- The 'snags, crashes, whirlpools and trailing edges' that'll be holding you back
- The 'propellers' and 'wormholes' you can use to help you upgrade

YOUR SELF-ASSESSMENT in Chapter 8 is based largely on a snapshot in time. It's a measure of the level at which you're currently operating in each of the four capacities. It's your perception of your current operating system.

Your current OS will be more sophisticated than it was when you were growing up. However, it's also perfectly possible that you're currently operating at a *lower* level in one or more capacities than you have in the more recent past. That's because, when human beings upgrade their operating systems, it's a more organic and less stable process than it is with computers and mobile devices. Progress

> "If opportunity doesn't knock, build a door."
>
> Milton Berle,
> actor and comedian[76]

comes in fits and starts and we sometimes find ourselves reverting to old, less helpful ways of thinking, doing and feeling.

Our focus in this chapter is on the deeper process of development that underpins our progress through the various levels in each of the four capacities. It'll help you understand your own journey to date and prepare for what's to come. You'll also find it useful if / when you take on the challenge in Chapter 15 and use this book to help others upgrade.

It's important to be clear on one thing before we start: you don't need to remember all the details. You won't need to memorise the distinctions between a 'snag', 'crash', 'whirlpool' or 'trailing edge'. It's enough to simply consider, recognise or *imagine* how these phenomena play out in your world. Once you've done that, you'll carry with you a sense of the psychology behind your own and others' development. That will be enough for you to spot a snag when it's interfering with your response to a situation; catch a crash before it happens; attend to your trailing edges; watch out for whirlpools that can drag you back to levels you thought you'd left behind.

A new analogy for the four capacities

The analogy of an operating system only takes us so far. When we're thinking about developing our individual capacities, it helps to imagine a flotilla of four boats. Each boat is one of the four capacities.

The development of the four capacities is like the movement of that flotilla from its coast of origin (your birth) across the ocean. The closer each boat gets to the opposite shore, the higher the level you've

reached in that capacity.

From a distance, the flotilla appears to be a single object. Close up, it's clear that some of the boats are further ahead than others, just as your capacity profile probably shows that you're more developed in some capacities than in others.

Let's call the owner of this particular flotilla 'Anne'. At this point in her life, Anne is operating somewhere between Level 1 and Level 2 in all four capacities.

By contrast, the capacity profiles of her colleagues, Brigitte and Charles (shown below), are more spread out. Hence their flotillas look a little different.

Brigitte is somewhere between Levels 2 and 3 in three of the capacities, but has a 'leading edge' when it comes to Perspective-shifting. That capacity is probably 'pulling her along' in her development.

Charles, on the other hand, has a 'trailing edge' when it comes to Self-relating. While he operates consistently at Level 2 in the other capacities, some of his ways of looking at and managing himself are more characteristic of Level 1.

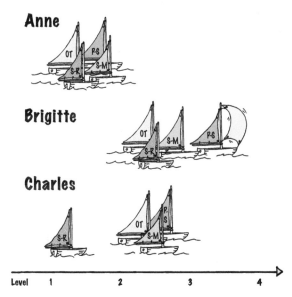

Trailing edges and snags – the things that hold us back

What causes a trailing edge? Usually it's just the fact that we simply don't develop perfectly evenly. There's no set curriculum for this kind of development – not yet anyway – so it's a little messy. Maybe something held you up in one area. Maybe your life or career simply hasn't given you an even spread of opportunities to develop all four capacities equally well. Maybe you've sought out one kind of opportunity and avoided others. Either way, like a muscle, the capacity you've used least might have failed to strengthen as much as the others.

Trailing edges make for good development opportunities. The patterns of thinking and behaving that characterise your trailing edge are sustained and repeated, meaning you and others will probably notice them in action. For example, you might notice that you're really good at making sense of layers of cognitive complexity you come across in calm, stable environments, but considerably less sophisticated in your approach when the stakes are higher or the pace of change increases.

In which capacity do you think your trailing edge lies?

....

What specific patterns of thinking or behaving convince you that this is your trailing edge? At which level do you think you are currently operating in this capacity?

....

....

....

....

Charles' capacity for Self-relating *may* continue to develop at the same pace as his other capacities but still remain a trailing edge. It might, even, 'catch up' with the rest – whether that happens naturally over time or through focused development. On the other hand, it could be that this trailing edge has actually been 'snagged'.

'Snags' are significant events or experiences in our past that echo into our present. When that 'snag' is triggered by an event in the present, we are likely to drop into outdated ways of thinking, feeling and/or behaving that we thought we'd left behind. We snag on a specific topic or type of event – and when we say 'we', we speak from first-hand experience (see 'A couple of our own snags', below).

Snags rarely resolve themselves without conscious effort. The thing you're snagged on sits immobile on the seabed. As your other strands continue their journey, the part of you that's snagged stretches out like the yarn of a sweatshirt caught on a door handle as you inadvertently walk away.

As you might expect, the two of us (Karen and Richard) have invested a fair amount of time and effort working on our most problematic snags. You kind of have to when your job involves helping others with theirs!

As a result, we're less 'had by' the patterns those particular snags created than we used to be. However, we do still 'have' them. Like anyone, from time to time, we still get tripped up by these (and other) outdated ways of thinking and feeling. We've never met anyone who doesn't.

What are the 2-3 biggest 'snags' in your life to date? What patterns have they created in your ways of thinking, feeling and responding to the world around you?

....

....

....

A couple of our own snags

From Karen: I have a snag associated with 'shaming' – I react viscerally to any deliberate attempt by people to belittle or undermine others. However far I've developed in other ways, any hint of humiliation in my social setting has a massive effect on me – especially if it's someone else who's being shamed. To this day, I cannot watch reality TV because of the acute stress it triggers when I see others being humiliated, or being placed in positions where they will humiliate themselves.

From Richard: like most people's, my biggest snag was triggered by a childhood experience. My father's death of a heart attack when I was seven years old was awful in lots of obvious ways, but it also left me with a number of persistent and unhelpful thought patterns that still trip me up from time to time. For example:

- My first reaction when something goes wrong is to blame myself. What's the link? My father used to encourage me to test my strength and his by punching him in the stomach, leaving me wondering after his death whether I'd punched him too hard and killed him.

- I've a strong compulsion to rescue people, even if they don't want rescuing or it's beyond my gift. I realised a few years ago that is me subconsciously trying to save my dad.

Crashes – the things that knock us back

As the name suggests, a crash is more immediate and surprising. It happens when something that is a 'hot button' for us triggers a loss of control and a lapse into less-developed, lower-level ways of thinking, feeling and responding to the world around us. For example, you might be operating at Level 3 in your day-to-day, then suddenly drop to Level 1.

We only notice crashes once we're deep within them, confronted with their negative impact, or when we're looking back on them from a calmer, sunnier place. They typically affect all four of the capacities  at once, too, unlike our snags and trailing edges, which typically relate to just one capacity at a time.

Common triggers include:

- A situation or behaviour that breaches our core values or fundamental assumptions about what's right and wrong (or how people should or shouldn't behave)

- Stress, fear, powerlessness and rejection

- Impatience, frustration and time pressure

- Ill-health, hunger, cravings or impairment through drugs or alcohol

- A situation / behaviour that's a strong match for a situation or event in the past

Values are a great source of crashes because they are typically rooted in a sense of identity that's generally been forming since we were very young. Brains are pattern recognition machines. When yours spots a pattern out in the world that looks familiar, it goes rummaging around in its memories for the quickest, easiest response. Stimulus, response; stimulus, response. Unfortunately, in looking to make life easy for you, it'll prioritise the response that can be implemented with the least conscious thought. This is typically the response that was laid down earliest.

The most obvious crashes are those that are associated with *negative* events in the past. However, a perfectly pleasurable association might trigger a similar temporary regression. If you've ever reconnected with friends from childhood you might have noticed how you or they quickly reverted to long-forgotten, less mature ways of operating.

Crashing at Christmas

Have you ever seen a family get-together become hijacked by a well-worn row about long-forgotten things? We often look back on these situations soon after and wonder how we let ourselves get caught up in patterns we'd normally associate more with our childhood than our current, adult selves – patterns like sibling rivalry and resenting our parents' demands. That's a crash.

What 'crashes' have you experienced in the past few months?

....

....

....

....

What 'hot buttons'[77] triggered them? How did you experience the resulting 'crash state'? What thoughts, feelings and behaviours showed up that are not part of your normal day-to-day ways of operating?

....

....

....

....

Which capacity or capacities were affected by the crash? When you think about how you felt and thought when you were in that 'crash state', what level do you think you slipped back into in each of those capacities? *(It could be that you slipped even further back, to a level before the ones we've focused on in this book, so it can help to think instead in terms of the question 'What age was I acting in that situation?')*

....

....

....

....

What 'crashes' have you seen in the people around you? What triggered them?

....

....

....

....

Whirlpools – the things that drag us down

There's a difference between a sudden, temporary regression to lower levels in these capacities and a long, persistent dip in our capacities for Sense-making, Perspective-shifting, Self-relating and Opposable Think-ing. We call those long dips 'whirlpools' as they're generally trig-gered by finding oneself in a situation, relationship, climate or organisational culture that prompts a slow spiral into less enabling ways of thinking, feeling and behaving.

Common causes include:

- A boss who, for whatever reasons, is operating at a lower level[a] than we'd prefer and ignores, punishes or belittles us whenever we try to introduce higher-level thinking

- A team, stakeholder relationship, organisation or family situation where the discourse is persistently and infectiously characteristic of a level from which we've previously moved on

- Difficult periods in our lives that cause us to question our choices or remind us of our mortality – redundancies, divorces, bereavements, etc.

---

a   In one or more of these four capacities.

The good news, at least where these capacities are concerned, is that when the contextual trigger passes we recover the ability to access the levels we could before. We might even find the experience has helped us move up a level in one or more of the capacities – *if* we're able to reflect on it and work it through in a productive way. After all, as grim as it can be, much of our development comes from dealing with adversity.

What 'whirlpool' periods have you encountered in your career / broader life in recent years?

....

....

....

When you think about your most significant whirlpools to date, in what ways did it reduce your effectiveness in one or more of the four capacities?

....

....

....

So, what do we do with these snags, crashes, trailing edges and whirlpools?

First and foremost, we work on becoming more aware of them. We familiarise ourselves with the 'hot buttons' that trigger a crash and the sensations that precede a drop out of our usual way of operating. We pay attention to the things in our past that have snagged us, and so on.

Secondly, we develop tactics for managing them in the moment. The best tactics will depend on the precise nature of the 'problem' you're dealing with, so it's best we don't attempt to cover them here.

Instead, we've suggested some approaches in the notes at the end of this book.[78]

Thirdly, we approach them more strategically. This means investing in loosening the hold of the patterns of thinking, feeling, and behaving that make us more susceptible to snags and crashes. It means actively working on the capacities in which our trailing edges lie. When it comes to whirlpools, it means working on our resilience, influencing skills and ability to spot the signals that there's one on its way and recognise that we might get sucked in.

Ultimately, all of these approaches leverage and rely on your capacity for Self-relating. They also remind us of another great metaphor:

One day, you're walking down the street and you fall down a hole.

The next day, you're on the same street. You see the hole coming but somehow you still manage to fall into it.

On day three, you see it, walk around it, smile widely, turn the corner and fall down a hole you've never encountered before.

Your attitude to the inevitability of 'day three' might depend on where you're at with regard to Self-relating. Sadly – or perhaps, happily – that's just the nature of human development!

Propellers and wormholes – the things that pull us forward

We've given a lot of attention to the things that hold us back and pull us back, but there are some enabling forces out there, too – some things that can  help one or more of your 'boats' move faster across the ocean.

We've taken to calling the most common cluster of enabling forces 'propellers' because they're like strapping a propeller to the back of your boat. Some of these propellers are natural events, like a new role or some major organisational change that offer a development opportunity and help carry you into the next level. You might even think of these as the equivalent of the Gulf Stream, propelling you along, if you'd rather stick with a softer, more natural and less mechanistic metaphor.

People can be propellers, too. Some help us intentionally, like the boss, mentor or coach who invests time and effort to help you upgrade in one or more of the capacities.

Others are accidental catalysts for our development. They might be role-modelling a greater capacity to manage complexity – like the

---

Richard has a propeller

Some years ago, I took on a mentor who has played an invaluable role in my development.

We have our different goals in life and our different styles, for sure, but he opened my eyes to entirely new ways of looking at my clients, myself and the world around me. Early on, it was the answers he provided that were most helpful. These hints, tips and tricks were rooted in his own considerable experience and added useful apps to my existing operating system.

Increasingly, though, it was the questions he posed and his analysis of my ways of thinking that proved most useful. Why? Because they were chipping away at my entire operating system. I could almost feel myself evolving, but I kept drifting back into old habits and ways of thinking. Little by little, I got better at reaching out for those higher-level questions in my mind, dragging myself forward by integrating what he'd taught me into my own ways of thinking, rather than relying on his frequent reminders.

colleague or boss who offers a new way of looking at the project, team, organisation, market, customer or end-user and encourages us to do the same. They might be shining a light on the limitations of our own current operating system – the flaws in our logic, the dogma and over-simplification, the hidden contradictions inherent in our current ways of thinking about ourselves, other people and the world in which we live.

Propellers come in other forms, too. They can be short events, like attending a meeting, reading a book or watching a film or a play. Anything that offers a glimpse of new ways of thinking, feeling or being that we're left itching to explore further.

Importantly, though, propellers can only carry us so far. Eventually, they leave us. Initially, we drift back a little, but then we find we're better prepared to continue the journey under our own steam.

Using the table below, identify the people, events or periods of your life to date that have acted as propellers for you. On which capacities did those experiences have the greatest positive influence?

Propeller	The influence it had on my development

Who else could you draw on to help you develop in each of the four capacities? *(Note their names in the table below. It needn't be a different person for each. However, it should be someone you feel is operating at your current level or, ideally, at a higher level.)*

Capacity	Who could help
Sense-making	
Perspective-shifting	
Self-relating	
Opposable Thinking	

What other tasks, projects, roles or opportunities could you take on or explore to help you develop in at least one of the capacities? *(These could be existing opportunities, ones you could create or seek out, or ones you could ask someone else to create with / for you.)*

....

....

....

....

In addition to propellers, there's a more fleeting force that helps us move forward. The sudden, inexplicable flashes of 'genius' we have in which we're momentarily accessing a higher level in one or more capacities. We call these 'wormholes', because they're windows to different ways of thinking, feeling and behaving that close as quickly as they open.

Karen opens up a wormhole

When I started my MSc training, I'd been 'playing' for some years with Level 4 Perspective-shifting. I was getting better at understanding the different subjective experiences which affected my world-view and at inquiring deeply into the world-views of others.

The wormhole came when my tutor introduced me to 'inter-subjectivity'. This is the notion that we're all continuously being created by (and creating) the experience of others around us. Thus we're more like clouds than billiard balls in the way that we make sense of the world[79].

This new concept was a revelation to me. It shook my confidence in my ability to ever discern 'my position' amid the messiness of any given relationship or group.

For a few weeks, I became an 'inter-subjectivity junkie', endlessly unpicking the question 'What is going on between us?', much to my friends' amusement (or horror).

Then, in the face of more pressing needs, the effect wore off and I returned to the comfort of the reciprocity of relating that was already 'in the muscle' for me.

Five years later, though, I returned to the idea of inter-subjectivity as part of my professional practice, and set about properly integrating it as part of my personal operating system.

We tried coming up with a boat-themed picture that would illustrate wormholes effectively without disappearing into the realms of science fiction. We even tried to come up with other names. We failed. So please do feel free to send in suggestions!

To clarify this metaphor, though, we can't technically pass through a wormhole. We can't use them to skip a level. We can't use them as a replacement for other development.

What we can do with wormholes is cling to the memory of them. We can use the fruits of those 'flashes of genius' as food for further thought. We can use our curiosity about them to fuel our explorations of what it means to operate at the next level.

What wormholes can you remember experiencing yourself? What insights did they bring?

....

....

....

....

What was going on in and around you that caused or allowed those wormholes to open? Bearing in mind your answers to the previous two questions, how might you increase your chances of experiencing further wormholes? *(You might focus on increasing your exposure to certain kinds of situations or people. You might even choose situations or people that are likely to trigger wormhole experiences that target a specific capacity.)*

....

....

....

....

Summary

Four mechanisms hold us back or pull us back into ways of thinking and behaving that are less well-suited to a VUCA world:

- Trailing edges: the least developed 'boats' in our 'flotilla' of capacities that, for whatever reasons, are behind our current centre of gravity

- Snags: significant events or experiences that anchor us to outdated ways of thinking, feeling and operating that we thought we'd left behind

- Crashes: hot buttons that trigger a loss of control and temporarily knock us back in one or more capacities

- Whirlpools: climates, situations or cultures that prompt a slower spiral into less useful ways of thinking and operating

We can accelerate an upgrade by capitalising on two things:

- Propellers: people and situations (including the practices in this book) that give us temporary access to a higher level in one or more capacities

- Wormholes: sudden, fleeting and inexplicable flashes of 'genius' characteristic of a level we've yet to reach

• ● •

10

Where to from here?

● ● ●

- The decisions you need to make now
- The difference an upgrade has made to others
- How best to use Part 4 of this book
- Where else to get help
- Are you one of 'the one in seven'?

MOST IF NOT ALL OF US live in an increasingly Volatile, Uncertain, Complex and Ambiguous world. At all levels – local, regional, national, societal, international, global – we face a host of VUCA challenges in a variety of different domains: organisational, social, commercial, political, technological, economic, environmental, cultural, epidemiological and more.

Your current place in that world will determine the 'VUCA-ness' of the challenges you and your people face day to day. That, in turn, will determine the extent to which you and your people will rely on the four meaning-making capacities at the heart of this book – and what level you'll need to be at if you're to survive, or truly thrive.

Whatever world you work in, we're pretty sure it needs its leaders, teams and organisations to be able to see, understand and

> "It's what you learn after you know it all that counts."
>
> Harry S. Truman, US President (1945 – '53)[80]

work with the complexities of their environment. It needs them to be able to switch through different perspectives, stepping back and back in pursuit of greater objectivity and a more expansive view. It needs them to understand and manage themselves effectively, despite what the world is throwing at them. And that world, your world, needs its leaders to work effectively with the polarities and interdependencies that sometimes threaten to tear us apart.

Like everyone else, you have a decision to make. You could stop here and skip the opportunity to upgrade, or pretend getting this far in this book is enough. That's fine if all three of the following conditions apply:

1. You're sure the capacity profile of the operating system you're using already matches or exceeds what's required by your working world

2. You're correct in that assessment

3. Conditions 1 and 2 will continue to apply for as long as you're still around

Of course, you, your people and your organisation could decide to stick with your current OS, choose simply to continue 'adding more apps' – investing time and money in traditional training in knowledge and skills, while sticking with the same, increasingly outdated operating system. If you take that approach, though, you run the risk of continuing to fill a cup that is already full when what's actually needed is a bigger cup. It doesn't matter how tasty the coffee is, how rarefied the beans it's made from, how artfully the barista brews and pours it. None of it will stay in the cup. If the cup is already full, pouring more coffee is pointless. It'll just spill across the table and floor[81].

Upgrading your operating system – moving up through the levels in each of the four capacities – enables you to swap the cup you have for a bigger one. It's making a conscious choice not to accrue the human equivalent of the 'technology debt' we referenced in Chapter 2.

Fail to invest appropriately in the right upgrades and there's a high probability you'll eventually meet a challenge you simply can't handle. That might mean you'll find yourself unable to fix an important or career-defining problem, or failing to capitalise on a ground-breaking opportunity. Maybe you'll hit a plateau or ceiling in your career, damage an important relationship or expose your team or organisation to unnecessary or poorly managed risk.

There's no telling what form that roadblock will take, but – unless you're already running a good enough OS and you avoid environments where VUCA is on an upward trajectory – eventually you'll run out of luck.

You might, of course, see upgrading more as an opportunity than the avoidance of some looming threat. You may not need any 'burning platform' to spur you on. You may simply enjoy the fact that that upgrading enables us to experiment with different ways of seeing, interpreting and interacting with the world. Thus, your next upgrade could well be one that opens new doors for you. It could be one that enables you to operate in ways, roles and environments you hadn't previously considered or had the confidence or courage to explore.

The difference an upgrade has made for people before you

If you're keen to continue upgrading yourself and others, then you're in good company. We've cited Bob Kegan before. He speaks of 'deliberately developmental' organisations[82], who are intentionally upgrading their people's individual and collective operating systems. They're reaping the rewards, both commercially and in terms of morale, employee engagement and their contribution to the world around them.

Three final case studies offer insights into the value upgrading these capacities has had both at an individual level and on whole teams and organisations. Unlike most of the case studies in Part 2, which were amalgams of real stories, each of these is a single, real individual or team.

Ben

Ben has a background in two of the world's leading consulting firms and is a very bright and driven man. Eighteen months into his role as Finance Director for a slice of one of the world's best-known companies, he was promoted to head of operations. Overnight, he became jointly responsible for two territories on opposite sides of the world. For perhaps the first time in his life, he was out of his depth and he struggled.

Ben's boss was keen to help him develop into a Vice President role in International Finance. He offered Ben a coach who introduced him to the concept of these upgrades. The levels brought him clarity but also triggered both curiosity and appetite for a genuine, radical change in the way he thought, worked and interacted with other people. Building his capacity for Perspective-shifting enabled him to better understand the impact he has on others – a key development need at the time. He switched from making assumptions about people to truly listening to them – seeking to understand rather than merely influence. Developing his Opposable Thinking helped him shake his reputation for dogmatism and being a bit of a 'know it all'. Similarly, the levels helped him appreciate what people really meant when they said he needed to 'be more strategic'.

Upgrading has increased trust and empowerment in his teams, and he's become much better at seeing and distilling complexity. He's been promoted twice in 3½ years – those promotions being all the more significant given the company's huge growth in that time, which will have made each role considerably more complex than it would have been otherwise. He now has financial responsibility for all territories outside the company's home country. He's at the top of the ladder where he is, which opens up a whole new world of opportunities – opportunities he'll approach with a more sophisticated eye thanks to his investment in Self-relating.

Mina

Mina was a senior technical adviser in a public sector organisation who was considered talented but very 'high maintenance'. Working with her coach, she realised her intellect (including Sense-making) far outstripped her skills in the interpersonal and intrapersonal domains (which are underpinned by our capacities for Perspective-shifting and Self-relating). Thus she relied on her IQ to see her through in high-pressure situations. This came at considerable expense to herself and others.

Mina's upgrade began with work on her capacity for Self-relating, introducing more reliable practices for observing herself and reflecting in the moment – especially when stressed. She became better able to cope with difficult situations (and some *very* difficult colleagues), radically transforming her reputation for reliability under pressure.

Building on this foundation, she and her coach focused on Perspective-shifting and Opposable Thinking. Previously she would come up with answers remarkably quickly but overlook the political factors involved. As she upgraded, she grew better at inquiring and helping others see the dilemmas and conflicts they were facing. Thus she earned a reputation for easily aligning disparate stakeholders in pursuit of a common purpose. It's little surprise, given these upgrades, that she progressed from being relatively junior to Director, then to a very senior role in Government, and now into a global role for a worldwide NGO.

An upgraded team

A year before they sold their business to venture capitalists, the founders of a tech company started working on an upgrade to their own personal operating systems. The founders and the rest of the leadership team knew the sales process and subsequent transition would bring a number of challenges – both commercial and relational. These included the planned departure of the founding CEO and the need to appoint a successor.

Karen helped each member of the team understand their 'capacity profile' and craft a programme of individual and collective sessions focused on everyone's chosen upgrades. When the sale and transition were complete, the CEO cited these upgrades as key to a smooth handover to the new owners and the lack of conflict when he chose an unexpected successor. The company's new owners also commented on the leadership team's maturity and self-awareness, which they experienced as significantly greater than in other digital start-ups.

Ben, Mina and that leadership team had coaches to help them. A book can't replace the personal attention that coaching can offer. However, part of the 'magic' that helped them upgrade was the practices they adopted – the kinds of practices you'll find in Part 4.

Crunch time

You've three decisions to make, for yourself and for (or with) the people you lead:

1. Is your current operating system (or capacity profile) sufficient to survive in this increasingly complex world?

2. Will your current capacity profile *remain* sufficient for survival for the foreseeable *and unforeseeable* future?

3. Is it enough to survive when there's a genuine opportunity to *thrive*?

If your answer to any of these questions is 'No', then you've a fourth decision to make: will you use the practices in Part 4 to help you and others upgrade?

It's a choice. No one can make you do this.

At the same time, if you know full well that you *need* to upgrade your individual or collective operating system, then we'd encourage you to heed this warning from Nick Petrie at the Center for Creative Leadership[83]:

"When cardiac patients are told by their doctors they will die if they don't change their lifestyle, eat less, and exercise more, only one in seven make changes. One in seven, seriously? If the threat of death isn't enough to make someone change, what is?"

So if we've one request of you at this point, it's this: be one of the one in seven.

Making the most of Part 4 to help ensure you're one of the 'one in seven'

Chapters 11 – 14 build on the questions we posed in Part 2, which encouraged you to reflect on and apply these ideas to your day-to-day. There's a chapter for each of the four capacities. In each, you'll find a set of practices to help you make whatever upgrade you want to make in that capacity. For each upgrade, we've offered three types of practice:

1. **Reflections** are for you to use on your own, to help you exercise the internal 'psychological muscles' that are core to the upgrade on which you're focusing. These will typically involve you taking a few moments to think. Some will require you to write things down. Some might require additional material, like everyday objects or simply a room to yourself in which you can move freely.

2. **Inquiries** involve some form of dialogue with others to help you access their different perspectives, experiences and ways of making sense of the world. Inquiries will typically involve targeted questions or topics of conversation intended to encourage shared learning and to help you understand how people see you or the world in which you operate. Sometimes your insights will come from the content they offer you. Sometimes it will be the *process* of the inquiry itself that triggers

new ways of thinking. Sometimes, it will be your own approach and reactions to that process that are the biggest source of insight.

3. **Experiments** require you to stick your neck out a little and use what you're learning in a real, live work context. Because of the added risk involved with publicly trying out something different, we've designed these so they're a little less of a stretch than the preceding inquiry.

We'd encourage you to use each Experiment at least three times. First in response to a reasonably 'safe' challenge, where you feel *comfortable enough* to focus on the Experiment itself without being distracted by worrying that it might go wrong. Then try it again where the stakes are a little higher, then again where the stakes are higher again. Each time, you should feel your comfort zone growing, but you should still feel at the edge of it.

For maximum return on the investment of your time and effort, your Experiment also needs to be 'robust'. So the context needs to be one that matters and reflects the reality of your day-to-day. If it's too abstract or removed, you're less likely to get a real sense of the experiment making a tangible difference.

The Sense-making practices are different

Upgrading in this capacity is a little different so we've taken a slightly different approach. For each upgrade we've offered a practice that you can use as a Reflection, Inquiry or as the basis for an Experiment.

Some words of advice for using these practices

Some of these echo the advice we offered in Chapter 3. Some will have a different ring to them now that you're about to get stuck in.

1. **Do NOT try to read chapters 11 – 14 from start to finish**	There are more than thirty separate practices here. Reading them all in one go would likely prove boring, frustrating, bewildering or all of the above. Focus on the sections that apply to the upgrade that you, personally, are working on.

2. **Some of these practices may seem a little weird / abstract / touchy-feely** Remember: with all of these practices, we're trying to achieve something unusual that requires accessing brain functions you're not currently using as much as you could. The more unusual they seem on paper, or as you're doing them, the higher the probability that you're truly developing that capacity. If a practice feels obvious, easy or predictable, then either you're missing something in that practice or you're already ready for the next upgrade.

3. **Racing ahead is admirable, but could be unhelpful** If you're currently at Level 2 in a given capacity it could be developmentally *unhelpful* to 'aim high' and start with practices aimed at the upgrade to Level 4. Doing so is a bit like deciding that, because you're a really good cyclist, you should enter a powerlifting competition without any prior training. You may, of course, learn something. However, you're unlikely to do the practice with the level of nuance that'll maximise the return on your investment. You risk simply completing an exercise, rather than truly taking yourself into new territory.

4. **It's okay to drop back to the level before the one you're working on** If the practices for a given upgrade are so 'out there' that you're simply not prepared to give them a go, we'd recommend starting with the practices for the previous upgrade. This will help you consolidate the development you've already done to reach that level, giving you a more solid foundation from which to approach the next.

5. **Work on just one or two capacities at a time** Trying to upgrade all four at once will prove very, very difficult. The more you focus your efforts, the more progress you'll see.

6. **Ground your practice in real, current events** Doing so will help you bed the learning in faster, deeper and more sustainably. It'll also help you integrate these new ways of thinking with your existing approaches to surviving and thriving in a VUCA world.

7. **Use this material with others**

If you have a coach or mentor, sharing these ideas with them will expand the shared language you have for discussing your development. Alternatively, you could ask one of your colleagues to be your development 'buddy', enabling you to discuss the book and its practices with someone else who's reading it and working on their own upgrade. The practices also work really well in 'action learning sets'[84]. Alternatively, you could use these practices in your work developing others. After all, teaching others accelerates our own learning. If you're looking to help others upgrade, we'd recommend you work through some of the practices yourself then draw on the advice in Chapter 15 to help you use them with others.

8. **Be curious and playful**

Upgrading can feel like very serious business. However, if we take it (or ourselves) too seriously it can lock us into our current ways of thinking. One reason young children develop so quickly is that they're more curious and playful than most adults. The more you engage that curious, playful side of yourself, the more open you'll be – particularly when it comes to the Inquiries and Experiments. The more curious and playful, the more you'll accelerate your upgrade to the next level in a given capacity.

9. **Enlist someone who's a few steps ahead of you to be your 'propeller'**

We develop more quickly and sustainably when someone we respect and see as 'ahead of us' on their own journey supports us and holds us to account. They don't necessarily need to be more senior or in the same organisation as you, but that often helps. Unless you've a really good reason not to do so, we recommend you choose someone suitable and approach them as soon as possible. It could be your boss or a mentor or coach. It could be someone else entirely.

What's essential is that it's someone:

- Whom you respect, and who respects you
- With whom you can have a relatively deep discussion about your development
- To whom you'll feel genuinely accountable, as it's very tempting and easy to wriggle out of pursuing an upgrade

Ideally, they'd be operating at least one level ahead of you in the capacities you're seeking to upgrade. However, it can also work well if they're a highly effective individual with the same capacity profile as you and an appetite for developing others.

Write their name below and consider how that person could best support your development in the capacities you've chosen. This might include:

- Giving feedback on your responses to the 'Reflection' practices

- Contributing to your Inquiries

- Supporting or even simply tolerating your Experiments

- Helping you step back and review your progress and its impact on your work and the people around you.

....

....

....

....

| 10. **Take a relatively structured approach** | Our day-to-day lives are rife with opportunities to develop ourselves. However, where conscious, proactive development is concerned, all too often day-to-day life gets in the way. It's worth using the development plan below to create a 'little and often' programme for yourself that spans a number of weeks or months. Include the actual dates so you don't lose track or accidentally let yourself off the hook. Pick a capacity and decide what level you're upgrading to. Then use the quick-reference guide on the following page (and repeated in Appendix 5, the final page of the book) to select the relevant Reflection, Inquiry and Experiment from Chapters 11 – 14. Decide when you'll do each of them, two or three times each, and record the page numbers in the relevant box in your development plan. It might sound rigid, but we promise it'll help you enormously. |

However you use Part 4, we strongly recommend you come back in 3 months' time to Chapter 16, where you'll review your progress and the impact it's had on you and others. You'll also find further help there, should you need it, including:

- Some tools to more formally 'assess' the level at which you and others are currently operating

- The use of these concepts at a team and organisational level

- Where to find further inspiration if you're moving beyond Level 4

	Week / Month 1 (....................)	Week / Month 2 (....................)	Week / Month 3 (....................)	Week / Month 4 (....................)	Week / Month 5 (....................)	Week / Month 6 (....................)
Capacity and target level						
Reflection						
Inquiry						
Experiment						
Signs of progress						

Finding the right practices for you

	Upgrading from Level 1 to Level 2	Upgrading from Level 2 to Level 3	Upgrading from Level 3 to Level 4
Sense-making	Combined reflection, Inquiry and Experiment: page 289	Combined reflection, Inquiry and Experiment: page 293	Combined reflection, Inquiry and Experiment: page 298
Perspective-shifting	Reflection: page 232 Inquiry: page 234 Experiment: page 235	Reflection: page 237 Inquiry: page 239 Experiment: page 244	Reflection: page 245 Inquiry: page 247 Experiment: page 250
Self-relating	Reflection: page 253 Inquiry: page 255 Experiment: pages 255 and 256	Reflection: page 258 Inquiry: page 260 Experiment: page 262	Reflection: page 263 Inquiry: page 267 Experiment: page 268
Opposable Thinking	Reflection: page 271 Inquiry: page 273 Experiment: page 273	Reflection: page 275 Inquiry: page 277 Experiment: page 278	Reflection: page 279 Inquiry: page 282 Experiment: page 284

PART 4

• ● •

How to upgrade each of the four capacities

Upgrading your Perspective-shifting capacity

• ● •

- Reflections
- Inquiries
- Experiments

THE CAPACITY TO SHIFT our perspective to take an increasingly expansive view of any situation or relationship is essential when it comes to navigating the complexities of any situation that involves other people. We witness it in kids as their approach to relationships with siblings, friends, classmates and adults evolves with age and experience. That evolution is easiest to see when we watch children of very different ages – and hence levels of development – operating within the same social group. The differences

> "If you are emotionally attached to your tribe, religion or political leaning to the point that truth and justice become secondary considerations, your education is useless. Your exposure is useless. If you cannot reason beyond petty sentiments, you are a liability to mankind."

Chuba Okadigbo, philosopher, political scientist and president of the Nigerian Senate[85]

we see aren't simply differences in levels of age-given authority or perceived intellectual development. They're qualitative differences in their ability to notice and respond to the varied views, needs and preferences of others – differences in their ability to 'stand in other people's shoes', which forms the basis of all effective attempts to negotiate and influence.

Those children of different ages are operating at different levels when it comes to Perspective-shifting, albeit levels that precede our Level 1. On average, the older kids will be operating at a higher level, which gives them an advantage over their juniors.

The same advantage applies in adulthood. The more we progress through the levels, the more able we are to shift perspectives from first person to second to third to fourth. The more able we are to do that, the better equipped we are to understand other people, relate to them, work with them, influence them, collaborate and co-create with them – even live with them. We're also increasingly able to notice and manage how our own internal processes help and hinder those activities – one reason why the development of this capacity dovetails so well with the development of Self-relating.

If you're an L&D professional using these practices

If you're familiar with NLP or Gestalt coaching, some of the practices in this chapter might remind you of techniques from those disciplines. They're similar, but different – sometimes in subtle ways. So we'd encourage you to attend to the detailed nuances in the descriptions given here. It might not always be immediately obvious why a given step is written the way it is, but we've tried numerous variations and what you have here is the benefit of us learning through trial and error how subtle changes in wording can cause a practice to either fully deliver or veer off course.

As children, we gradually upgraded this capacity through some combination of interpersonal conflict, advice, admonishment, role-modelling and encouragement from our parents, teachers and peers. It's a slow and sometimes painful process. The practices in this chapter offer you the opportunity to take a more proactive, conscious approach to upgrading this capacity into its adult form, rather than leaving your development to chance. Used regularly, they will transform your relationships with your colleagues, seniors, stakeholders, friends and even your family.

Choose a relationship to work on

Whichever upgrade you are working on, focus your attention on a close and long-standing relationship in which you're currently having some form of difficulty. Don't go too far, though: it shouldn't be a difficulty, issue or conflict that is so emotionally 'hot' that you'll find it too hard to step back and take a relatively neutral perspective on it. The relationship should, however, be one which matters to you and one where you know you have some strongly held beliefs about the relationship and your own part in it.

From Level 1 to Level 2

Reflection

1. Once you've decided on the relationship difficulty you're keen to examine, choose someone to act as an 'imaginary advisor' from the list below:

   - A good friend

   - A trusted colleague

   - A coach or mentor

   - Someone you consider to be a role-model, ideally for their approach to relationships

(You won't actually be interacting with that imaginary advisor. They'll be part of a 'thought experiment' in which you imagine how this positive but neutral observer might see the situation. So it doesn't need to be someone who is actually present in your life at this point. They could be someone you've valued and lost, someone you used to know – even a fictional character, as strange as that might sound.

Whomever you choose, though, they should be someone you like but who is different from you and would thus likely take an alternative view regarding the relationship difficulty you've chosen for this practice.)

2. Make a note of the person's name and ask yourself the following questions:

What would this advisor say about how I'm behaving in the relationship I've chosen for this practice?

....

....

....

What would this advisor say about the person I'm having this difficulty with? What would they say about the quality of the relationship between my 'problem person' and me?

....

....

....

How else would my advisor see the situation differently?

....

....

....

What advice would this imaginary mentor give me?

....

....

....

Inquiry

1. Use the following structure to prepare for a conversation with the person you are having this current challenge with.

   a. How will you 'frame' the conversation (either at the start or beforehand)?

   (e.g. your intention for the conversation, what you'd like it to achieve, how you'd like both of you to feel at the end of it, why you feel it's important to have it now)

   ....

   ....

   ....

   b. What's your perception of the situation?

   (e.g. the impact it's having and the sequence of events that led to the current state of play)

   ....

   ....

   ....

c. How will you ask about their perception of the situation?

(e.g. the impact it's having on them and/or their stakeholders; the sequence of events they believe led to the current state of play)

....

....

....

d. What, from your current point of view, is the most useful thing you could do that would help both you and the person with whom you're having this difficulty?

(Be prepared to adapt this potential course of action to integrate what you hear from them in the conversation.)

....

....

....

2. Now have that conversation, and note down the outcomes and your reflections below

....

....

....

Experiment

(It's really important that you include the physical movements and 'speaking out loud' that we've included in this Experiment. The muscle you're working is heavily reliant on the felt experience elicited by doing so.

It won't develop nearly as effectively if you treat this as a quiet, stationary or purely intellectual exercise.)

As strange as this may sound, get yourself a room with two chairs in it[86]. It's best to choose a room no one else can see into. Place the chairs so they're facing each other, about an arm's length apart. Decide which chair is 'you' (Chair 1) and which chair is 'the person you're having some form of relationship challenge with' (Chair 2). Then...

1. Sit in Chair 1 and imagine the other person sitting in Chair 2

2. Talk to them (ideally out loud, but at least in your head) about the current state of your relationship

   Share what you think is working, what is difficult and any specific recent incidents that have affected you

3. Stand, move to the other chair and sit down in it

4. Settle into their position in this relationship.

   Imagine you're looking at yourself through their eyes, from where they sit in this relationship. Imagine the events that have led to this difficulty, as they would have experienced them over those critical days, weeks or months. Imagine how they might have interpreted those events differently and what might have caused them to act the way they did. Now think about the things they've seen you do (and not do), the things they've heard you say and the impact those things might have had on the way they think and feel about you

5. Use 2-3 sentences to articulate, in summary, the things they believe you've said, done and not done and the impact it's had on them

6. Stand aside so you can look at the space between the two chairs.

   It might seem strange to do so, but visualise yourself and the other person talking to each other. This time, imagine (from this slightly removed third position) that the two of you are discussing your relationship and the issue that is causing difficulties between you. As objectively as you can, focus on watching the interaction between these two people

7. Still standing there, looking at these two people, consider the following:

   a. What do you notice about the dynamic of the relationship?

   b. What do you see and hear in the way each person is expressing themselves?

   c. What is helping and what is not?

8. Note down the insights you've gained

   Note, too, the actions those insights suggest you could take to enhance the quality of this relationship.

....

....

....

From Level 2 to Level 3

Reflection

The following process has proven a helpful tool for deeply understanding others, particularly for people who are quite task-focused and tend to view empathy and feelings as uncomfortably touchy-feely.

In some places, this process relies on you knowing things about the person you've chosen to focus on. If you don't know them, allow yourself to hypothesise and extrapolate from the things you *do* know. It's important that you do the work, not that your answers are entirely accurate. After all, Perspective-shifting isn't mind-reading. It's best approached as a generation of hypotheses about another person, which we then test through observation and enquiry.

Steps 1 and 2 are optional, but we'd highly recommend them. They're designed to increase the accuracy of the data you get from the rest of this practice – in part by reducing the natural biases you'll otherwise bring to the practice. It'll probably help to close your eyes throughout, although you'll need to open your eyes to read what comes next!

1. Bring to mind a particularly difficult interaction you've had with this person

2. Take a few moments to picture the person you've chosen to focus on

   Recall their facial expression the last time you saw them; the clothes they were wearing; the way they held themselves; the way they moved. Then hear the sound of their voice; the pace at which they spoke; the volume and the kinds of phrases they used that last time you interacted. Them when you've got that visual and audio going...

3. Zoom in on that person until you're so close that you can 'step inside' them and inhabit their body

4. Consider their day as it led up to that interaction with you

   The things they'll have done, the people they'll have interacted with, the challenges they'll have faced and overcome.

5. Consider the days and weeks that came before, then the earlier years of their career.

   Think about how those experiences could have affected the way they showed up in that last interaction you had with them.

6. Come back to their present and consider the people around them in their working lives

   Include the people above them, the people they lead (if they lead), their peers and various other stakeholders – including you. Notice how it feels to be them in those relationships – the positive and negative; the give and take.

7. Turn your awareness to the people in their life outside of work

   Consider the impact those people might be having on the way this person feels and thinks about their life at work.

8. Start attending to the future they have ahead of them

   Attend to their hopes and expectations about the coming weeks and months; their aspirations for the years ahead of them.

9. Notice how all these things in this person's past, present and future affect their approach to working with you

   Focus in particular on the way they've been approaching the situation you're focusing on in this reflection.

10. Capture your insights below

....

....

....

....

....

Inquiry

For this Inquiry you'll need to engage someone you trust and respect. It needs to be a third party who knows you and the person you're focusing on equally well, who has goodwill towards you both and favours neither of you over the other.

This person is going to act as your 'Witness' for the practice, giving you a sense of what it is like to have your own internal fourth-person witnessing perspective. So they must also favour neither of your *positions* on this particular matter. Their interest must be in helping you improve the quality of the relationship you've chosen as the subject for this Inquiry.

1. Arrange four chairs as in the image below

   Each chair represents one of the first, second, third and fourth-person perspectives. You are the Inquirer. The 'Subject' is the other person you're focusing on for this Inquiry. In case it's not obvious, that person is not present. They're represented by the chair.

2. Sit in Chair 1 and invite your Witness to sit in Chair 4

3. Ask your Witness to take this book and lead you through the process of Inquiry using the following script

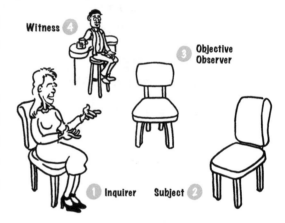

As the Witness, sitting in Chair 4, your role is to use the following script to help the person in Chair 1 (the Inquirer) better understand the person represented by Chair 2 (the Subject of this Inquiry).

You've a second role, though: to observe how well the Inquirer is able to put their own emotions and preconceptions about the Subject to one side. When you ask them to move from chair to chair, how able are they to objectively put themselves in the Subject's shoes or take an entirely neutral 'Objective Observer' position to look at the situation?

What follows is a script to be read aloud. Please stick to the script as it includes some subtle nuances designed to extract maximum value from this practice. Replace "[Subject's name]" with the name of the subject of this Inquiry, and "[Inquirer's name]" with the name of the person who's actually physically present, whom you're guiding through this process. We recommend you read it through to the end at least once before starting.

The numbered bullets are the 13 instructions for you to give the

Inquirer as they go through the practice. The italicised text under each bullet offered further explanation of that step, also intended for you to read aloud.

1. Take a few moments to picture the Subject of this Inquiry, sitting in the chair opposite [Chair 2]

   It'll probably help to close your eyes to do so. See their facial expression the last time you saw them; their hair and the clothes they were wearing; the way they held themselves; the way they moved. Then hear the sound of their voice; the pace at which they spoke; the volume and the kinds of phrases they used that last time you interacted.

2. From your own perspective, briefly describe the relationship as it stands and the events that have led to this point

3. Describe the behaviours you've seen [Subject's name] demonstrate and the impact those behaviours have had on you

   (The thoughts those behaviours have evoked in you and the emotions they've triggered.)

4. Now move to Chair 2

   You'll find it helps to close your eyes and keep them closed until I tell you to open them.

5. Firstly, as [Subject's name], tell us your three greatest strengths or best character traits

6. Now, take a moment to settle into what it's like to be [Subject's name]

   Think about the nature of their role, the responsibilities you (as [Subject's name]), have on your shoulders and the people around you who are either helping you meet those responsibilities or seem to be getting in the way.

7. Now, tell us what challenges you (as [Subject's name]) are currently facing elsewhere in your life and working life, other than in this relationship

8. Now picture [Inquirer's name], sitting opposite (in Chair 1)

   Picture [Inquirer's name]'s facial expression the last time the two of you interacted. See his/her hair, the clothes s/he was wearing, the way s/he was sitting.

9. Now, keeping your eyes closed, and maintaining [Subject]'s perspective, briefly describe the relationship as it stands and the events that have led to this point

10. Describe the behaviours you've seen [Inquirer's name] demonstrate and the impact those behaviours have had on you

    (The thoughts those behaviours have evoked in you and the emotions they've triggered.)

11. Now say what you, as [Subject's name], need [Inquirer's name] to do to create a positive change in this relationship / situation

12. Now open your eyes and move to Chair 3

    In this chair, you're an objective observer. You're someone who knows [Subject's name] and [Inquirer's name] but has no preference for one or the other.

    It's up to you whether you choose a specific third party from among the people who know you both, or use an imaginary third party. As long as this observer is truly neutral.

13. Tell me what you notice about the way these two parties are interpreting and responding to this relationship

    If you'd prefer to write this down initially, then share, then you're welcome to do so.

Now, as the Witness, offer the Inquirer feedback on the extent to which you truly believe they stepped out of their own way of looking at the situation and saw it from the Subject's and Objective Observer's perspectives. Anything you offer will be valuable here, as long as you're able to leave any biases of your own to one side.

Then hand the book back to the Inquirer to record (below) the insights they've had from this process.

As the Inquirer:

a. What did you notice about your ability to truly set your own emotions aside to adopt the Subject's perspective on the situation?

....

....

....

....

b. What biases and assumptions did you notice creeping in when you took the Objective Observer role?

....

....

....

c. What new insights did you gain from the feedback of your Witness?

....

....

....

d. How might you develop the ability to hold an internal Witness who would give you similar, unbiased, feedback about your relationships?

....

....

....

Experiment

For this Experiment – similar to the Inquiry above – you'll need to engage someone you trust and respect. Ideally, as before, it will be a third party who knows you and the person you're focusing on equally well and has goodwill towards you both. The most important thing, though, is that they've no vested interests and they don't favour either of you over the other. For the purposes of this Experiment, we'll call this person your 'partner'.

The Experiment is a reverse role-play. Your partner plays you. You play the person you're looking to understand better – the person you're having these current challenges with, i.e. the 'Subject' if this were the Inquiry above.

1. Brief your partner on the situation just enough that they'll be able to bring some reality to the situation

    It's obviously best if you can brief them as objectively as possible! You might also brief them on the approach you think you'll take to your next conversation with this person.

2. Ask them to start the reverse role-play

    Remember, this is a conversation between you (played by your partner) and the person you're having the issue with (played by you).

3. After 5-10 minutes, pause the action and ask your partner for feedback

    The question to focus on when seeking this feedback is "How

balanced is my depiction of this person?"

You might also give them feedback on how accurately you think they're playing you, but that should not be the focus and should only be done in service of the next step...

4. Run the reverse role-play again

    This time you need to work even harder on seeing things truly from the perspective of the person whose role you are playing.

    You need to truly set aside your own attitudes to them and the emotions they've evoked in you to date. If it helps to dip back into the earlier processes for this upgrade – the Reflection and Inquiry above – then do so.

5. Ask your partner (who has been playing you throughout this reverse role-play) to give you some advice on how they think you might handle this situation more effectively in real life

There's an advanced version of this practice, which we'd recommend using only once you've tried the original version at least once. Having run the reverse role-play, stay in your role and share what it's been like *as that other person* to be on the receiving end of you. This is you articulating what it is like for that person to be in this relationship with you. It is *not* you sharing what it was like to play that person in a role-play – although you could do that as well, if you like, at the end.

From Level 3 to Level 4

Reflection

1. Looking back over the last couple of years, identify 2-3 work relationships that have been difficult (or included some ups and downs) and 2-3 relationships that have been smoother or required less energy to 'manage'. Write their names or initials in the table below.

More challenging	Easier / smoother

2. What common patterns do you see in your interactions with the people in each of those two columns?

More challenging	Easier / smoother

3. When you really think about it, what beliefs, assumptions and expectations have influenced your approach and response to the relationships in each of those two columns?

More challenging	Easier / smoother

4. Using the table below: what needs (of your own) have driven your behaviours in those relationships? What needs have the people in each of those two columns met / failed to meet for you?

(Avoid assuming that the relationships on the right will have met needs that those on the left haven't. It could easily be the other way around. Also, the deeper the need you explore, the more insight you'll gain. It's one thing to realise that having a difficult relationship with Bill meets your 'need' to requisition 11 paperclips from Bill's department. It's far more profound and useful to realise you're sustaining a pattern of quiet conflict with Bill because you need to feel more powerful or intellectually superior to him, or to feel that your values are more 'right' than his.)

More challenging	Easier / smoother

Inquiry

Pick one of the least helpful patterns you identified in the reflective practice above. Tell 2-3 trusted colleagues that you're working on that pattern. These are your 'Witnesses'. It's probably best not to name the relationships you listed above.

Then share your observations of that pattern with them – either with one of these 'Witnesses' at a time, or with all of them at once if you're prepared to do that. In doing so, it's essential that you take a 'third-person' perspective, as if you're a neutral observer standing outside of yourself and looking in. It can be hard to maintain this perspective, so tell your Witness(es) what you're doing and why, and ask them to listen first as you work through the thinking out loud. Tell them you'll ask them for feedback afterwards, not just on the pattern but most importantly on the extent to which they think you've been able to stick with that neutral, third-person description of the pattern.

We'd recommend working through the following questions or handing this book to your Witness(es) so they can take you through them. The latter approach will have them most actively engaged, so they might prefer it.

Tip: if your Witness leads you though the questions below, it can help you stay in the third-person perspective if your Witness substitutes 'you' in the questions below with your name. Thus it would be "What events trigger this pattern in Eva?" if your name was Eva, rather than "…in you?"

Questions 1-8 are for *you*, the Inquirer, to answer. Those that follow are for the *Witness*, to help them give you useful feedback.

1. Describe the pattern as it plays out, using a couple of recent examples.

2. What impact do you see that pattern having on others?

3. What impact does that pattern have on you in the short term, and in the medium-to-long term?

4. What are the benefits you get from maintaining that pattern?

   Keep digging on this one as they may be far from obvious, and don't stop after the first 1-3 benefits as they'll be the easy ones to spot.

5. What events, contexts, unmet needs and 'types of people' trigger this pattern in you?

   Dig into all of these and take your time. This may be hard to work out.

6. What does the fact that you're repeating that pattern tell you that you must (consciously or unconsciously) believe about:

   a. The people you're repeating that pattern with?

   b. The nature of relationships?

   c. People in general?

   d. Who [Inquirer's name] is in these relationships?

7. Where in your history might this pattern have first formed? What does that tell you about its relevance in the present?

8. What small changes could you make that will make it easier for you to avoid falling into this pattern the next time you are tempted to do so?

Questions for the Witness:

9. How objectively do you think the 'Inquirer' answered the previous questions?

10. What would an even more objective exploration of this particular pattern have looked / sounded like?

11. In what ways did they judge themselves too harshly?

12. In what ways did they seem a little too generous towards themselves?

13. What other feedback could you give them on the impact of this pattern?

14. What other theories do you have as to what triggers this pattern and where it might come from?

As the Inquirer, use the space below to note down your insights into your ability to take and maintain that objective third-party perspective. Then record the insights you've gained on the pattern itself.

Observations regarding my ability to take and maintain an objective, third-party position on myself	Insights regarding the pattern itself

Experiment

It's important to keep in mind that the conversation at the heart of this Experiment is *not* a role-play.

It's a genuine conversation between you and the person you have this relationship with. You are practising your ability to act as a neutral Witness to a relationship difficulty and you are asking for their assessment of your capacity to do this.

If you're unwilling to give the Experiment a go, ask yourself what that resistance is telling you. It could be that the relationship is the wrong one to choose, in which case choose another that's stronger, a little less disrupted or less important to you. If your resistance is to the Experiment itself, then it might be that you're not quite ready for this upgrade, or at least not ready to start trying it out in the real world – in which case, if you've not already done so, we'd recommend the preceding Reflection and Inquiry practices and/or the Experiment for the upgrade from Level 2 to Level 3.

1. Choose a working relationship that's usually really good but is in a bit of a dip at the moment – where, for whatever reason, you're going through a period of *relative* difficulty

    We're not looking for a huge, hot conflict or painful disconnection, just a wobble.

2. Engage that person in a conversation about the current situation

    Start by setting a positive frame for the discussion[a]. *Then share the following:*

    a. *Your position on what's currently happening in this relationship; how that compares to what the relationship was like before; what*

---

a   This might include your reasons for speaking now or your desire to hear their views and continue to invest in the relationship. The frame should include whatever you think, in your preparation for the conversation, is going to set the right tone for what follows.

might have triggered the change

b. *What you think their position is regarding the current state of the relationship; how that compares to how it was before; what might have triggered the change*

c. *What you think an objective third person would think of what's going on in this relationship at the moment, in the context of what's come before*

3. Ask the other person to give feedback on what you've said about all three positions

If they feel unable to do so, suggest a course of action based on the things you've just shared – and heard from them – and ask them for feedback on that.

If you try this Experiment and can't get it to work as described, we recommend seeking out a third party who can facilitate the conversation on your behalf using the structure we've provided above.

●●●

12

Upgrading your Self-relating capacity

● ● ●

- Reflections
- Inquiries
- Experiments

SINCE DANIEL GOLEMAN'S seminal work on emotionally intelligent leadership[87] triggered an explosion of interest in 'EQ', many competency frameworks and leadership orthodoxies now put 'self-awareness' near the top the agenda for anyone seeking to work more effectively with others. Unfortunately, while many people in organisations have bought into the importance of self-awareness, most writers and trainers are surprisingly shy when it comes to telling us how to develop it. They also too often make it seem like a quality or inherent gift rather than, as we see it, the result of ongoing attention to observing ourselves from the inside as we go about our day-to-day lives.

Access to clear, challenging and unambiguous feedback from others is obviously a key element, especially where we have unacknowledged blind-spots. Other than

> **"Until you make the unconscious conscious, it will direct your life and you will call it fate."**
>
> Carl Jung, psychiatrist and psychoanalyst[88]

that, though, simply being told to 'reflect on yourself more' is probably worse than useless – particularly as, for some people, that Reflection can turn into paralysing rumination and have a negative impact on confidence. In reality, if your Self-relating muscle is relatively under-developed, then what you need is some simple and effective daily practices to help you start lightly working that muscle and gradually strengthening it. If your muscle is already working well but you're looking to take it to the next level, then you'll be looking for guidance on how best to exercise that muscle so it's supporting peak performance.

Thus the practices in this chapter are designed to help you shift your ability to actively observe and, eventually, change your ways of operating day-to-day – especially the limiting beliefs, unhelpful emotional reactions and other psychological patterns that may be getting in your way.

Many people have an immediate emotional reaction to doing this kind of work that often manifests in a little voice in their heads shouting "You've no time for this stuff; do some emails!" Hence, we've chosen practices that are simple, quick and easy to turn into habits.

From Level 1 to Level 2

The focus in these practices is twofold:

1. Helping you identify any habits, needs, mind-sets and emotional responses that could be reducing or limiting your effectiveness at work – whether that's in VUCA situations or more straightforward ones

2. Enhancing your ability to notice these things happening in the moment and choose an alternative course of action

You'll find these three practices increase your resilience. Life at work rarely involves the level of 'hot' emotion that we sometimes experience in other environments, but the emotional load can still wear us down if we're not managing it well. The ability to manage our moods and understand how they shift in response to what is happening within and around us is key to maintaining a healthy and effective equilibrium in difficult circumstances.

These practices will also enhance the quality and clarity of your thinking. The psychology of decision-making shows that the majority of the decisions we make are based not on conscious logic but on subconscious and unconscious assumptions, biases, short-cuts and emotional pre-dispositions. Thus, the practices will help you decide the right direction, maintain your own commitment and manage your own intellectual and emotional capacity. That in turn will make it easier for you to direct others, secure their commitment and harness the capacity they have to offer.

Reflection

1. Use a notebook (or something similar) to keep a journal for the next week, including the days you're not at work

2. At the end of each day, take five minutes to draw a timeline to show your mood as it went up and down during that day in response to the various things you did and things that happened to you

    You can decide for yourself what constitutes a positive or negative mood for you – there are no cut-and-dried definitions! There's an example below, using a scale from minus 5 to plus 5 as a measure of

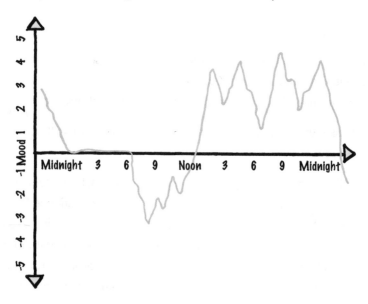

your mood, but you can use whatever scale feels most appropriate or useful. We do recommend you label each of the spikes and 'triggering events' so it's easier to interpret when you come back to it.

3. At the end of the week, re-read the journal and review the timelines. What triggered those up and down movements in your mood?

....

....

....

Inquiry

1. Choose 3-5 friends and family members and ask them what they notice about your moods and how your energy levels move up and down at different times of day, during the course of a week, month or year

    For instance, you might ask them:

    a. *What patterns they see*

    b. *What situations, events or people seem to trigger specific kinds of negative emotions (like frustration, sadness, loneliness or dips in confidence)*

    c. *What they think gives you pleasure or lifts your energy*

2. Use the space below to capture what emerges:

....

....

....

Experiment 1

Most people working on this upgrade want practices that help them solve a specific problem. Experiment 2 fits that category. This first Experiment is more a door to a potential new opportunity. We'd recommend trying this before Experiment 2.

1. Looking back at the Reflection and Inquiry practices above, choose one of the things that lifts your spirits

2. For four weeks, do that thing just one more time per week than you currently do

   That might mean one more conversation with your best friend than you'd usually have in a week; one more swim or run; one more breakfast, dinner or bath-time with your kids; one lunch away from your desk; one more meeting that's dedicated to generating ideas with no pressure for any of those ideas to bear fruit. It doesn't matter what it is, as long as it's something that has a significant positive impact on your mood.

3. What have you noticed as a result of conducting this Experiment?

   ....

   ....

   ....

Experiment 2

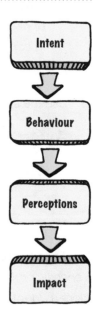

We can't *not* have an impact. Even if someone sits in motionless silence for the entirety of a meeting, that will have an impact.

It might not be the impact they intended. That's because of the sequence of events shown on the right. Their *intent* drove them to demonstrate certain *behaviours*. You then interpreted those behaviours, forming your own perceptions – which are rooted in your own beliefs, assumptions and expectations. It's those *perceptions* that created the *impact* that person's behaviours had on you. It's not the behaviours themselves.

Bearing that model in mind, pick one of the less-helpful emotional patterns you've identified through the Reflection or Inquiry above. Then choose one of the triggers that kicks off that pattern for you. It could be a person, context or specific event.

Next time you're faced with that trigger, Experiment with pausing and using this 'Intent-to-Impact' model to dissect and articulate your experience.

It's a good idea to choose a fairly low-stakes situation to start with – one with a person or people that you trust and who will be willing to listen to your immediate response to the trigger event. The practice is to state out loud:

1. The situation / trigger's emotional *impact* on you.

   It can feel less exposing / touchy-feely if you start the sentence with something like "The impact this is having on me is…"

   Alternatively, if stating these things out loud feels too risky for now, you could start by simply writing down your responses to this and the subsequent steps in this practice.

2. The *behaviour(s)* that triggered that impact

3. How you *interpreted* their behaviour and the various reasons you made that interpretation

   In doing so, it's important that:

   a. *You acknowledge the possibility that you misinterpreted their intent*

   b. *You recognise that your interpretation is rooted in your own beliefs, assumptions and expectations about a whole load of things*

   c. *You make no assumptions about the intent behind their behaviour*

4. Your hypotheses as to the original *intention* behind their behaviours

   This step takes you into the realms of Perspective-shifting, too. It's important that you offer new hypotheses regarding the person's intentions, not just the ones you started this practice with.

Once you've completed the practice, note your reflections below.

What do you notice about your ability to articulate the behaviour, your interpretation of it and the emotional impact that situation had on you?

....

....

....

If you did choose to voice your observations out loud, what do you notice happened when you did so?

....

....

....

From Level 2 to Level 3

The focus in these practices is twofold:

- Helping you start to notice some of the psychological patterns that are personal to you. Some you might definitely want to retain because they feel core to your identity; others may feel more limiting and unhelpful

- Leveraging your increasing ability to notice your patterns playing out in the moment and to choose alternative courses of action that are more consistent with the 'you' you want to be going forward.

You'll find this increasing awareness and ability to self-manage in the moment enhances both your resilience and the quality and clarity of your decision making. This in turn will make it easier to define your own identity at work and to make a real difference to your team, your organisation and your other stakeholders in an increasingly VUCA world.

The uncertainty and turbulence of VUCA environments can leave us feeling less able to cope – not least because other people's anxieties in those environments can be highly infectious. The more you can notice and deal with your own triggers, unhelpful belief patterns and emotional reactivity, the more resilient you'll be in challenging situations. You'll find it easier to maintain focus and engagement, and thus easier to be a beacon for others.

Similarly, the more proactively you define your own identity, the easier you'll find it to imagine a unique, authentic direction for your part of the organisation – a direction that will enthuse both you and the people around you.

Reflection

Identify 5-6 different roles you have, 'hats' you wear or groups you're in (e.g. boss, subordinate, finance team, executive team, company choir / rock band). It's fine for this to be a mix of roles, hats and groups. What matters is that they're all-important to you in your working life.

1. What do you appreciate about how you *are* in each of these contexts?

....

....

....

2. What things about your current ways of thinking, feeling or responding in each of those contexts bother you or cause you to question yourself?

....

....

....

3. What is it about those situations that can trigger those ways of thinking, feeling or responding?

....

....

....

4. Which of those contexts or triggers remind you of environments or incidents earlier in your life (e.g. in your family, at school, in your teenage peer groups)?

....

....

....

Inquiry

1. Choose 3-5 trusted friends

   These could be people who only experience you in one of the various roles or groups you occupy in the course of your work; or they could be people you see in a variety of different contexts.

2. Ask them to talk about any patterns they see in your behaviours and the ways you seem to think about situations

   This Inquiry works best if you frame this with them as follows:

   a. *It's really important that they don't try to be balanced in their feedback. Instead, they should imagine they're your coach and that their sole focus is on raising your awareness of the ways you think, behave and react to the people and situations around you*

    b. *If they experience you in multiple roles or groups, or wearing a few of your different 'hats', then ask them in what ways they experience you as being consistent across contexts and in which ways they see you showing up differently*

    c. *Ask them not to make comments about your authenticity or guess at your intentions in those different situations. They should focus purely on the different behaviours they observe and any differences in the apparent beliefs, assumptions and expectations you bring to the different contexts*

3. Resist the temptation to justify or explain your behaviours. You'll get far more value from the conversation if you stay curious and treat it as a data-gathering exercise, not a performance appraisal

4. Harvest your learning using the following questions:

    a. What additional insights has this Inquiry brought you regarding the patterns of thinking, feeling and responding that limit your effectiveness and/or happiness?

    b. What patterns has the Inquiry highlighted that you're glad to have in your repertoire?

c. How did the patterns in questions 1 and 2 form in the first place?

(e.g. which did you inherit from others, and which did you create – intentionally or unintentionally – for yourself?)

....

....

....

d. What alternative patterns would you like to create? What would it take to create them?

(It's worth bearing in mind that some of your more problematic patterns may be perpetuated by the beliefs, assumptions and expectations that you or significant others hold about 'who you are' or 'how you should behave'. Your existing patterns will also meet certain needs for you, and changing some patterns may require others to change their own habits or find other ways of meeting certain needs.)

....

....

....

Experiment

1. Pick a role or context in which you believe you're operating at your best or truly thriving

2. In the left-hand column of the table below, write down the behaviours you display in that situation

3. In the right-hand column, record the attitude, beliefs or assumptions that you hold in that role or context that make it easier for you to

display those positive behaviours

Behaviours	Attitudes, beliefs, assumptions

4. Choose a role or context in which you believe you're currently significantly less effective

   Pick one of the behaviours from the table above, and/or the associated attitudes, beliefs and assumptions.

5. Seek out the role / context you identified in Step 4 and experiment, in *that* situation, with:

   a. Holding the attitudes, beliefs and assumptions there from Step 3

   b. Porting across the behaviours from Step 2

   c. Demonstrating new, healthier behaviours that are based on the same attitudes, beliefs and assumptions but even more suited to thriving in that particular situation

From Level 3 to Level 4

The focus in these practices is to help you:

- Further enhance your ability to notice long-standing patterns of thinking, feeling and behaving that are continuing to limit your enjoyment or effectiveness at work

- Start to unlock some of those patterns

- Identify the strongly held aspects of identity that sustain the patterns you're already noticing

- Enable you to more consciously choose which aspects of that identity you wish to keep and which to evolve or discard

You'll find these practices provide an opportunity to weave together some of the seemingly disparate insights and questions about yourself that you've been accumulating in recent months or years. The more complex the environment we work in, the more we need to be able to examine our responses to what is going on around us. Doing so increases our independence from any group-think or unhelpful, contagious emotions.

The better you understand yourself, the more flexible and adaptive you can be. As you'll no doubt have found in the past, this benefits the people around you as much as it benefits you. They'll profit from your enhanced ability to help them manage their own anxieties. You'll also be role-modelling an attitude to self-Reflection that should, for many, inspire an open curiosity into their own unhelpful beliefs and assumptions about themselves.

Reflection

This practice is inspired by Robert Kegan's work on 'competing commitments', beautifully laid out in his book (with Lisa Lahey) *Immunity to Change*[89]. We have outlined a somewhat different, simplified version here which is easier to use on your own, but the practice uses a similar underlying principle of 'mining for the assumptions' that maintain puzzling patterns of behaviour.

1. Choose a long-standing habit or pattern of behaviour that you've been keen to change about yourself and write the *desired* behaviours in the space below

    They need to be stated in positive terms, i.e. the habit or behaviour you would like to be demonstrating but currently aren't. For example, "Managing my time / boundaries effectively", "Focusing on strategic

rather than operational issues", "Standing my ground with senior stakeholders".

....

....

....

2. Write down all the things you're currently doing instead of the thing you've written above

   For example, "Saying 'yes' to additional work when I know I already have too many things on my plate", "Checking every detail in the work done by my team". Really push yourself on this. You're only finished when you've gone past the easy ones to write, have really struggled to come up with more, and have then written things you're embarrassed / ashamed of.

....

....

....

....

....

....

3. The list you've just created is essentially a list of habits that are the antithesis of the behaviour you're keen to see in yourself. Looking at that list, what needs are those habits meeting for you?

   Dig deep here, going beyond the obvious. When you get to needs like "To feel safe, significant, competent, in control, liked..." then you know you're onto something.

....

....

....

....

....

4. What other ways could you find to meet those needs while also doing the thing you're aspiring to in Step 1?

....

....

....

5. Again, looking at that list of counterproductive habits in Step 2, what are the beliefs, assumptions and expectations that make those habits make sense?

    These could be beliefs and assumptions about you, about other people, about potential consequences, etc.

....

....

....

....

....

....

6. What alternative, equally logical and evidence-based beliefs could you hold that would allow you to let go of the habits in Step 2 and start making a habit of the behaviour(s) you're aspiring to in Step 1?

....

....

....

Inquiry

1. Find a partner for this Inquiry. You'll need someone you believe fits these criteria:

   - Operates consistently at Level 4 when it comes to Self-relating (if it helps, refer to the summary on page 187, which also appears at the back of the book in Appendix 4, on page 351)

   - Doesn't have a vested interest in you behaving in a particular way or making certain decisions

   - Doesn't want something from you or have power over you (your boss wouldn't be a good choice, nor would your partner or spouse!)

2. Ask for their perspective on an unhelpful pattern you identified in the Reflection above (or another if you prefer)

   The following questions should help focus the conversation:

   - *What benefits do you think I could be getting from maintaining the unhelpful habits that support this way of operating (or pattern of thinking, feeling or behaving)?*

   - *I can see that this behaviour / way of thinking / way of feeling is limiting me, but I wouldn't be doing it if it didn't make some kind of sense. So what assumptions must I be holding that make this pattern make sense?*

3. Notice your response to their answers to these questions, and use the space below to capture your reflections during and after the conversation

   The more emotional your response, the closer they've landed to the core things that are locking that pattern in place. In fact, if their replies irritate or upset you, they are probably getting pretty close to what's really going on!

   ....

   ....

   ....

Experiment

1. Using the pattern you chose for the Inquiry above, pick one of the beliefs or assumptions that may have created that pattern or might be maintaining it

2. For one day, practice 'being' someone who believes the opposite to be true, which means really getting into how that person would operate, think and feel

   This will probably prove quite difficult because:

   - *It may mean stepping into the imaginary shoes of someone you might not like at all or whose values you don't agree with*

   - *For that day, all of your decisions and behaviours must be consistent with that opposite belief*

   As they say, though: 'No pain, no gain'! This ability to Experiment with flexing your core beliefs is a vital one for your development if you're set on upgrading to Level 4 in this capacity.

   If you really can't bring yourself to fully embrace the Experiment, it could be that you're not yet ready for this Self-relating upgrade. Bear in mind, though, that you can try this Experiment in any context where the pattern you've chosen applies: at work, at home, in a social environment, in pursuing a hobby, with complete strangers where no one will know who you are, and so on.

3. Use the space below to capture the insights that Experiment brings

....

....

....

....

• ◉ •

Upgrading your Opposable Thinking capacity

• ● •

- Reflections
- Inquiries
- Experiments

IN A SERIES OF EXPERIMENTS, Michael Hall and Kaitlin Raimi from

the University of Michigan's Ford School for Public Policy showed that our confidence in the superiority of our beliefs over others' is *inversely* correlated with the extent to which we actually know what we're talking about[90]. Not only that, but the more confident we are that we are right, the less likely we are to seek out data that supports the *opposing* position.

"That all opposites – such as mass and energy, subject and object, life and death – are so much each other that they are perfectly inseparable, still strikes most of us as hard to believe. But this is only because we accept as real the boundary line between the opposites."

Ken Wilber, *No Boundary: Eastern and Western approaches to personal growth*[91]

Fortunately, Hall and Raimi's research also suggests that this over-confidence and confirmation bias can be reduced by feedback that shows us our knowledge on a given topic isn't as great as we thought it was. Knowing about Hall and Raimi's research itself makes a significant difference!

The practices in this chapter will help you upgrade your Operating System to reduce your chances of falling into these and other traps when working with conflict, dilemmas and valid differences of opinion. They're practices designed to improve fluid thinking, which underpins creativity, and to enhance collaborative thinking, which is even more important in a complex world than collaborative *doing*. Developing this capacity can mean covering some pretty tough terrain: each upgrade requires us to challenge our existing beliefs, some of which we'll have been holding pretty tightly for quite some time. That's why we've chosen to tackle this capacity after the previous two: if you've been working on either or both of those already, you'll have warmed up your muscles in preparation for these practices.

From Level 1 to Level 2

We spend a great deal of our development at school and work accumulating knowledge and solidifying our beliefs in 'what we know to be true'. As useful as this process is, there comes a point when we start to notice that having a rigid set of beliefs and ideas makes us less adaptable to new information and stops us negotiating freely with other people. Upgrading our capacity for Opposable Thinking means holding our beliefs less tightly – which requires us to first work out what those beliefs *actually are*!

Reflection

1. Identify one real, current problematic situation you're facing

    It can be as big or small as you like, but it needs to feel significant.

2. Write down the one personal quality you believe you absolutely must live up to in this situation – regardless of what the actual solution to the problem turns out to be

    This needs to be a quality you feel you have to demonstrate if you're to be able to look yourself in the eye afterwards. If you're struggling to think of one, you might find it helpful to refer to the list of values in Appendix 2.

    ....

3. What *plausible* evidence could there be that holding onto that quality so tightly is actually the wrong thing to do in this situation?

    ....

    ....

    ....

4. What evidence is there that holding that quality too tightly might cause you to demonstrate behaviours that *aren't* consistent with being the person you want to be?

    For example, Richard places a great deal of importance on being responsible. However, when he grips that too tightly, he risks taking on too many responsibilities. If he falls into that trap, it can mean he's less fun, less generous, less free to live a diverse life and has less time for creativity and exercise. All of those are qualities that characterise the person he wants to be.

    ....

    ....

    ....

Inquiry

1. Identify a work colleague you trust to give you some honest and valuable feedback

2. Ask them what values and 'shoulds' you seem to hold most strongly and defend most passionately

    They might find it helpful to refer to the values in Appendix 2. 'Shoulds' are strongly held principles like "A boss should protect their subordinates from the chaos above them" and "People shouldn't lie".

3. Ask them to tell you:

    a. What they appreciate about the way you apply these values / shoulds

    b. About times when adhering to these values or principles seems to get in your way, make it harder for them / the team, cause delays or have other negative implications

    c. Whether they see evidence that your commitment to holding onto those values / principles means other people *fail* to take due responsibility for delivering on those values / principles themselves and leave it up to you

4. What insights have you gained from this Inquiry and how can you use them?

    ....

    ....

    ....

Experiment

1. Identify a position, proposition or point of view that you've been strongly advocating at work

2. The next time it comes up, rather than continuing to argue for it, ask with genuine curiosity for other people's views – especially for views that differ from your own.

   Really seek to understand why they hold the views they do. For instance, find out:

   - *What matters to them in relation to this issue*

   - *What benefits they think it would offer the team, organisation, customer, client, end-user, shareholder, etc.*

   - *What they are worried might happen if other people ignore their perspective or overrule their preferred course of action*

3. Listen carefully to each of the different views, then summarise those different positions out loud and ask if you've understood them well enough

4. Imagine a solution that draws the best from all of those positions

   Whether you then share that solution and seek their views on it is up to you.

5. Record your experience by answering the following questions

   a. What do you notice about your approach to this Experiment and your experience of doing it?

   ....

   ....

   ....

   ....

   ....

   ....

b. What do you notice about the impact of your Experiment on others and on the outcome of the conversation?

....

....

....

From Level 2 to Level 3

Once we've started to be able to question our own positions and beliefs, the next step is to recognise that many of the positions we hold are connected to their opposites. Moving from Level 2 to Level 3, we realise we've tended to favour our own positions on topics, rather than genuinely exploring the validity of the 'opposing' position.

This upgrade to your Opposable Thinking capacity also means noticing the contradictions in your own belief system and contradictions between the things you believe and the things you actually do. So these practices can be quite disorienting or confronting, hence difficult to embrace with 100% conviction. Nevertheless, they are crucial steps on the way to fluid and flexible thinking. So they'll help you become more effective, even in the most ambiguous and uncertain situations.

We're indebted to Barry Johnson[92] here as these practices are rooted in his work on managing polarities.

Reflection

1. Identify a position, proposition or point of view that you've been strongly advocating at work

2. Choose a position that is the polar opposite of the one you've been advocating

   It could be a position that someone else holds, but it could equally be

the case that no one is entirely opposed to your position so you have to come up with this opposing view yourself. For example:

- *Structure – Flexibility*
- *Investment – Cost-cutting*
- *Long term – Short term*
- *Speed – Quality*
- *Stability – Change*
- *Outsource – Build our own*
- *Honesty – Diplomacy*

- *Now – Never*
- *People – Profit*
- *Staff – Customers*
- *Growth – Consolidation*
- *Justice – Mercy*
- *Localise – Centralise*

3. List the benefits of that opposing position and the risks of your own position

Benefits of the opposing position	Risks in my own position

4. Identify ways to adapt your own position, proposition or point of view so it, too, has some or all of the benefits you've listed above

....

....

....

5.   How else could you adapt your own position, proposition or point of view in order to minimise, mitigate or eradicate the risks you've listed above?

....

....

....

Inquiry

1.   Identify a topic on which you hold a view to which you are strongly attached

2.   Choose three to five colleagues who hold very different positions from your own and to each other on that same topic

For instance, one of those people might hold views that are the polar opposite of yours; another might typically take the middle ground or seek to mediate between the two of you; another might believe the topic, discussion or debate isn't worth discussing or shouldn't be discussed (perhaps because it's too sensitive or political).

3.   Using a sheet of paper or flipchart, work with them to capture the content of the conversation

In doing so, work through the process described in the Reflection above.

4.   Afterwards, use the space below to record:

   a.   How it felt to set your own agenda to one side and seek to truly understand those other people's perspectives in the moment

   b.   What you did well

   c.   What you struggled with

   d.   How you can use that learning in other situations

....

....

....

Experiment

1. Identify a topic on which you hold a view to which you are strongly attached

    If you're ambivalent, the Experiment may not challenge your underlying beliefs enough, so you'll find it less useful.

2. Find an opportunity to argue publicly for both your position and the opposite position, presenting the two 'poles' as a dilemma / polarity that you see in the situation

    When putting forward those two positions, take care to do full justice to both: be totally fair, base each on the strongest supporting evidence you can find (critiquing that data equally thoroughly) and discuss them with equal passion.

3. Afterwards, ask the people present to give you feedback

    The feedback should focus on your ability to stay impartial while presenting those two positions, rather than falling back into advocating your preferred position.

4. What did you notice in yourself when conducting this Experiment?

    ....

    ....

    ....

5. What impact did it have on the other people present? What feedback

did they give you?

....

....

....

6. What other strongly held positions could you use for future iterations of this Experiment?

....

....

....

From Level 3 to Level 4

Opposable Thinking matures further when we are genuinely able to 'step outside' a given polarity or dilemma to look at the underlying dynamic of beliefs. In doing so, we find we're no longer trapped in simply oscillating between one belief and the other.

When working through a problem where there are strong and valid opposing views, the development of this capacity underpins an increasing ability to find a way forward that no one would have foreseen. This new direction surfaces and pulls together all of the threads, differences, biases, assumptions and choice-points without seeming judgemental or taking sides.

The practices in this section might require you to dig increasingly deeply into beliefs you might feel are core to your identity. It's important, throughout, that you are aiming to fully understand a belief or position. You may still choose to disagree with it, but the more you can try to let go of your own position, the more effective your thinking will be.

Bear in mind that the cognitive difficulty of organising your thinking around an underlying polarity can be particularly taxing or confusing. Again, stick with it: even if the route you take is a tricky one, the insights you gain will reward your perseverance.

Reflection

You'll want some space for this practice, which is influenced by John Whittington's[93] work on 'coaching constellations'.

Setting up the practice

1. Choose a polarity that you notice within yourself, where you as an individual tend to oscillate between two poles, preferences, opinions, behaviour patterns or extremes.

   You might sometimes attach firmly to one end, sometimes to the other. Alternatively, perhaps you never commit to either due to the strong pull each of those poles exerts on you, but at the same time you find the 'midpoint' doesn't work. That might be because that midpoint feels like a theoretical concept that doesn't really exist in practice, or just leaves you deeply dissatisfied. For example:

   - *Being assertive vs Being humble*
   - *Doing what's best for the business vs Looking out for my own needs'*
   - *Diversifying vs Focusing on our core offerings'*
   - *Challenging my boss's inappropriate behaviour vs Ensuring I keep my job in the longer term*
   - *Involving the team in shaping direction vs Showing decisive leadership*

2. Create a physical representation for each of the two sides of that polarity

   Any objects found at home or in the office can work. It's best if they're

objects that resonate with those two positions, but it might be more of a felt, intuitive resonance than an obvious, logical one.

Running the practice

In describing this practice, we'll use X and Y to refer to the two objects and the poles they represent. You'll obviously have your own names for them and it doesn't matter which is X and which is Y.

1. Hold X and take a few moments to see and hear what it's like when you fully embrace that position with regard to this polarity

    Attend to the things you're doing and saying; the way you carry yourself; the things other people say about you; the way they react. Feel what it's like to fully occupy that position.

2. Articulate the beliefs and assumptions you hold when you're full embracing X

    You'll find the practice is more effective if you're prepared to speak these thoughts out loud, rather than in your head.

3. Ask yourself:

    a. What am I attached to here?

    b. What constraints does full embracing X bring when it comes to choosing a direction with regard to my career, life, team and/or organisation?

    c. What impact does embracing X have on my commitment and the commitment of others?

    d. What impact does it have on my performance and the performance of the people around me?

4. Put X down on the floor and repeat Steps 1 to 3 with Y

5. Put Y down on the floor and step back from both X and Y to a third place where you can see each equally well

What do you notice now, looking at both, that you'd not noticed previously?

6. Ask yourself "What would it take for me to be more open to new possibilities?"

7. Gradually move X and Y closer together, to the point where they're almost touching, noticing:

    a. What it is that connects the two positions

    b. The weaknesses and learnings in X that have given rise to Y (and vice versa)?

    c. What it's like to loosen your grip on the two positions – to step back from them and recognise that both are valid in their own ways, and both contribute to a larger, more complex and more resourceful whole

8. Ask yourself what it would look and feel like to operate from this third position (c) instead, simultaneously drawing on the best of both X and Y while shedding the downsides of both?

Capture your reflections below.

....

....

....

Inquiry

This Inquiry is something of a 'thought experiment', rather than an actual discussion, as the intention is for you to do this from afar, rather than with the people whose views you'll be working with.

1. Identify two or more people, organisations or groups who hold opposing views on a topic to which you aren't emotionally attached

For example, two competing newspapers, a panel of politicians debating a hot topic on TV or the radio, two sides of a division battling it out on social media. It could be people you actually know, but we'd still recommend doing your first Inquiry from a distance, rather than engaging with them directly.

2. 'Mine' for the dilemmas

    As you listen or read about the debate, make as full a list as you can (on a separate sheet of paper) about the polarities and dilemmas that people are referring to – the ones that really underpin the differences of view.

3. Look at that list, noticing where *you* stand on each one, and make any useful notes below

    It's important to properly invest in this step. If you don't, you won't be building a muscle you'll need when it comes to applying this and other related practices to something that is important to you in your own life.

    Useful questions for yourself here include "How clear is my own position on each polarity?", "How does that drive my level of agreement with one side or the other?" and "What dilemmas (if any) seem neutral or unimportant to me? Why is that?"

    ....

    ....

    ....

4. Take some time to listen to (or read about) the views that seem to underpin each polarity, doing further, deeper research where necessary

    Get beneath the surface conversation to understand the individuals or groups involved, considering their different histories, hopes, fears, needs, assumptions and expectations.

5. Working on paper – whether that's writing or drawing – weave the poles of this debate together into something new

You're looking for a third way that favours neither but grows out of both, to find a new starting point for conversation. This will not be some bland compromise in which each of the parties sacrifices something for the good of the other. It will be a way of connecting the ideas together into a larger whole.

This is a difficult step, as it requires genuine insight into the underlying dynamics of the ideas. It sometimes helps to leave this step 'on the back burner' of your mind for a day or two. Your brain will be processing it in the background. The freer, 'associative' approaches it'll take while you're focused on something else are more likely to come up with a better solution than you might think.

Experiment

Here you're taking the Inquiry above and running it for real.

Setting up the practice

1. Find your 'participants'

You might choose people at work who have opposing views. You might prefer a different, 'safer' environment in which to run the Experiment for the first time – for example, a community group or a social situation where the topic isn't too sensitive or laden with emotion.

2. Identify a core dilemma that these people differ on, one that they care enough about to hold quite strong positions on

The following questions can help you identify that dilemma. They're inspired by the work of David Campbell[94], as is the whole of this Experiment.

a. *What are the 'stuck' conversations in the organisation / group / team? What subjects keep looping around, coming back to haunt you?*

What do you keep meeting about that never seems to get resolved?

b. *What issues cause repeated friction between different individuals, teams or business units? What do you find it hard to move forward on?*

c. *What decisions keep getting put off?*

The answers to those questions will be the symptoms *of a dilemma.*

3. Running this Experiment means facilitating a conversation between these people

You are the passionately detached enabler, not a participant like everyone else. You're helping elicit the needs and mind-sets beneath the views people are sharing on the surface, deepening the various parties' understanding of each other's positions.

4. Hence, in preparing for the discussion, it might help to review the practices we've offered above for the upgrade from Level 2 to Level 3

You'll likely find inspiration there for the kinds of questions it'll be helpful to ask during or before the conversation.

Running the practice

When you feel ready, bring the people involved together and take the following steps:

1. Invite them to agree on definitions for the two ends (or 'horns') of the dilemma

These definitions must be expressed in positive terms that highlight the value of each polarity. Thus 'Gung ho' and 'Risk averse' would be inappropriate judgements of two polarised positions. More valid definitions that focused on the positive value of those same positions would be 'Maximise revenue for the company' and 'Minimise our exposure to risk'.

2. Take two flipcharts and place them at opposite ends of the room with empty space between them

3. Write one of the polarities on one flipchart and one of them on the other

4. Ask everyone present to place themselves somewhere on that line between the two polarities, as shown below

5. Ask each person to describe, in detail, what makes them take that position, what it means to them and how it feels to be in that position

6. Invite the group to discuss:

   a. The history of the dilemma

   b. The impact of this dilemma on the group, team or organisation as a whole

   c. The impact that keeping this dilemma unresolved is having on relationships between different parts of the business and on decision making[a]

   d. The positive contribution each polarity makes to the success of the whole

   e. The risks and downsides of each polarity

   f. The signs that each polarity has been taken too far

   g. The signs that each polarity hasn't been taken far enough

7. Help these people weave the poles of this dilemma together into something new

---

a   Most long-lasting dilemmas result in an 'us vs them' mentality that breeds all kinds of beliefs, assumptions and expectations about the people we consider 'us' and those we consider 'them'.

As with the Inquiry above, this third way should favour neither side and tick everybody's boxes, rather than meeting in the middle in a compromise that leaves both sides dissatisfied.

8. Once you've run this Experiment, use the space below to capture your reflections

....

....

....

....

....

....

In helping these people through this challenge, you'll also be working the muscles that will help you weave together the polarities within yourself – the dilemmas, contradictions and hypocrisies that are such a common ingredient in the human psyche.

●◉●

Upgrading your Sense-making capacity

•●•

- One adaptable practice per upgrade
- One tool per practice
- Where to find additional tools

OF THE FOUR CAPACITIES,

Sense-making is perhaps the hardest to develop intentionally. It usually just evolves through repeated exposure to increasing degrees of complexity. Of all the capacities, it's also the hardest to self-assess, because it's hard to spot the flaws in one's current ways of thinking by using that same kind of thinking to *look at* one's ways of thinking.

It's like looking at your eyes *through* your eyes in the hope that doing so will show you the parts of the colour spectrum you can't currently see – infrared, ultraviolet, etc.

It's for that reason that upgrades to this capacity often involve a fair amount of stuckness and confusion. We're faced with not knowing 'the answer', which can make us feel stupid or incoherent. So, in this chapter, you'll need to hold onto the curious playfulness we've suggested you bring to

"Out of intense complexities, intense simplicities emerge."

Winston Churchill,
Prime Minister of the UK
(1940 – '45)[95]

all of the practices in this book. The good news is that you will probably, at some point, start to enjoy the slightly cloudy feeling of being 'at your edge' in your thinking. Rather than retreating from that cloudiness, you'll recognise that the cloudier it feels the more certain you can be that you're entering new territory, doing useful and important work on your existing operating system and making progress towards your next upgrade.

You'll also want to work your Sense-making 'muscles' using a problem or opportunity that is current, important and meaningful to you. For each practice, we'll offer a tool that triggers the new kinds of thinking associated with the relevant upgrade. You'll then apply that tool to a current situation.

Unlike in previous chapters, there's just one practice per upgrade. It's a practice you can use to reflect, as a tool for Inquiry with someone else, or as the basis for an Experiment.

You'll find additional tools for each upgrade in the notes at the end of this book.

From Level 1 to Level 2

The 'Fishbone' or 'Ishikawa' diagram[96] is really useful for this upgrade[a]. It focuses on identifying root causes, encouraging us to think beyond the obvious. You'll want a large sheet of paper, laid out in landscape fashion. If you're using a flipchart, use the usual, thick flipchart pen for Steps 1 and 2, then do the rest of the work in a normal pen (like a biro). That way you'll get maximum benefit from the additional space.

---

a   There are many other tools and models that can help here, too. Their ability to build your muscles in this area depends on two things. Firstly, whatever tool you choose, it must be focused on non-linear problem-solving or strategising where the intention is to move from 'single path' to 'multiple path' thinking. Secondly, you'll only really benefit from using that tool if you work though its component techniques with all of your attention, taking enough time to allow new ideas and connections to emerge as you go. If, instead, you rush it or prioritise capturing all the stuff you *already* know, you'll reap *some* rewards, but they'll be relatively superficial, and you'll make little actual progress in developing this capacity.

1. Articulate the problem

   Draw a line across the centre of the paper, with a triangle on the right-hand side, as shown below. Then, in the triangle, write a single sentence that sums up the problem itself. While it might sound obvious, this 'statement of the problem' should focus on the problem and its impact, not potential solutions or causes. Those come later.

2. Identify the major potential causal factors

   Look to draw out as many potential causal factors as possible and make these the 'bones' of the fish, as shown below. At this point, it doesn't matter whether these actually are the causes, only that you're covering as many different domains of potential causal factor as you can.

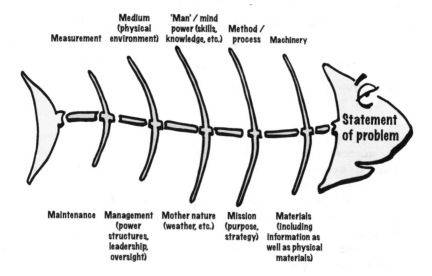

The potential causal factors in the example above are based on the most commonly used factors in manufacturing[97]. There are equivalent industry standards in other sectors, too. For instance, product marketing often uses 'Eight Ps': product (or service), price, promotion, place, process, people (or personnel), physical evidence and performance[98]. Then there's the more general purpose 'PESTLIED' model that draws our attention to Political, Economic, Social, Technological, Legal, International, Environmental and Demographic factors.

3. Drill down to the root causes

For each of the broad potential factors you identified in Step 2, brainstorm actual root causes. These are shown as smaller lines coming off the main 'bones' of the fish. You might even identify finer 'causes of those causes'. In which case, represent them as even smaller bones.

You'll notice there are more root causes against some domains than others. That's absolutely fine. There might even be nothing against one or two domains in your own diagram and that's fine, too – as long as you've exhausted all of your thinking. We've included

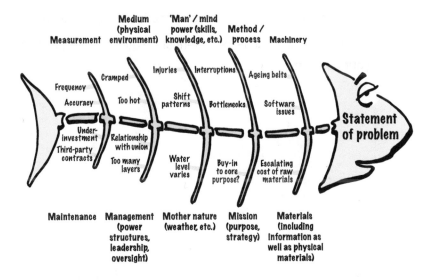

one causal factor ('buy-in to core purpose') that ends with a question mark. This is to show that, in this example, there's a sense that this might be an issue, but there's no certainty as to whether it is.

4. Identify the core challenges and quick fixes

   Label each of the root causes to indicate the following:

   a. *The probability that this is a major cause of the problem (High, Medium or Low). You might choose to use H, M, L for short, or Red, Amber and Green*

   b. *The effort, High, Medium or Low, you believe would be required to fix or control that root cause*

5. Decide what happens next

   You might choose to take immediate action to resolve things – for instance, on those root causes that are highly likely to be major causes and require least effort to fix or control. Alternatively, you might start further investigations, to test your thinking or hypotheses (like our hypothesis that 'lack of buy-in to core purpose' could be a contributing factor).

6. Review your use of this practice using the following questions:

   a. What new links, ideas or potential solutions emerged through your use of this tool?

b.   What did you notice about your approach to using the tool?

....

....

....

c.   In what ways could this tool continue to enhance your thinking and day-to-day work?

....

....

....

You'll find other great tools for this upgrade online and in other books. You'll find suggestions in the notes at the end of this book[99].

From Level 2 to Level 3

When we're making this transition, we're starting to notice the wide range of influences that affect the success of any response to a complex adaptive problem. We're developing the mental muscles required to understand and respond to situations with multiple interconnected causes, options and potential outcomes.

Mind-maps and scenario-planning are common, helpful tools for building this capacity. We've found the combination of a 'relationship map' and a 'power map'[100] particularly useful, so that's what we'll focus on here. It's a combination we've seen help clients better understand the complex dynamics in one-to-one and group relationships – dynamics that can affect an organisation's response to a complex situation. This understanding is a core feature of Level 3 Sense-making.

1. Get three large sheets of paper

2. Decide on the real, current challenge you're keen to make progress on through this practice

   It'll need to be a situation in which you have a preferred overall course of action but – for whatever reasons – you're finding it difficult to make that happen.

3. On one sheet of paper, list the people involved

   Include anyone who has an interest in the problem or idea you are considering. It's best if you're able to focus mainly on individuals. If you do include groups, avoid generic groupings like whole departments. Instead, try to focus on the key individuals or specific, clearly defined teams.

4. Identify the key players and how much influence they have

   Choose the individuals and groups that have greatest influence over the change you are keen to make. Then take a clean sheet of paper and write their names on it, leaving as much space between the names as you can.

   Then draw a circle around each of the names to show the amount of influence each 'player' has over the challenge you've chosen, as shown below. The larger the circle, the more influence they have.

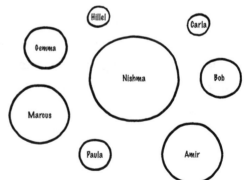

5. Map the connections

   Draw lines between the people on your map to show whatever alliances and linkages seem relevant to the challenge. We find it helps to use the thickness of the line to show the strength of each alliance – the thicker the line, the stronger the alliance.

6. Note down the insights this map has offered you so far

....

....

....

7. Map the extent and direction of influence

On a third, clean sheet of paper, take each of the people on the map you've just drawn and place them on your own version of the axes below. The vertical axis shows the amount of influence each person has. The horizontal axis shows the extent to which they are 'for' or 'against' the direction you're keen to take in this situation.

If there is an individual or group who does not seem engaged or interested in the change that you propose, place them outside the diagram – these people are bystanders.

8. Add the alliances

Use lines to link any individuals or groups who have strong alliances with each other. Then add yourself to the map.

9. Looking at the patterns in the two maps you've created, record what you notice that you'd not noticed before

It might help to compare your own map with the map below, which shows how each of seven positions can look, and how best to leverage them.

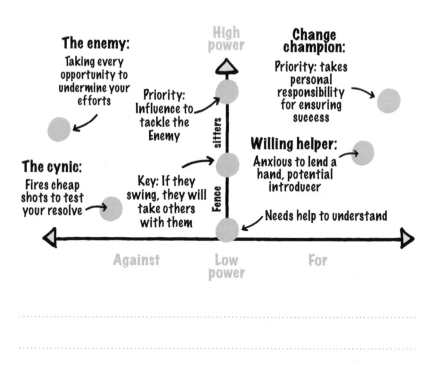

10. Decide a way forward, making a note of the actions you'll take

For instance, how can you give the 'champions' and 'helpers' more energy or ask for more support? How could you influence the 'fence sitters' to take positive action or be more curious and informed about the course of action you're proposing? How could you encourage the 'bystanders' (outside the map) to get involved? How could you reduce the energy or influence given to the 'enemies' and 'cynics'? How could you use their opposing views to strengthen your own proposition?

11. Review your use of this practice using the questions below:

    a.   What new links, ideas or potential solutions emerged through your use of this framework?

         ....

         ....

         ....

    b.   What did you notice about your approach to using the framework?

         ....

         ....

         ....

    c.   In what ways could this practice continue to enhance your thinking and day-to-day work?

         ....

         ....

         ....

You'll find a treasure trove of other techniques for building this capacity in Daniel Kim's book Systems Thinking Tools[101].

From Level 3 to Level 4

The more complex our environment or situation, the more the events and outcomes we experience have multiple causes. The clearer we are as to the nature of those multiple causes, the more effectively we can respond to the situation. Level 3 Sense-making brings with it an enhanced ability to understand relational complexity. As we upgrade to Level 4, we're building on that foundation, developing the capacity to understand and work with the wider, deeper and messier *systemic* forces that help or hinder people's collective responses to an adaptive challenge.

Thus the practice we recommend to help access Level 4 Sense-making has at its heart a 'multiple cause diagram'. These diagrams are extremely useful for:

- Clarifying and organising our thinking regarding an event or sub-optimal state[b]

- Tracing the sequence of cause and effect through a complex situation or system

- Identifying potential intervention points

- Understanding what is making a persistent problem (or pattern) so difficult to solve (or change)

- Identifying feedback loops and reinforcing cycles that could maintain any change we're looking to implement

- Stimulating discussion, debate and shared understanding – when we use these diagrams with others

---

b E.g. "We didn't win the bid" (an event) or "Our win ratio on bids is consistently lower than our competitors'" (a state)

Preparing for the practice

The easiest way to introduce the approach is with examples. The example below summarises a 20-page document produced for the health sector – which shows how effectively this tool can capture complexity without destroying an entire rainforest.

Whether you agree with the findings doesn't matter at this point. What matters is the process itself. Importantly, the meaning of the arrows joining the items is 'causes or leads to', not just 'causes', and there's no value judgement placed on any of the arrows. They're intended as objective observations of what appears to be happening in the system.

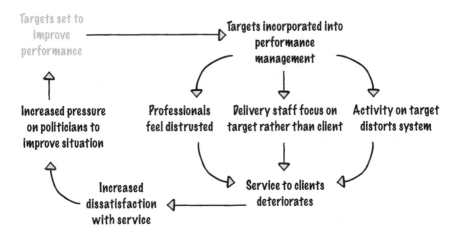

This process is also far more effective than reams of text when it comes to spotting feedback loops – self-perpetuating cycles, shown (on the left of this example) as a sequence of arrows heading in the same direction that eventually create a circle.

Our next example comes from a call centre. 'Maurice', the executive who created the diagram, had noticed that he and many of his predecessors typically took simplistic approaches to improving call waiting times and that these always failed to have lasting positive impact. He'd started to wonder whether it was a more complex problem than it might first appear. Hence the multiple cause diagram you see here.

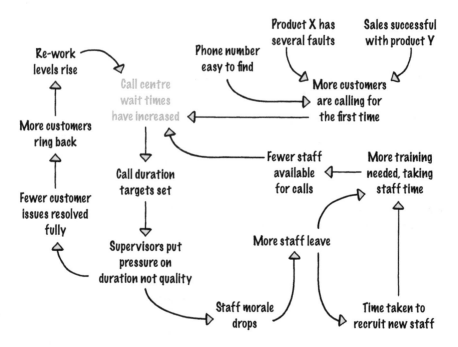

Maurice's approach exemplified some key things to bear in mind when creating one of these diagrams, i.e.

- Focus on the sequence and mining for complexity, rather than rushing to solve the problem

- Remember that elements in a system can be connected in ways that are not immediately apparent

- Between 10 and 20 items per diagram gives a workable level of detail

- Items in the diagram are usually variables (things that can change), although they can also be events

- For every item, take time to think of as many causal factors as possible rather than settling for the obvious

Running the practice

1. Choose a current unresolved situation

    It doesn't need to seem complicated or complex at first glance. However, it should be one that is relatively long-standing – something you and your colleagues have tried to solve in a variety of ways, none of which are working. Plus, you need to be open to finding deeper levels of causal complexity.

2. Take a large sheet of paper – flipchart is best – and start in the centre with the event or current sub-optimal state that you want to understand better

    For instance, 'This committee is held in low regard' was the topic for one of our clients.

3. Ask yourself what causes this event or sub-optimal state (X) and write those things on the page, joining them to X with an arrow

    So, in this example, the causes of the committee being held in low regard were identified as a lack of challenge and a lack of understanding of the programme.

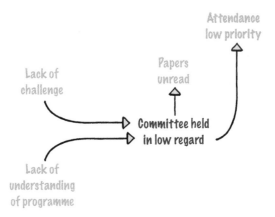

4. As in the example above, identify what X leads to

   In the example, it was that papers went unread and attendance was a low priority for members of the committee and their stakeholders.

5. As shown below, work outwards from the causes and effects you've identified

   It's important to note the interactions between causal factors (like the 'culture of silo working' and 'lack of corporate thinking'). We'd also advise looking for other causal factors for each of the effects you've spotted (e.g. the irrelevance of most agenda items to the individuals attending).

   Keep going until you've a sequence of 2-3 links in a causal chain coming into your starting point (X) and 2-3 links in a chain of effects coming out of that starting point.

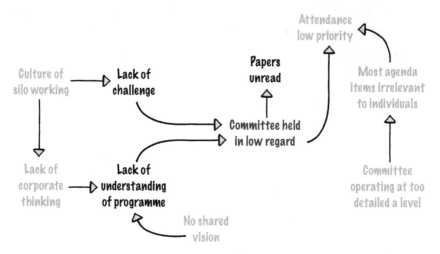

6. Look for any feedback loops you might be missing (see below)

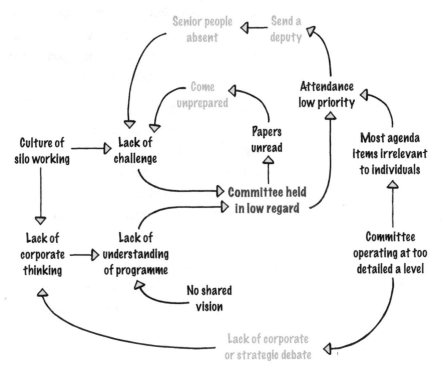

7. Look for opportunities to intervene and create a significant sustainable change to the status quo that will have positive, reinforcing ripple effects through the whole system

   Generally these come from one or more of four sources:

   a. *The pivotal item(s) in the diagram* i.e. the items that have the most arrows (causes and effects) going in and out of them – like 'lack of challenge' in the example above

b. *'Originating' items that only have arrows leaving them*   i.e. the starting items that cause and maintain everything else in the diagram – in our example, these are 'no shared vision', 'culture of silo working' and 'committee operating at too detailed a level'

c. *Feedback loops*   e.g. the loop running through 'committee held in low regard', 'papers unread', 'come unprepared' and lack of challenge' then back into 'committee held in low regard'. Look for ways to strengthen any loops that are helpful and weaken or break those that are counterproductive

d. *Any parts of the diagram that are particularly interesting, intriguing, worrying or opaque and warrant expansion*   e.g. 'send a deputy' could be worth exploring as there may be something the committee could do differently when it comes to deputisation

8. Make a note of the actions you are keen to take based on your analysis of your multiple cause diagram

....

....

....

....

9. Review your use of this practice using the following questions (and feel free to add your own):

   a. What new links, ideas or potential solutions emerged through your use of the multiple cause diagram?

   ....

   ....

   ....

   b. What did you notice about your approach to this practice?

   ....

   ....

   ....

   c. In what ways could this practice (or your own, adapted version of it) continue to enhance your thinking and day-to-day work?

   ....

   ....

   ....

As with the upgrade to Level 3, if you would like additional tools to help you upgrade to Level 4, Daniel Kim's book *Systems Thinking Tools*[102] is a rich resource.

● ● ●

PART 5

• ● •

Mining this book for more

Helping others upgrade

● ● ●

- How best to help others upgrade
- The ethics of upgrading others
- Using the practices in Part 4 with others

ONE OF THE THINGS
that separates good leaders and good managers from those that are average (or below average) is that the good ones help their people learn. Increasingly, organisations seeking to develop their people call on everyone to take a hand in developing each other, whether that's:

- Peer-to-peer

- Senior leaders mentoring new recruits and the leaders of tomorrow, or

- Younger generations acting as a source of insight and inspiration to people two or three times their age

Sometimes that's by working one-on-one. Sometimes it's by working in groups and teams, enabling a mix of individual and collective development.

You'd probably not be reading this

> **"...the mind is not a vessel that needs filling, but wood that needs igniting..."**
>
> Plutarch, biographer, philosopher, magistrate[103]

chapter if you didn't have an interest in developing others. It could be the focal point of your profession – if you work in HR or Learning & Development, perhaps as a coach, mentor or trainer – or it could be something you do alongside your official 'day job'. Wherever you're coming from, our intention here is to feed that interest, to offer some suggestions for using this book to help other people upgrade.

In doing so, we're respecting the fact that you'll have a range of other tools at your disposal. Many of those will work really well alongside the ones we're offering here. At the same time, thinking in terms of these capacities and levels might help you see why some of your tried-and-tested tools work perfectly with some people but don't land nearly as well with others. Often, a tool's effectiveness depends heavily on the extent to which it matches the capacity profile of the person you're using it with.

We're also aware that there are a number of different types of people you might be keen to help upgrade. It could be someone you lead, coach or mentor. It could be someone you've 'buddied up with' to read this book together. Perhaps you're looking to use the practices on a leadership programme or to take an action learning set or coaching supervision group to a whole new level. They're all valid contexts in which to use the practices, and each will bring its own nuances when it comes to framing, setting up and debriefing a given practice. We can't cover all of those nuances in detail, but we've tried to bear them in mind throughout.

Upgrades by invitation, expectation or stealth?

We – Karen and Richard – have had quite a debate about this.

We believe these four capacities are essential if people, teams and organisations are to survive and thrive in an increasingly VUCA world. That does present something of a conundrum. After all, if these capacities are that important, doesn't that mean it's fair to expect people to upgrade if failing to do so would be to the detriment of everyone else?

It's a question that provokes at least three ethical dilemmas and beneath each lies at least one polarity:

1. It may be acceptable to require people to keep their knowledge and skills up-to-date. Is it also acceptable to demand that they change the ways in which they think; how they relate to different aspects of their world; the lens through which they interpret themselves and the people around them?

2. As people progress through the levels, their motives for developing change. So, too, do their beliefs about what 'development' means and looks like. For some it's about accumulating or refining knowledge or skills; for others it's about changing deeply ingrained habits. For some it's about becoming a better version of oneself; for others, it's something else entirely. So, if we're expecting people to upgrade, aren't we at risk of privileging our beliefs about development over theirs?

3. Rather than demanding an upgrade, you could quietly engineer one through a series of conversations and developmental experiences. What right, though, does one human being have to decide an upgrade is required and try to 'rewire' someone else's brain without their consent? Even a highly-qualified brain surgeon wouldn't operate without a patient's permission, but then maybe it's wonderful that 'white hat' hackers are out there surreptitiously upgrading the security on thousands of people's Wi-Fi routers to protect them from all kinds of electronic mischief...

You'll have your own response to each of those dilemmas. Ultimately, though, when we refer to '*helping* people upgrade' that is exactly what we mean. You'll find it much easier if it's a joint endeavour, and much more rewarding, too.

A five phase approach to using Part 4's practices with others

Human development is rarely a linear process. However, we've found Richard's Five Phase Framework[104] (see right) helps people bear in mind the various critical ingredients. It's also as applicable with groups and teams as it is with individuals – you simply put the group / team in the 'them' box at the centre of the diagram.

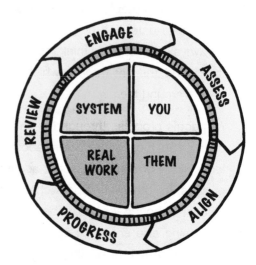

At the heart of the framework are four essential elements:

1. You – the person trying to help an individual upgrade

2. Them – the individual, group or team you're seeking to help

3. The system around them – which can help or hinder an upgrade

4. The requirement to develop by doing real work

The five phases form the outer ring. They fall in a natural sequence and we'll explain each in more detail shortly. However, there are times when you'll find yourself looping back to an earlier phase, typically for one of three reasons:

*   Things have changed in the wider system

*   The development agenda has evolved

*   The needs of that earlier phase weren't met as well as they might have been

The latter is most likely when we've neglected one of the four essential elements at the heart of the model. For instance, if you've not *engaged* someone's wider system in their development, then you'll probably lack some useful data to *assess* the level at which that person is currently operating across the four capacities. It'll just be your opinion and theirs.

Similarly, if the system's not engaged and aligned, then when the person you're trying to help attempts to *progress* with some changes to the way they operate, they'll meet more resistance from the people around them. After all, those people have grown used to this person operating in a certain way. In order to maintain their own status quo, they'll often act as an 'immune system' rejecting those new ways of working.

Engaging people with these practices

If you're working with someone who hasn't' previously encountered the 'vertical' approach to development that underpins this book, then we'd recommend drawing on Part 1 of this book. How they'll respond will depend a lot on the level at which they're currently operating, particularly with regard to the Self-relating capacity. So it's worth bearing in mind the following when encouraging others to pay attention to their development in this space.

Those at Level...	Will typically engage if they believe these practices...
1	Have had a demonstrable impact on your ability to solve difficult problems
2	Have enabled you to fulfil stretching goals, overcome seemingly intractable challenges or find creative workarounds that enable you to be more efficient and effective

Those at Level...	Will typically engage if they believe these practices...
3	Have increased your awareness of patterns and previously-hidden processes playing out in the team or organisation
4	Could help them create transformational shifts in people, teams and organisations

The thing that gives most people a sense that they might want to upgrade is a 'heat experience'. It's a term Nick Petrie at the Center for Creative Leadership uses to describe those situations when an individual[a]:

"faces a complex situation that disrupts and disorients his habitual way of thinking. He discovers that his current way of making sense of the world is inadequate. His mind starts to open and search for new and better ways to make sense of his challenge."[105]

So if you've a sense that someone might benefit from an upgrade, look for the heat experience they are currently in the midst of. For instance, look at how they're feeling about, or responding to:

- A new, bigger role or project

- A major setback, failure or negative piece of feedback

- A seemingly intractable or perpetually recurring problem

- An inner conflict, or conflict with others, that they're struggling to resolve

- A challenge they've never met before, where the road ahead is unclear and littered with hazards

It's anything that could confront them with the realisation that 'What got

---

a   From our perspective, groups and teams (as well as individuals) can also have heat experiences me here won't get me where I want to be.'[106]

Whatever the heat experience, they'll need to know you're an ally. It needs to be clear that you're not judging them, that you're there to help. They'll need to feel this is something you're doing together, not something you're doing *to* them.

They'll need a sense that the work you're doing together is purposeful, too. So focus the attention on the 'real work' you'll place at the core of whichever practice(s) you choose to use with them. Ideally, ask *them* to choose that real work, rather than choosing it for them. The more responsibility they take the better.

Assessing the upgrade required

If you're going to keep them engaged, it's best to approach this as a joint exploration of their needs and aspirations. In doing so, bear in mind that:

- Most people overestimate the level at which they're operating – the case studies and self-assessments in Part 2 can help off-set that, as can feedback from others or recordings of oneself in action

- Many of us are inclined to believe we are functioning as well as humanly possible given the situation in which we find ourselves. This can blind us to the need or opportunity to try upgrading our underlying operating system. If you're trying to help someone you think might be caught in that pattern, it can help to remind them of the developmental journey they've already been on. Then suggest that there are further interesting and exciting ways of looking at things that could potentially offer them alternative ways of approaching their situation. They'd still have the option of sticking with what they're doing, of course, but at least they might get some new ideas

- If people struggle with a practice it's usually because it's a level (or two) up from their current way of operating. So, as long as you can keep them engaged, it's not a disaster if you start with a practice that's at too high a level. If it doesn't work, you can simply step back from it, drop down a notch, and try another

- If the person you're helping is convinced their current level ways of working don't reflect the level at which they'd usually operate if it weren't for certain situational factors, remember you can draw on the concepts of snags, crashes, whirlpools and trailing edges (Chapter 9)

Aligning on the best way forward

When you're working one-on-one, aligning is likely to be about choosing the practices that match the upgrade they want to make (from the table back on page 228[b]). In doing so, we'd recommend you encourage them to:

- Build from Reflection through Inquiry to Experiment within a given upgrade

- Focus each practice on *real work* – e.g. for Perspective-shifting ask them to name three relationships they're keen to improve, then do the practices bearing those relationships in mind

- When using the Inquiries, seek people with different views. They're intended to provoke new thinking, not reinforce an existing mind-set. So the more diverse (and even conflicting) those views are the better

- Plan their approach over a period of weeks and months, using each of the chosen practices two or three times to work the necessary muscles. There's a downloadable copy of the planning sheet from Part 3 on the Upgrade Resources page at www.leaderspace.com

- Focus on one (or at most two) capacities at any one time – any more and they're likely to stall

---

b   There's also a quick reference guide to the practices in Appendix 5, on page 352.

Progressing with the practices

When using the **Reflections**, your role is fairly simple – although some bits might require you to rein-in your own well-meaning but unhelpful urges:

- Introduce them to the practice

- Briefly share your own experience of doing it or a similar practice (focusing on what you learned, rather than the content itself)

- Agree whether they should do the Reflection there and then or come back to you when they've done it. If the latter, agree when to reconvene and suggest they do the Reflection 2-3 times between now and then

- Listen (*attentively and deeply*) to them reporting back when they've completed the practice

- Offer your own observations on their process, not the content

- Explore the learning and agree next steps (which could be a repeat of this practice, progression to the Inquiry, or stepping back a notch and taking a practice from the previous upgrade)

The process with the **Inquiries** is similar, with two additional ingredients:

- Observe and help them reflect on their response to any feedback they receive through the Inquiry – especially if the response is a tendency to catastrophise or get defensive. You will need to help them find a curious and neutral position in relation to any feedback – this is often development in itself

- Help the learner make sense of the data they're gathering from others. This is a process of integration so it can take some time and might involve discomfort and the occasional backwards step

The **Experiments** are the first acid test of their learning in action. Here, the key to successful facilitation is to help them ensure the experiment[107]:

- Is safe enough for them to engage wholeheartedly in it without too much fear of it going wrong – some people choose non-work experiments initially

- Is sufficiently rooted in (or sufficiently replicates) their real work, so the outcomes and activities matter

- Will provide meaningful feedback (verbal or non-verbal)

Reviewing the work you're doing together

We've built a review process into each of the individual practices. You'll also want to periodically review the progress made by the person you're helping upgrade.

When doing so, we recommend focusing on exploring:

- What they themselves are noticing about their approaches to situations

- The impact that's having (e.g. on them, other people and on the quality of their work), ideally including feedback from others

- The knock-on effect on their development in other capacities

> "The problem with most workplaces is not the lack of developmental opportunities, but that no one is learning anything from them."
>
> Nick Petrie, US Center for Creative Leadership[108]

- Any snags, crashes or whirlpools they've been noticing or experiencing

- How their sense of themselves is changing

- How their progress means their ongoing development should evolve

How do I help my whole team upgrade together?

Given the impact of developing these capacities at an individual level, there's clearly an opportunity for marked improvements in groups' and teams' thinking, creativity, collective decision-making, strategising, stakeholder management and so on. The quality of these collective endeavours is directly dependent on the level of the conversation or 'discourse' those groups and teams are having. This is not just about 'getting on better together', it is about finally being more than the sum of our parts – rather than less, which is sadly most often the case when groups of people come together.

Most of the practices in Part 4 can be run with whole groups, with each person working independently or with pairs helping each other. As we mentioned in Part 1, we've also designed a set of practices for groups and teams to work on together, but they've proven too much to include in this book.

Importantly, those additional practices aim to raise the level of the group's *collective discourse* where these capacities are concerned. It's pretty common for there to be a mismatch the level at which a team operates collectively and the levels at which its members operate individually. Hence, upgrading the team will likely require a combination of individual and collective work. When it comes to working on that collective discourse, we're hoping to share the aforementioned practices in the not-too-distant future. So feel free to contact us for further details.

Summary

When you're helping an individual to upgrade there are four essential ingredients:

1. You

2. The person you're helping upgrade

3. The system in which they operate

4. Real work to act as the focus for the development

While no development is truly linear, it helps to bear in mind five 'phases' of activity:

1. **Engage** their appetite for an upgrade

2. **Assess** the level at which they're currently operating

3. **Align** around an agreed approach to the upgrade and the practice(s) you'll use from Part 4 of this book

4. **Progress** using the relevant practice(s)

5. **Review** your use of the practice(s) and its enduring impact

Each of the five phases needs to attend to all of the four essential ingredients.

●●●

16

Where you're at three months on... and what comes next

• ● •

- Your progress to date
- The impact it's had
- The foundations you're laying
- Further resources

WELCOME BACK!
If you're reading this chapter three months after you read Chapter 10, then you're using this book as it was intended.

If you're a little earlier or later, that's fine, as long as you've made some sustained use of the practices in Part 4.

The intention in this chapter is twofold. Firstly, to help you recognise the progress you and others have made in the intervening weeks. Secondly, to help you lay the foundations for taking things further, should you wish to do so.

Take a moment to review your reflections in the summaries at the ends of Chapters 4, 5, 6 and 7, and the work you did in

"There is nothing like returning to a place that remains unchanged to find the ways in which you yourself have altered."

Nelson Mandela, President of South Africa (1994 – '99)[109]

Chapters 8 and 9. What do you notice with the benefit of hindsight and by asking yourself those questions again in relation to more recent situations?

....

....

....

What shifts have you seen since in your own 'capacity profile'? *(We'd recommend using the image below to give you a visual sense of your progress.)*

Sense-making   Perspective-shifting   Self-relating   Opposable Thinking

Level 4
Level 3
Level 2
Level 1

What impact have these shifts had on your leadership and day-to-day work?

....

....

Which of the practices in Part 4 most appealed to you? What was it about them that most appealed, and why?

Which practices did you most dislike or feel most uninspired by? How could you use your answers to the previous question to help you adapt these practices to suit you better?

What successes have you had when it comes to helping others upgrade?

Who else might benefit from this work, whether they were doing it with you or by themselves?

What's next for you where these capacities are concerned?

....

....

....

• ● •

Seeking help beyond this book

We've been keen to make this book as useful as possible. That's made it longer than we intended, but we've still had to leave a lot out. If you're keen for more, there are a number of approaches you might want to take.

Using a more 'formal' assessment of your own and others' capacity profiles

Chapters 4 through 8 offer plenty of material to help you gauge the level at which you and others are currently operating with regard to these capacities. At the same time, these are new concepts for most people and it's hard to assess ourselves accurately, particularly given that one of the capacities *is partly about* how accurately we understand ourselves.

While there's currently nothing out there that measures these four capacities directly, there are tools you can use as data points to help you work out your own and others' capacity profiles.

> We're developing a 360-degree feedback tool that measures people's current levels in each of the four capacities. If that's of interest to you, do get in touch.

Harthill's *Leadership Development Profile* (LDP), Torbert's *Global Leadership Profile* (GLP) and Cooke Greuter's *Leadership Maturity Assessment Profile* (MAP) each offer a means of assessing your current 'overall stage of development'. All three tools are rooted in the work of

Jane Loevinger, one of the original giants in this field – as is Terri O'Fallon's STAGES model, which you might also find helpful.

The combination of an LDP, GLP or MAP report and a good debrief with a trained professional can help you estimate your *average* level when it comes to the four capacities – the mid-point of the flotilla of boats, if we're thinking in terms of the analogy in Chapter 9. A *really* good debrief could even offer insights into which level you're at when it comes to the individual capacities of Sense-making, Perspective-shifting and Self-relating – and *maybe* Opposable-Thinking.

Cognadev's *Complexity Processing Profile* is an imaginative and surprising tool that will help you understand your capacity for Sense-making. It assesses how well you process complex information in an unfamiliar and challenging environment. It provides a comprehensive and detailed readout of your cognitive styles and the ease with which you analyse, synthesise and transform complex data. It also offers a number of tips for developing your capacity in this area.

Applying these capacities and practices to groups and teams

There's huge benefit in upgrading the discourse you're having as a group or team and we've created a number of practices to help with this. However, there's simply not been room in this book to include them.

We're planning to share them in a subsequent book focused entirely on groups and teams. If you're interested, please either look out for it or get in touch.

Building these capacities at an organisational level

It's tempting to brand a whole organisation with a capacity profile that says it's at Level X in one capacity, Level Y in another and so on. However, as with groups and teams, it's the *discourses* between the people in those organisations that are characterised by being at one level or another.

Thus, an organisation might operate at Level 1 in Sense-making when it comes to certain topics, but approach less emotionally-charged topics at Level 3.

These discourses will include conversations between different groups and teams across and around the organisation. There are other forms of 'discourse', though, such as the ways in which people in power make decisions, and the creation of structures and processes that enable or inhibit the organisation.

All of these discourses combine to shape people's individual and collective beliefs about *how* things are done, *what* things are done and *why* they should be doing them.

In addition, everyone involved in those discourses will be interpreting them and engaging with them through the lens of their own internal operating systems. Some people's OSs will be aligned with the dominant level of discourse. Some won't.

Some people will be operating at the highest level they've achieved in the relevant capacities. Others may have suffered a crash – perhaps due to the emotions that discourse has awakened in them. Others might be caught in a whirlpool that's dragged them down a level or two – perhaps something in their relationship with their boss or the climate in their team or the organisation that has temporarily robbed them of higher-level thinking.

If you want to explore ways of using the four capacities and the levels within them at an organisational level, three books could prove useful sources of inspiration for you:

- Kegan and Lahey's *An Everyone Culture*[110]

- Laloux's *Reinventing Organizations*[111]

- Fisher, Rooke and Torbert's *Personal and Organisational Transformations*[112]

None of these books explicitly targets our four capacities, so it will be a case of you weaving together what you've learned from our book with the ideas in theirs.

None of these books explicitly targets our four capacities, so it will be a case of you weaving together what you've learned from our book with the ideas in theirs.

> "I not only use all the brains that I have, but all that I can borrow."
>

Further reading

A number of other books offer great insights into the ways we make meaning in organisations. The work of Barry Oshry[114] is particularly enlightening when it comes to spotting patterns in organisations and other complex systems. We'd also recommend books by Peter Senge[115], Otto Scharmer[116], Chris Argyris[117], Gareth Morgan[118] and Glenda Eoyang & Royce Holladay[119].

Richard has drawn on a number of these authors' ideas to create his own tool for understanding complex systems, the 'Systems Wheel'. If you're keen to add that to your own repertoire, you'll find it in Routledge's *Practitioner's Handbook of Team Coaching*[120].

If you're interested in exploring the world beyond our Level 4 in these capacities, we'd recommend Wilber's *Integral Psychology*[121], Kegan's *In Over Our Heads*[122] and Maslow's *The Farther Reaches of Human Nature*[123].

Obviously, none of these sources reference the capacities directly, but you'll see the links if you look for them.

Hands-on help from us

If you'd like help developing your leaders, team or organisation, then we recommend you contact Richard and his team via www.leaderspace.com.

If you're a practitioner in leadership development seeking to integrate this work into your own practice, essentially 'teaching' the four capacities independently of us, then Karen is likely to be your best option. You'll find her at www.velopconsultation.com.

Into the great beyond

If you're reading this chapter, you're mining this book for all it has to offer. You'll have been on quite the journey since Chapter 1, particularly if you've also been using these practices with others. We're confident you (and your colleagues) will continue to benefit if you dip in and out of the book over the coming months and whenever you're ready for your next upgrade.

It'd be good to hear from you, even if it's just to share the most valuable nuggets you've taken from this book.

For now: best of luck. It's a messy world out there and it needs people who are prepared to go the extra mile and make it a better place – however they choose to do so.

All the best

Karen and Richard

● ● ●

Acknowledgements

•●•

Thanks from Karen

It is always difficult to list all of the people with whom we have thought in the development of our ideas. Numerous clients and colleagues have been alongside me over the last 15 years and I have played with them and with the theories and techniques outlined here. A number of people have been there for the long haul, though, and each has provided something totally unique to my thinking or my general wellbeing. So, I would like to thank:

Judith Ward for her perceptiveness, her late-stage wisdom, her humane grappling with the whole world and her willingness to play with these ideas, often long into the night. Jenny Isaac for years of grounded practical support and love, as well as many jolly dog walks. Julie Allen for her intellectual stimulation, poetic imagination and for turning me on to metacognition. Matt Gott for working with me on the interface between vertical development and innovation/design thinking and for being tenacious in the building of our creative relationship. Chris Lawrence-Pietroni for helping me to think through the implications for movement building and narrative leadership. David Bolger and Joe Simpson for helping me (and allowing me!) to apply the ideas at a practical level with hundreds of senior public sector leaders – especially when the ideas were controversial in the early days. Jonathan Males for his long-standing fellow traveller role, his groundedness, solidity and emphasis on the all that is best in human nature (especially when I have been at my most cynical). Jane Sassienie for our early collaboration and co-development as we found our own ways through the various capacities, with daily support calls about our joyful and painful noticings. Philip Hayton and David Rooke at Harthill for their technical and practical knowledge of applying constructivist development with clients and for giving me places to play in. Last, but by no means least, in that sphere: Mike Vessey and the consultants at MDV (especially Carol Jefkins and Jo Hennessy) for playing along, being willing guinea pigs, contributing their own ideas and being willing to apply the new ideas and practices with clients so we could 'road test' them in development programmes and executive assessment.

Finally, of course, I want to thank Alex Bailey for coming along with me on this journey over the last 12 years, as companion, kin and co-conspirator – for his unfailing interest in, and support for, my work and for the long weekend walks where I would chatter along about meaning making and, gradually elucidated, the ideas that are at the heart of this book. Thanks Alex.

Thanks from Richard

My first acknowledgement has to be to Karen, for inviting me to partner on another fascinating journey. It's been great getting to know each other, fusing and refining ideas; snatching moments to tease or iron things out; conjuring cartoons that capture what we're talking about.

Dick Willis and Peter Hawkins were the first to alert me to the concept of 'vertical development' – my gateway drugs, so to speak – so I owe them thanks for the initial nudge in that direction. Back then it was mainly Bill Torbert's name I was hearing associated with the topic, so due thanks to him, too. I'd also echo Karen's thanks to David Rooke and Mike Vessey for the roles they've played in this journey.

Thanks to all the clients whose requests, challenges and development have helped me learn – about this stuff and everything else. Thanks to those who've allowed me to experiment with new material, too, particularly when testing out the ideas in this book. Clinton Stewart and Anton Zelcer at BHP deserve special mention on that front and on so many levels.

My daughter Evie played a bigger role than ever with this book. Previously, it's been her patience with my absences and distractedness that's been the focus of my gratitude (and a fair amount of guilt). This time, she contributed directly, helping me distil the essence of the upgrades in each capacity into the simple, one-stop-shop descriptions you'll find at the start of Chapter 8 and towards the back of the book. Her challenge, precision and insight were beautifully enjoyable and wonderfully helpful.

My friends Paul Hamilton and Scott Gibson have been a real asset, too. They've contributed nothing to the content of the book, but they've had me crying with laughter on multiple occasions during its creation. That's been a fundamental piece of vertical development in its own right. It's also been a huge boon when it comes to simultaneously writing a book, consulting, running a business, running stupidly long distances and trying to be a half-decent husband and father.

Last but the opposite of least, there's my wife Jane. Without her, I might never have met Karen and I might never have written my first book (outside of fiction), let alone three. Here's hoping my own vertical development turns me into a higher-level husband someday. You're the perfect combination of inspiration and enabler, Jane. 'Thank you' will never do it justice.

Thanks from both of us

Credit where credit is due to the team who turned the manuscript into the book you hold in your hands today. Jackie King as editor and Ali Rayner for layout, both on round three with Richard. Jason Flinter for the cover and graphics. Jenni Boston for helping proofread the book, which is always a sticky part of the process!

A number of friends and colleagues took time out of their ludicrously busy lives to offer their perspectives and comments on early drafts of the book. For their collective blend of insights, ideas, reassurance, challenge and hilariously frank criticism, huge heartfelt thanks to Andrew Fox, Anna Heywood, Anuj Kapoor at NTT Data, Caroline Britton, Catherine Poyner, Claire Davey, Daneel Siddiky, Danielle Lewis and

Matt Hale at Southampton Football Club, Dave Tansley, Gareth Rogers at Farnborough, James Taylor, Jenny Kidby, Jess Dooley, Lida Da Sie, Mark Griffiths at Workplace Systems, Michael Borthwick at Claranet, Nick Prangnell at Iron Mountain, Nick Sandall, Peter Young, Phil Hayes at Management Futures, Rebecca Stevens at Clarks, Rupert Howe, Sabrina Lakhani, Stephen Amos and Tim Patterson. Without your help and the significant upgrades you encouraged and enabled us to make, this book simply wouldn't have been the book it is today.

● ● ●

Appendix 1: Additional notes and references

●●●

Based on feedback on previous books, we've listed references in full where they appear in notes that are some distance from each other. Where they're repeated in notes that are closer together, we've pointed you back to the nearest note that includes a full reference. It's more usable than the traditional "ibid" and "op. cit." approach.

1   Clancy has been quoted in numerous places, but we've been unable to find the original source. One example, close to home where this subject matter is concerned, is on Page 125 of Garvey Berger, J. & Johnston, K. (2016) *Simple Habits for Complex Times: powerful practices for leaders.* Stanford Business Books.

2   To be fair, 'So what?' and 'Now what?' are fairly common responses when people receive feedback from psychometric test results, too.

3   Page 7 of Petrie, N. (2013) *Vertical Leadership Part 1. Developing Leaders for a Complex World.* Colorado Springs, Colorado: Center for Creative Leadership. Petrie uses the term 'stage', which is prevalent in the literature he's working with and some of the literature we've drawn on. For a number of reasons, we've chosen to speak of 'levels' of development where these capacities are concerned, rather than 'stages'.

4   Lawrence, J. & Steck, E. (1991) *Overview of Management Theory.* Intended to be Chapter 2, Army Command and Management: Theory and Practice, (1991-1992 Edition) United States Army War College, Department of Command, Leadership, and Management (DCLM) Carlisle Barracks, PA. USA.

5   Corporate Research Forum (2018) *Facing Disruption.* CRF discussion paper.

6   See, for example, Kurtz, C.F. & Snowden, D.J. (2003) The New Dynamics of Strategy: Sense-making in a complex and complicated world. *IBM Systems Journal, February, 42(3),* pp 462 – 483. Snowden did later change 'Simple' to 'Obvious'. We've kept both terms because they're both helpful and because some readers might be familiar with either the earlier or later versions of his work.

7   Page 11 of DDI (2014) *Ready-Now Leaders: 25 findings to meet tomorrow's business challenges.* DDI Global Leadership Forecast.

8   For the full list, see Chapter 2, note 4 on Page 290 of Kegan, R., Lahey, L.L., Fleming, A., Miller, M. L. & Helsing D. (2016) *An Everyone Culture: becoming a deliberately developmental organization.* Boston: Harvard Business Press.

9   The list of things people were better at comes from Page 72 of Kegan et al (2016) – see note 8. The study they cite is Eigel, K. (1998) *Leader Effectiveness.* PhD dissertation, University of Georgia.

10   You'll find some really good supporting statistics on Page 174 of Kegan et al (2016) – see note 8. The three companies they studied were Bridgewater (hedge fund managers), Decurion (which manages cinemas, real estate and homes for the elderly) and Next Jump (focusing on e-commerce)

11   Contextual Intelligence is defined as "the ability to quickly and intuitively recognize and diagnose the dynamic contextual variables inherent in an event or circumstance and results in intentional adjustment of behavior in order to exert appropriate influence in that context" on Page 23 of Kutz, M. (2008) Toward a Conceptual Model of Contextual Intelligence: A Transferable Leadership Construct. *Leadership Review, Kravis Leadership Institute, Claremont McKenna College, Vol. 8,* Winter, pp 18-31.

12   According to DDI, leadership agility blends "leader capability in VUCA... environments with effectiveness in four foundational skills underlying leader readiness for these challenges: communicating/interacting, managing change, inspiring others, and fostering innovation" – Retrieved from https://www. ddiworld.com/leadership-practices/making-leadership-agility-a-priority on 19 March 2019.

13   Leadership agility is cited as key in DDI (2014) – see note 7. Contextual intelligence is flagged in many places, including in Oxford-Saïd Business School and Heidrick & Struggles (2016) *The CEO Report: embracing the paradoxes of leadership and the power of doubt.* University of Oxford. Heidrick and Struggles is a worldwide executive search firm, specialising in chief executive and senior level assignments.

14   DDI (2014) – see note 7.

15   The notion that uncertainty requires us to develop the ability to attend to not just what's *probably* going to happen but all the things that could *possibly* happen is tabled in Garvey Berger, J. & Johnston, K. (2016) – see note 1.

16   DDI (2014) – see note 7.

17   The data we have – which doesn't measure these capacities specifically, but assesses closely related constructs – suggest that approximately two thirds of adults average out across the four capacities at around Level 1 or 2. A significant number will not yet have reached Level 1. It seems around 11% operate at an average of Level 3 across the capacities. Perhaps 7% operate consistently at

Level 4 and above. For more, see Cook-Greuter, S. (2004) Making the case for a developmental perspective. *Industrial & Commercial Training, 36(7),* pp 275-281 and Fisher, D.; Rooke, D. & Torbert, B. (2000) *Personal and Organizational Transformations Through Action Inquiry.* Edge\Work Press.

18   Kahneman, D. (2012) *Thinking, Fast and Slow.* New York: Farrar, Straus and Giroux.

19   Peters, S. (2012) *The Chimp Paradox: the mind management programme to help you achieve success, confidence and happiness.* London: Vermilion.

20   Goleman, D. (2013) The Focused Leader. *Harvard Business Review, December.* Retrieved from https://hbr.org/2013/12/the-focused-leader on 19 March 2019.

21   Oxford-Saïd Business School and Heidrick & Struggles (2016) *The CEO Report: embracing the paradoxes of leadership and the power of doubt.* University of Oxford.

22   For this short-lived acronym we cannibalised Julie Allan's "SCSU", meaning Stable, Certain, Simple, Unequivocal. "Unequivocal" is a great word for it, but as we're not dwelling on the SCSC/U thing beyond this chapter we thought we'd opt for "clear". See Allan, J. & Ellis, K. (2017) *What in the world is going on? Mapping Vertical and VUCA beyond the bandwagon.* MDV Research and Innovation Alliance.

23   Page 241 of Galbraith, J.K. (2001) *The Essential Galbraith.* Boston, Mass.: Houghton Mifflin Company. We were reminded of this quote by Garvey Berger, J. & Johnston, K. (2016) *Simple Habits for Complex Times: powerful practices for leaders.* Stanford Business Books.

24   We've based our description on Chapter 10 of Hawkins, P. (2014) *Leadership Team Coaching: Developing Collective Transformational Leadership. (2nd Ed)* London: Kogan Page.

25   Loevinger, J. (1966) The meaning and measurement of ego development. *American Psychologist,* 21(3), 195.

26   Cook-Greuter, S.R. (2004) Making the case for a developmental perspective. *Industrial and Commercial Training, 36(7),* pp 275-281. Retrieved from https://doi.org/10.1108/00197850410563902 on 19 March 2019.

27   O'Fallon, T. (2011) StAGES: *Growing Up Is Waking up - interpenetrating quadrants, states and structures.* Paper presented at the Integral theory Conference, 2011, San Francisco CA.

28   Rooke, D; Torbert, W. (2005) Seven Transformations of Leadership. *Harvard Business Review, April.* Watertown, MA: Harvard Business Publishing.

29   Joiner, B. & Josephs, S. (2007) *Leadership agility: five levels of mastery for anticipating and initiating change.* San Francisco: Jossey-Bass.

30   Jaques, E. (1986) The Development of Intellectual Capability: a discussion of

stratified systems theory. *The Journal of Applied Behavioral Science, 22(4)*, pp 361-383.

31   Jaques, E. & Cason, K. (1994) *Human Capability: study of individual potential and its application.* London: Gower.

32   Cook-Greuter, S. R. (1999) Postautonomous Ego Development: a study of its nature and measurement. (habits of mind, transpersonal psychology, worldview). *Dissertation Abstracts International: Section B: The Sciences and Engineering, 60(6-B)*, p 3000.

33   O'Fallon, T. (2011) – see note 27.

34   Kegan, R. (1982) *The Evolving Self. Problem and Process in Human Development.* Cambridge, MA: Harvard University Press.

35   Garvey Berger, J. (2013) *Changing on the job: Developing leaders for a complex world.* Stanford, CA: Stanford Business Books.

36   Laske, O.E. (2011) *Measuring Hidden Dimensions. The Art and Science of Fully Engaging Adults. (2nd Ed.)* Gloucester MA, USA: IDM Press.

37   Martin, R. L. (2007) *The Opposable Mind: how successful leaders win through integrative thinking.* Boston, Mass.: Harvard Business School Press.

38   The Leadership Development Framework and related Profile are available through Harthill Consulting. The Global Leadership Profile is available through Bill Torbert and his associates. The two frameworks share common origins. The four stages we've mentioned in this chapter are the ones from those frameworks that are the most aligned to the four levels we're talking about in this book. However, it's a far from perfect match.

39   The Australian Strength & Conditioning Association defines 4 broad physical capacities and sub-capacities: strength (strength endurance, hypertrophy, speed strength, max strength, control & stability), speed (reaction, acceleration, agility, max speed, speed endurance), endurance (aerobic, lactic & alactic) and flexibility (static, passive, dynamic, PNF, ballistic). If you'd like to explore this further, visit www.strengthandconditioning.org

40   One of our friends, Dave Tansley, likens the failure to keep upgrading these four capacities to the 'technology debt' accrued by many organisations. The pace of technological progress means many are rushing to launch a host of new digital products and services while others are too cash-strapped or cautious to do so and focus instead on adding just enough to avoid falling too far behind the curve. Unfortunately, those in both camps typically underinvest in upgrading their underlying IT infrastructure – accruing the aforementioned technology debt. It's the equivalent of adding shiny new kitchens and bathrooms to your home, all wired up to the Internet of Things, then decorating everything beautifully, while completely ignoring the fact that the plumbing and wiring are a hundred years old.

Eventually, your pipes spring a leak and you realise your electrics simply can't handle all those fancy gadgets. Unfortunately, to get at the piping and wiring, you need to rip out much of your kitchen and bathroom. The organisations that accrue the biggest, riskiest technology debts typically do so because the people making the investment decisions are fairly confident that they'll no longer be around when the outdated infrastructure fails and brings all of the organisation's IT systems crashing down, or when the risk of that happening is so high that the need for an immediate, expensive upgrade is undeniable. When it comes to upgrading your own OS long after you've accrued that 'debt' and lagged behind, you might not have that luxury.

41   Scaffolding and trellising are technical terms from the world of learning and development. Some people prefer one over the other, often based on their preference for either mechanistic or organic metaphors for learning. Others use both terms, using each to refer to different kinds of activity that support people's development.

The purpose of scaffolding, after all, is to allow the people working on a building to contribute more easily to its construction or renovation. The work itself is done by others from the outside and the scaffolding remains on the outside of the building. Thus, if you're using the practices in this book to support the development of others – or someone's using them to support your development – they're scaffolding.

A trellis, on the other hand, supports the growth of a plant by offering it something to lean on and cling to as it grows. The plant grows around it, doing the work itself. Once that plant is strong enough to support its own weight, the trellis can usually be removed – assuming you can find it! If you're using the practices in this book on yourself, then you're using them as trellising. Each practice will be working your muscles in one of the four capacities, helping you grow stronger to the point where the trellis is no longer required. However, you're unlikely to be able to extract the practices from yourself once you've used them!

42   Eigel, K.M. & Kuhnert, K.W. (2005) Authentic Development: leadership development level and executive effectiveness. *Authentic Leadership Theory and Practice: origins, effects and development. Monographs in Leadership and Management, 3,* pp 357–385.

43   Page 366 of Eigel, K.M. & Kuhnert, K.W. (2005) – see note 42.

44   This is one of Richard's favourites, supposedly of Irish origin although his Irish friends say otherwise!

45   The actual quote is taken from Covey, S.M.R. with Merrill, R.R. (2008) *The Speed of Trust: the one thing that changes everything.* London: Simon & Schuster. However, this is the latest in a long line of similar quotes going back at least as

far as Page 383 of Nevins, W. (1836) *Select Remains of the Rev. William Nevins with a Memoir*. New York: John S. Taylor.

46   Cook-Greuter, S. (2005) *Ego Development: nine levels of increasing embrace*. Wayland: II Psychology Center.

47   O'Fallon, T. (2011) – see note 27.

48   Cook-Greuter, S. (2005) – see note 46.

49   O'Fallon, T. (2011) – see note 27.

50   The poem *If* first appeared in the 1910 edition of Kipling, R. (2007) *Rewards and Fairies*. Fairford, Glos.: Echo Library.

51   Kegan, R. & Lahey, L.L. (2009) *Immunity to Change: how to overcome it and unlock potential in yourself and your organization*. Boston, Mass.: Harvard Business Press.

52   Garvey Berger, J. (2013) – see note 35.

53   To get to the true nub of this capacity we had to chisel out Opposable Thinking from a number of related concepts. Opposable Thinking is related to Otto Laske's 'dialectical' thinking, with human development in this capacity progressing through 'positivistic' through 'relativistic' and finally (within our four levels) 'dialectical'. Laske's dialectic is pretty extensive, drawing in matters of context, relationship, process and transformative thinking. If you're interested, the most accessible summary of his work can be found in Laske. O. (1999) An Integrated Model of Developmental Coaching. *Consulting Psychology Journal 51(3)*, pp 139-159.

Opposable Thinking also borders on other concepts like 'integrative', 'transformative' and 'fluid' thinking. However, these are used in a variety of ways, often overlapping with creative thinking, 'intuition' or the development of insights to transform our own and others' thinking. We've avoided those terms in this book as our aim here is to streamline a complex literature to ensure these capacities are as digestible as possible.

54   From the sales pitch for the book *The Opposable Mind*, retrieved from https://rogerlmartin.com/lets-read/the-opposable-mind on 19 March 2019

55   Page 69 of Fitzgerald, F.S. (1993) *The Crack Up*. New York: New Directions Publishing. Originally published in 1931 by Charles Scribner's Sons.

56   From the sales pitch for the book *The Opposable Mind* – see note 54.

57   See, for example: Rollwage, M.; Dolan, R. J. & Fleming, S. M. (2018) Metacognitive Failure as a Feature of Those Holding Radical Beliefs. *Current Biology, 28 (24)*, pp 4014 - 4021. The study in question found that people with radical political beliefs have less insight into the correctness of their beliefs and decisions than less radically-minded people. They were also less likely to recalibrate their confidence in their beliefs when presented with contrary evidence. Importantly, this applied

not just to political beliefs but to situations with an objective right answer – in this case estimating which of two clusters of dots contained the most dots.

58   Laske, O.E. (2011) *Measuring Hidden Dimensions: the art and science of fully engaging adults. (2nd Ed.)* Gloucester MA, USA: IDM Press.

59   Retrieved from https://www.ccl.org/articles/leading-effectively-articles/are-you-facing-a-problem-or-a-polarity/ on 19 March 2019.

60   One good source is Johnson, B. (1992, 1996) *Polarity Management: identifying and managing unsolvable problems.* Amherst MA: Human Resource Development Press. Johnson also has a website at www.polaritypartnerships.com

61   Technically, Johnson calls it 'polarity management', rather than Opposable Thinking.

62   Peters, T. J. & Waterman, R. H. (1982) *In Search of Excellence: lessons from America's best-run companies.* New York: Harper & Row.

63   Collins, J. C. & Porras, J. I. (1997) *Built to Last: successful habits of visionary companies.* New York: HarperBusiness.

64   Page 5 of Johnson, B. (1998) *Polarity Management: a summary introduction.* Retrieved from www.jpr.org.uk on 19 March 2019.

65   If you're keen to know what those seven polarities are, we recommend you take a look at Pascale, R.T. (1991) *Managing On The Edge: how successful companies use conflict to stay ahead.* London: Penguin.

66   Martin, R.L. (2007) How Successful Leaders Think. *Harvard Business Review, June.* Retrieved from https://hbr.org/2007/06/how-successful-leaders-think on 19 March 2019.

67   Page 17 of Holt, J. (1982) *How Children Learn.* New York: Merloyd Lawrence, Delat-Seymour Lawrence.

68   If you're well-versed in the literature on complexity or management theory, you might (for instance) be wondering where the work of Elliott Jaques and Bill Sharpe's Three Horizons come in. Their concepts are related, for sure, but we've opted to limit the number of concepts and models we try to cover in this book.

69   Jaques, E. & Cason, K. (1994) *Human Capability: study of individual potential and its application.* London: Gower.

70   Jaques, E. (1998). *Requisite Organization: a total system for effective managerial organization and managerial leadership for the 21st century (Rev. 2nd ed.).* Arlington, VA: Cason Hall. In case you're familiar with Jaques' work, in constructing our descriptions of this capacity and the upgrades within it, we've drawn on the range of his levels that is most commonly demonstrated by people in supervisory, management and leadership roles. Jaques calls these 'Stratum II-V'.

71   'Deliberately developmental' is a phrase taken from Kegan, R., Lahey, L.L., Fleming, A., Miller, M. L. & Helsing D. (2016) *An Everyone Culture: becoming a deliberately developmental organization.* Boston: Harvard Business Press.

72 Brain imaging shows that grandmasters' brains are literally working differently – the neurons involved are organised and used differently from those of amateurs. See, for instance, Amidzic, O., Riehle, H.J., Fehr, T., Weinbruch, C. & Elbert, T. (2001) Patterns of Focal γ-bursts in Chess Players: grandmasters call on regions of the brain not used so much by less skilled amateurs. *Nature, 412* (6847), p 603.

73 Sady, M-H.S. (1808) *The Gûlistân, or Rose Garden.* Translated by F. Gladwin. London: W. Bulmer & Co. We've used the more common spelling of Saadi's name in the quote for our book. It appears slightly differently in the source material.

74 Boston, R. (2014) *ARC Leadership: from surviving to thriving in a complex world.* London: LeaderSpace.

75 Line-ups are a brilliant on-the-spot way of understanding the range of opinions in a group, especially on divisive or contentious issues. They provide a direct visual display of how people differ and where the weight of opinion lies. They often give clues as to possible reframes or changes which can resolve or dissolve the conflict. You simply identify two opposing views and state each one in terms that reflect the view of its strongest supporter. Then draw an imaginary line across the room, with one position at each end. People then spread out along the line and, in turn, tell the rest of the group why they have positioned themselves where they are. Often, someone will stand off the line or walk up and down it. This can be misinterpreted as them not 'playing ball' with the exercise. However, they may have useful different perspectives to share on the issue, too. There are numerous variants on the approach, but even the (often surprising) distribution of opinion and the simple sharing of views can open up a conversation in a totally new way.

76 We've struggled to find the original source of this quote.

77 A great starting point where 'hot buttons' are concerned is Evans, S. & Suib Cohen, S. (2000) *Hot Buttons: how to resolve conflict and cool everyone down.* London: Piatkus.

78 The best way to approach these patterns is through coaching, action learning sets or therapy. If you'd rather focus on books for now, we'd recommend the following – each arguably demanding a higher level of Self-relating than the last. Peters, S. (2012) *The Chimp Paradox: the mind management programme to help you achieve success, confidence and happiness.* London: Vermilion. Neenan, M. (2009) *Developing Resilience: a cognitive-behavioural approach.* London: Routledge. Davanger, S., Eifring, H. & Hersoug, A.G. (Eds.) (2008) *Fighting Stress: reviews of meditation research.* Oslo: Acem. Hood, B. (2011) *The Self Illusion: why there is no 'you' inside your head.* London: Constable & Robinson. Berne, E. (2004) *Games People Play: the basic handbook of transactional analysis.* New York: Random House.

79   This felt understanding of inter-subjectivity drives the development of the fifth-person perspective beyond Level 4 Perspective-shifting

80   The quote has been attributed to many sources over the years, including Truman, baseball coach Earl Weaver and basketball coach John Wooden. Wooden most often gets the credit and Weaver's biography carries the title. There's little hope of verifying the source, so we've opted for the one born first.

81   A metaphor used in Petrie, N. (2013) *Vertical Leadership Part 1. Developing Leaders for a Complex World*. Colorado Springs, Colorado: Center for Creative Leadership.

82   Kegan, R. et al (2016) – see note 71.

83   Page 4 of Petrie, N. (2013) – see note 81.

84   Action learning is a methodology we love that focuses on learning through action. Participants come together in a 'set' (i.e. group) of around five or six people, ideally with diverse backgrounds, often with a facilitator who is typically an experienced coach trained in the action learning approach. Each brings a real, current challenge to the discussion – usually one that is complex (in the way we've talked about complexity in this book). Participants take it in turns to occupy the 'hot seat' and while they're in it, the others seek to help them. That help comes in a number of forms, including enabling them to better understand the challenge, exploring the dynamics at play in the wider system, questioning underlying assumptions, and harnessing lateral thinking to generate more creative solutions. The participant in the hot seat leaves with concrete actions, which they report back on in the next session – usually a few weeks later. All members of the group are encouraged to reflect on their own inner processes, both when in the hot seat and when trying to help the others. You're welcome to contact Richard if you'd like to know more about action learning. If you'd rather explore the methodology on your own, two key references are Revans, R. W. (1982) *The Origin and Growth of Action Learning.* Brickley, UK: Chartwell-Bratt; and Revans, R. W. (2011) *ABC's of Action Learning.* Burlington, Vermont: Gower.

85   Inyang, I. (2017) Fani-Kayode urges Buhari to take Okadigbo's advice. *Daily Post, Nigeria*, 23 October. Retrieved from http://dailypost.ng/2017/10/23/fani-kayode-urges-buhari-take-okadigbos-advice/ on 18 April 2018.

86   The inspiration for this experiment comes from the 'empty chair', in the Gestalt approach to coaching, and techniques used in NLP (Neuro-linguistic Programming).

87   Goleman, D. (1999) *Working With Emotional Intelligence.* London: Bloomsbury. It's important to emphasise that plenty of other authors have also worked on this topic.

88   Jung, C.G. (1967, 1991) *The Development of Personality*. London: Routledge.

89　Kegan, R. & Lahey, L.L. (2009) *Immunity to Change: how to overcome it and unlock potential in yourself and your organization*. Boston, Mass.: Harvard Business Press.

90　Hall, M.P. & Raimi, K.T. (2018) Is belief superiority justified by superior knowledge? *Journal of Experimental Psychology, 76,* pp 290-306. This particular piece of research focused on people's beliefs on socio-political topics, but the same effect has been found in a range of other domains, including people's assessments of logic or grammar.

91　Wilber, K. (2001) *No Boundary: Eastern and Western approaches to personal growth*. Boulder, Colorado: Shambhala.

92　Johnson, B. (1992, 1996) *Polarity Management: identifying and managing unsolvable problems*. Amherst MA: Human Resource Development Press.

93　Whittington, J. (2012) *Systemic Coaching and Constellations: an introduction to the principles, practices and applications.* London: Kogan Page.

94　Campbell, D. & Grønbæk, M. (2006) *Taking Positions in the Organization.* London: Karnac Books.

95　Page 623 of Churchill, W. (1931) *The World Crisis, 1911-1918*. New York: Free Press.

96　The underlying concept of the fishbone diagram goes back to the 1920s, but it was popularised in the 1960s by Japanese organisational theorist, Professor Kaoru Ishikawa. He worked in the engineering faculty at the University of Tokyo and is credited with pioneering quality management processes in the Kawasaki shipyards. You can find more on his work in K. Ishikawa (1976) *Guide to Quality Control*. Asian Productivity Organization.

97　Some proponents of the fishbone model in manufacturing have expanded beyond the original 'Five Ms' to 'Eight Ms'. See, for instance, Bradley, E. (2016) *Reliability Engineering: a life cycle approach.* CRC Press.

98　For instance, Bradley, E. (2016) – see note 97.

99　If you're looking for a book, it's worth taking a look at Evans, V. (2014) *25 Need-To-Know Strategy Tools.* New Jersey: FT Press. You'll also find a host of other tools at https://www.mindtools.com/pages/main/newMN_STR.htm (retrieved on 19 March 2019)

100　You can find out more about power mapping at https://en.wikipedia.org/wiki/Power_mapping (retrieved on 19 March 2019). It's a Wikipedia entry that has been flagged for flaws as it appears to have been created by a politically-motivated organisation, so treat it accordingly. However, as a starting point, this entry is sufficient as a source of inspiration when it comes to the process of power mapping.

101　Kim, D.H. (1994) *Systems Thinking Tools: a user's reference guide.* Cambridge, UK: Pegasus.

102 Kim, D.H. (1994) – see note 101.

103 Plutarch was writing in the First Century CE and this quote comes from *On Listening to Lectures.* A similar quote is often ascribed to Socrates, who lived centuries before. However, there's no agreed source and the words ascribed to Socrates may in fact be pure paraphrasing by a 19th Century commentator on the works of Plato. You'll find further information at https://citacoes.in/ citacoes/1844164-socrates-education-is-the-kindling-of-a-flame-not-the-fill/ (retrieved on 19 March 2019)

104 This image and framework first appear in a slightly different iteration in Boston, R. (2018) *The Boss Factor.* London: LeaderSpace. Then in Boston, R. (2019) From Good to Great at Southampton Football Club. In Clutterbuck, D; Gannon, J; Hayes, S; Iordanou, I; Lowe, K. & MacKie, D. (Eds.) (2019) *The Practitioner's Handbook of Team Coaching.* London: Routledge. The framework is rooted in the GROW model (Whitmore, J. (2009) *Coaching for Performance: GROWing human potential and purpose – the principles and practice of coaching and leadership (4th Ed.).* Nicholas Brealey); Hawkins' CID-CLEAR (Hawkins, P. (2011) *Leadership Team Coaching: Developing Collective Transformational Leadership (1st Ed.)* London: Kogan Page); Kotter's models for organisational change (Kotter, J.P. (1996) *Leading Change.* Harvard Business School Press); Prochaska's work with addiction (Prochaska, J.O. & Velicer, W.F. (1997) The transtheoretical model of health behavior change. *American Journal of Health Promotion, 12(1),* pp 38–48); and Gestalt approaches to behavioural change.

105 We're unsure whether Petrie technically coined the term 'heat experience', but it is consistently attributed to him. This quote is from Page 3 of Petrie, N. (2015) *The How-To of Vertical Leadership Development – Part 2. 30 Experts, 3 Conditions, and 15 Approaches.* Colorado Springs, Colorado: Center for Creative Leadership. In that article, he says the description quoted here is derived from the work of Bob Eichinger and Michael Lombardo but he doesn't cite a specific reference. Apologies, on Petrie's behalf, for the "he" and lack of "she".

106 A term popularised in Goldsmith, M. & Reiter, M. (2007) *What Got You Here Won't Get You There: how successful people become even more successful.* New York: Hachette.

107 The 'safe and robust' aspects of the experiment come from Kegan, R. & Lahey, L.L. (2009) *Immunity to Change: how to overcome it and unlock potential in yourself and your organization.* Boston, Mass.: Harvard Business Press.

108 From Page 14 of Petrie, N. (2015) – see note 105.

109 Mandela, N. (1994) *Long Walk to Freedom: the autobiography of Nelson Mandela.* Boston., Mass.: Little Brown & Co.

110 Kegan, R., Lahey, L.L., Fleming, A., Miller, M. L. & Helsing D. (2016) *An Everyone*

Culture: becoming a deliberately developmental organization. Boston, Mass.: Harvard Business Press.

111   Laloux, F. & Wilber, K. (2014) *Reinventing Organizations: a guide to creating organizations inspired by the next stage in human consciousness.* Nelson Parker.

112   Fisher, D., Rooke, D. & Torbert, W.R. (2000) *Personal and Organisational Transformations: through action inquiry.* Boston, Mass.: Edge\Work Press

113   In a speech to the National Press Club on 20 March 1914. Cited in *The Independent, Volume 77.* Independent Publications Inc.

114   A good starting point is Oshry, B. (2007) *Seeing Systems: unlocking the mysteries of organizational life.* Oakland, CA: Berrett-Koehler, 2007.

115   Senge, P.M. (1994) *The Fifth Discipline Fieldbook: strategies and tools for building a learning organization.* New York: Currency, Doubleday.

116   Scharmer, C.O. (2018) *The Essentials of Theory U: core principles and applications.* Berrett-Koehler Publishers, Inc.

117   Argyris, C. 1993. *Knowledge for Action: a guide to overcoming barriers to organizational change.* San Francisco: Jossey-Bass.

118   Morgan, G. (2006) *Images of Organization.* Newbury Park, CA: Sage Publications.

119   Eoyang, G.H. & Holladay, R.J. (2013) *Adaptive Action: leveraging uncertainty in your organization.* California: Stanford University Press.

120   Boston, R. (2019) Spinning the Systems Wheel: turning the magic of 'systems thinking' into a practical tool for team coaching. In Clutterbuck, D; Gannon, J; Hayes, S; Iordanou, I; Lowe, K. & MacKie, D. (Eds.) (2019) *The Practitioner's Handbook of Team Coaching.* London: Routledge.

121   Wilber, K. & Wilber, K. (2000) *Integral Psychology: consciousness, spirit, psychology, therapy.* Boston, Mass.: Shambhala.

122   Kegan, R. (1994) *In Over Our Heads: the mental demands of modern life.* Cambridge, Mass.: Harvard University Press.

123   Maslow, A.H. (1971) *The Farther Reaches Of Human Nature.* New York: Viking Press.

124   The so-called Big Five factors of personality are the most consistently found (and used) dimensions in personality research and have become the industry's gold standard. The Big Five, each measured on a continuum on which each of us is deemed to fall, are: Neuroticism, Extraversion, Openness, Agreeableness and Conscientiousness. For more information, see Costa, P.T. & McCrae, R.R. (1985) *The NEO Personality Inventory Manual.* Odessa, Florida: Psychological Assessment Resources; or McCrae, R.R. & Costa, P.T. (2004) A Contemplated Revision Of The NEO Five-Factor Inventory. *Personality and Individual Differences, 36(3),* pp 587–596.

125 The most common tool for slicing up personality into different types is the Myers-Briggs Type Indicator (MBTI), a trademark of The Myers-Briggs Company headquartered in the USA. It helps users decide which of sixteen four-letter types best describes them, based on their preferences on four dichotomies: Extraversion-Introversion, Sensing-Intuition, Thinking-Feeling and Judging-Perceiving. Explaining these further would mean creating an appendix to an appendix, so instead we recommend you turn to Google for further information.

126 Bennet, A.A. (2010) *The Shadows of Type: psychological type through seven levels of development.* Lulu. The book is based on her PhD work, the thesis being Bennet, A.A. (2011) *Using Psychological Type for Developmental Coaching: The Inclusion of Intrapersonal Type Dynamics, Effectiveness Related to Aspects of Ego Development, and the Individual's Capacity for Development.* London Metropolitan University.

127 Bennet, A.A. (2010, 2011) – see note 126. Given that they're rooted in the same 'adult constructivist' research as our work, you'll see some parallels between Bennet's developmental stages and the four levels we've described for the four capacities. As with other stage approaches, we'd advise against simply mapping from her model to ours, but by all means use Bennet's model as a source of inspiration when seeking to upgrade.

● ● ●

Appendix 2: Values

• ● •

The following list of values is drawn from Richard's book *ARC Leadership*, where he offers a guided exploration of your values as a means of better understanding what it means for you to be authentic.

We've included it here as a resource to support some of the practices in Part 4.

Importantly, these are just examples. You may find other words better represent your values. Hence the empty row where you can add more.

Accountability	Achievement	Advancement
Ambition	Arts	Authenticity
Balance (of...?)	Beauty	Being admired
Being liked	Change	Clarity
Collaboration	Comfort	Commercial success
Commitment	Community	Compassion
Competence	Conflict resolution	Continuous learning
Contribution	Co-operation	Courage
Creativity	Culture	Dependability
Discipline	Efficiency	Enthusiasm
Environment	Equality	Ethics
Excellence	Excitement	Fairness
Family	Financial gain	Forgiveness
Freedom	Friendships	Future generations
Generosity	Growth	Harmony
Health	Helping others	Honesty

Humility	Humour/fun	Inclusion
Independence	Influence	Initiative
Innovation	Integrity	Intelligence
Interdependence	Intuition	Involvement
Job security	Kindness	Leadership
Listening	Logic	Love
Loyalty	Making a difference	Meaningful work
Mission focus	Obedience	Open communication
Open-mindedness	Openness	Order/structure
Peace (at a global level)	Peace (at a personal level)	Perseverance
Personal fulfilment	Personal growth	Physical fitness
Physical pleasure	Politeness	Power
Privacy	Quality	Recognition
Relationships	Religion	Reputation
Respect	Responsibility	Risk taking
Safety	Security	Self confidence
Self-discipline	Simplicity	Spirituality
Stability	Status	Success
Sustainability	Tidiness	Tolerance
Trust	Truth	Variety
Vision	Wealth	Wisdom

•••

Appendix 3: Personality and the four capacities

• ● •

YOU MIGHT BE FAMILIAR with the most commonly-used methods of describing personality: the Big Five model[124] and tools based on the work of Carl Jung, like the Myers-Briggs Type Indicator (MBTI®)[125]. If so, you might wonder whether people with certain personality traits or preferences are more likely to reach or get stuck at a particular level in one or more of the capacities (see 'Know your MBTI?' for examples).

The reality, though, is that all personality types can be found operating at all four levels in all four of the capacities.

Know your MBTI?

If you know the MBTI well, Level 1 Sense-making might seem quite 'Sensing, Thinking and Judging'. In some capacities, Level 2 might initially remind you of stereotypes associated with a combination of Extraversion, Thinking and Judging.

At the same time, you might suspect the capacity to 'put yourself in someone else's shoes' would come more easily to people with preferences for Feeling and perhaps Intuition.

You could equally look at the common Level 3 Opposable Thinking and Sense-making challenge of 'seeing all the complexity but struggling to find a way through it' as a familiar challenge for people with preferences for both Intuition and Perceiving.

We need to be wary of these judgements, though, for the reasons we'll share in this chapter.

Our own findings on that front are supported by extensive work done by psychologist Angelina Bennet[126] into links between personality and the stages proposed in the various theories of adult constructivist development that were the original inspiration for our four levels.

Your personality will influence the way you use the four capacities

People with the same 'capacity profile' but different personalities may well 'show up' differently. Take Amar and Pia. When we met them, both were at the same level of development in all four capacities. For example, they both had their own fixed, concrete way of viewing reality, which put them at Level 1 when it came to working effectively with polarities.

In personality terms, they were very different. Amar was all about people and Pia was all about getting the job done. For Amar, this manifested as a strong moral core he learned from his parents and applied to every decision and every interaction. Those who shared his moral compass were inspired and cared for and thrived under his leadership. However, he was quick to judge anyone whose values weren't aligned with his own, and quick to ostracise those who accidentally or intentionally breached his moral code.

For Pia, that same level of development manifested as a relentless focus on finding the right answer to increasingly difficult problems. She was an intelligent woman with a wealth of knowledge, who was frequently disappointed in the rigour of others' thinking. She found it incredibly difficult to delegate because she knew there would always be errors in people's work. Thus, her trust in others usually went down with every encounter rather than up.

Amar and Pia are just two examples of someone's personality interacting with their capacity profile. If you'd like to learn more about how each of the sixteen MBTI types looks, sounds and feels when operating from a given *stage* of development, then we'd highly recommend

Bennet's book *Shadows of Type*[127]. She is looking at 'whole self' stages, rather than at levels within separate capacities. However, if you're familiar enough with the MBTI and interested in taking things further, her book will offer useful food for thought.

Your personality will also influence the way you develop these capacities

As we said briefly in Chapter 2, personality may well be a factor when it comes to upgrading from one level to the next. For example, these kinds of transitions require us to let go of the habits, needs and mindsets associated with one level, then invest effort in moving to the next. Our willingness to do so is heavily dependent on our openness to new experiences and ideas, one of the Big Five traits that make up personality.

Experience tells us two other Big Five traits will have an impact, too – albeit a more complex one. Anxiety (technically referred to as 'neuroticism') is one. On the one hand, being more anxious than other people could make you more attuned to the limitations in your existing operating system and thus more likely to seek an upgrade. On the other hand, high anxiety could make you more reluctant to let go of your existing world view and travel through the unknown to the next level.

Similarly, a high score on a scale of 'conscientiousness' could make you more committed to improving yourself. However, it might also encourage you to cling ever-more tightly to an OS that has helped you be successful – and stay out of trouble – in the past.

At a more granular level, your personality will influence your attitude to the very idea of *levels* of development. The more competitive you are, the more likely it is that you'll want to outperform others by getting to a higher level than them. If you're also overly confident in yourself, you'll be at risk of thinking you're currently at a higher level in one or more capacities than you actually are.

If you're more egalitarian in your outlook, you might have an initial aversion to the idea of levels of development, preferring flatter ways of looking at the different ways people think and operate. As much as it could limit your willingness to engage with the levels, there's something powerfully positive in that mind-set. It'll help you avoid judging those who've yet to upgrade to the same levels as you. After all, being at one level or another doesn't make someone a better person. It simply helps them be more effective at dealing with a VUCA world.

Your personality will also influence the nature, causes, frequency and intensity of the 'snags, crashes and whirlpools' that could make it harder to upgrade a given capacity or temporarily drag you back into a less resourceful level than the one at which you usually operate.

The most obvious is a consistent pattern of high anxiety, which means our natural stress response is more likely to be triggered in relatively benign situations. That stress response switches off the higher functions of the brain to focus us on meeting our most immediate, basic needs. This can trigger the kind of crash we discussed in Chapter 9, causing us to temporarily slip backwards from the level of development we've reached in one or more capacities, back into the previous level or even beyond.

Every one of us has our own unique set of 'hot buttons' that can trigger these crashes. We've acquired them from a range of different sources, but many are relatively easy to predict from a basic personality profile.

● ● ●

Appendix 4: In a nutshell

● ● ●

Sense-making
What on earth is going on here?

❹ Re-framing
GOODBYE: uncertainty about how to handle a myriad of complex options
HELLO: weaving disparate threads into a single, coherent, co-created and adaptable set of strategies

❸ Connecting
GOODBYE: pursuing single, pre-set goals
HELLO: spotting numerous, interconnected ways forward and possible valuable outcomes

❷ Diagnosing
GOODBYE: relying on tried-and-tested rules and processes when seeking to understand and respond to the situation
HELLO: focusing on action, incremental improvement and results

❶ Analysing

Perspective-shifting
What more can I see when I step back and back and back from my own, first-person perspective?

❹ Co-Creating
GOODBYE: having my objectivity hijacked by my own 'baggage' and 'hot buttons'
HELLO: finding creative ways to step back from my own and others' viewing points to see how our subjective realities affect each other

❸ Inquiring
GOODBYE: inadvertently filtering my 'objectivity' through deeply held beliefs and biases
HELLO: noticing how and why my beliefs and biases affect my attempts to see the world through others' eyes

❷ Co-operating
GOODBYE: seeing other people in terms of simple categorisations that are, I now realise, really just stereotypes
HELLO: recognising that people are complex and have multiple reasons for doing what they do

❶ Acknowledging

Obviously there's a lot more to the capacities and upgrades than we could distil into Chapter 8's 'bare bones' summaries, but they're repeated here so you can find them easily.

Self-relating
How could I best 'show up' here?

Self-determining
GOODBYE: being hijacked by my own 'hot buttons', limiting beliefs and unhelpful patterns of behaviour
HELLO: aligning my life with my principles / preferences; managing the tension if I can't; genuinely reinventing myself to be what my context demands

Experimenting
GOODBYE: treating my identity as a single, stable, logically-coherent thing
HELLO: being increasingly aware of my unhelpful patterns of thinking and feeling, and increasingly able to shift those patterns over time

Balancing
GOODBYE: typically only noticing afterwards when I've been hijacked by my emotions, or by my most rigidly-held values and beliefs
HELLO: striking a balance between meeting others' expectations and living up to my own, individual values and beliefs

Noticing

Opposable Thinking
How do I best respond to dilemmas and conflicting views regarding the nature of the problem and how to proceed?

Integrating
GOODBYE: feeling discouraged by the absence of any objective 'truth' and the reality that some dilemmas are simply unresolvable
HELLO: integrating both poles' underlying 'truths' into a mutually attractive way forward; challenging my own internal polarities in the moment

Mediating
GOODBYE: treating polarities as 'either/or' debates
HELLO: finding polarities everywhere, including in my own thinking; noticing their causes and divisive effects; finding creative ways beyond mere compromise

Negotiating
GOODBYE: believing in one correct, black or white answer
HELLO: starting to see shades of grey and believing the 'best answer' can vary depending on context

Upholding

Appendix 5:
Finding the right practices

• ● •

	Upgrading from Level 1 to Level 2	Upgrading from Level 2 to Level 3	Upgrading from Level 3 to Level 4
Sense-making	Combined reflection, Inquiry and Experiment: page 289	Combined reflection, Inquiry and Experiment: page 293	Combined reflection, Inquiry and Experiment: page 298
Perspective-shifting	Reflection: page 232 Inquiry: page 234 Experiment: page 235	Reflection: page 237 Inquiry: page 239 Experiment: page 244	Reflection: page 245 Inquiry: page 247 Experiment: page 250
Self-relating	Reflection: page 253 Inquiry: page 255 Experiment: pages 255 and 256	Reflection: page 258 Inquiry: page 260 Experiment: page 262	Reflection: page 263 Inquiry: page 267 Experiment: page 268
Opposable Thinking	Reflection: page 271 Inquiry: page 273 Experiment: page 273	Reflection: page 275 Inquiry: page 277 Experiment: page 278	Reflection: page 279 Inquiry: page 282 Experiment: page 284

CPSIA information can be obtained
at www.ICGtesting.com
Printed in the USA
BVHW092023101121
621196BV00003B/64